Presence in Absence

Beneath Shakespeare's Poetic Surface

written by

S. W. Stout

© 2010

Presence in Absence

Beneath Shakespeare's Poetic Surface

S. Wade Stout

Copyright © 2010

ISBN-13: 978-0-9784483-4-9

Library and Archives Canada Cataloguing-in-Publication

Stout, S. W. (Sidney Wade), 1955-
Presence in absence: beneath Shakespeare's poetic surface / written by S.W. Stout.

Includes bibliographical references.
ISBN 978-0-9784483-2-5

1. Shakespeare, William, 1564-1616--Stories, plots, etc.
2. Shakespeare, William, 1564-1616--Criticism and interpretation. I. Title.

PR2976.S763 2010   822.3'3   C2010-905516-0

To

Janice Mackett

"Here come and sit, where never serpent hisses
And being set, I'll smother thee with kisses"

Venus and Adonis, (*ll.* 17-18)

"The jewel that we find, we stoop and take't,
Because we see it; but what we do not see,
We tread upon, and never think of it."

W. Shakespeare
Measure for Measure
(2.1.24-26)

TABLE OF CONTENTS

Presence in Absence
Beneath Shakespeare's Poetic Surface

Presence in Absence
Beneath Shakespeare's Poetic Surface

Introduction

These essays are a continuation of my exploration into ideas that are structural in Shakespeare's work. Each essay stands alone but can be read as a part of an unfolding program that I introduced in my first book *In Sheep's Clothing; The Arcane, Profane, and Subversive in Shakespeare* (2008).

The ideas, the source material, I explore in this work generally lie outside of Shakespeare's text. What I mean by that is that the works which influence Shakespeare's ideas and poetry are often hidden and cannot be seen directly in his text. Influence of one writer on another, without direct acknowledgement, is difficult to show. For instance it is difficult to demonstrate that Plutarch's *On Isis and Osiris* influenced Shakespeare's *Antony and Cleopatra*. Subject matter and a shared historical setting help to make connections but influence is still hard to prove. The influence lies outside the text but at the same time guides the text. The source work becomes mirrored in Shakespeare's work but Shakespeare does not quote directly from it, their influence is conceptual and therefore indirect.

The advantage of looking at source material is that often this work is very clear about the ideas it wishes to communicate. The source material was generally written for instruction and unlike poetry does not obfuscate its purpose. This overt content can often provide insight into understanding 'the purpose' of Shakespeare's play. Examining these works can suggest reasons why Shakespeare was drawn to them in the first place and can help us answer the question as to why he felt that their inclusion was necessary.

Indirect influence is difficult to prove but not impossible. Sometimes the ideas in the source work lie so far outside the norms of the times that to see even a slight reference to such ideas is both shocking and revealing. The uniqueness of an idea can tie it to its source. Such ideas, at times, stand out in Shakespeare's plays and immediately alert us of a source that is furnishing Shakespeare with his concepts. When these or other ideas from the same work occur in one or more plays we can be fairly certain that Shakespeare was well acquainted with the work. Such repeated allusions to a particular source work begin to reveal aspects of his education and philosophies that he thought worth preserving.

Throughout the following essays you will see examples of Shakespeare alluding to certain authors and sometimes personifying certain concepts from their works in his. Sometimes these sources are unique to a particular play and sometimes their contribution can be noticed in several of his plays. Generally Shakespeare would combine the learning of the ancients (classical texts) with the discoveries of the moderns. He brought these disparate views together to create a new world view, one that expanded on the old ideas of who we are. At the same time he managed to hide contentious modern ideas in traditional clothing.

Consistently Shakespeare chose plot structures that would integrate with the ideas he was interested in exploring such that the two would reinforce one another. These conceptual 'mash-ups' created a synergy in his work and made it possible to create very unique reinterpretations with established materials.

The danger Shakespeare faced by using plots supplied by other artists, living or dead, is that some of this source material carried with it its own baggage. Some of this Shakespeare could control and some he couldn't. Some meaning from those pre-existing plots, their mythic baggage, their tradition in folklore, always crept over. Recognizing the existence of these contributing works and the changes that Shakespeare made to them can help us see which aspects of the story were important to him and that he felt were worthy of expanding upon and which were incidental to his purpose. Shakespeare's 'new' contributions to the text can then be understood as intentional and his new ideas can be examined. The remnants of the old plot along with their associations can also be separated out and understood as either contributing to Shakespeare's new intent or as a source of traditional prejudices that Shakespeare was willing to accept as a type of 'cultural cost' for using these pre-existent structures.

If Shakespeare's poetry is the flower then this book can be said to explore its roots. The source work I examine is not the flower but that which gives life to the flower by providing it with nutrition and stability.

The hidden source work provides material for the poetry to improvise on. The poetry, the surface beauty, is what we all initially see, it is easy to be distracted by. Like a parable it is easy to get caught up in the story and lose track of its deeper meanings.

The purpose of these essays is to take the reader deeper into Shakespeare. To show them the roots, the ideas that make the plays worth seeing and talking about. The poetry is beautiful but it is the roots that provides the food for thought and make these plays the repository of such profound knowledge.

Abstract for *Timon of Athens*

The Mean Spirit in Timon

The argument put forth in this essay is that the characters that embody *Timon of Athens* find their source in Aristotle's *Nicomachean Ethics* and that the central metaphor comes from Aeschylus' *Eumenides*. Aristotle and Seneca can both be seen as source material for Shakespeare's understanding of virtue and gratitude.

The Mean Spirit in Timon

Introduction

Timon, on the surface, appears to be in the tradition of morality plays. The plot reveals the folly of an overly generous man who is exploited and ruined by ungrateful 'friends'. This violation of his trust results in his subsequent hatred of all men.

The play consists of two distinct halves. The first reveals Timon's excessive trust he places in mankind and the latter his excessive hatred for mankind. Timon is not a character of moderation but swings wildly between the two extremes. He is a character of narrow focus.

The broad strokes used to create the play seem to deny any subtlety in the contents. This lack of nuance begins with the characters which are more like types than people. This should alert us to the prospect that the play is not so much about character as it is about their actions. The play is an armature to investigate other concerns.

Aristotle Characterizes Timon

Aristotle's *Nicomachean Ethics* can be seen as the source book for most of the characters or types that appear in *Timon of Athens*. In a few pages Aristotle outlines the characteristics that Shakespeare will embody in Timon, Alcibiades, and the Senators.

Aristotle's book of ethics examines many aspects of virtue that are relevant to understanding the play (*Nicomachean Ethics,* Book III.i.1).

Virtue however is concerned with emotions and actions, and it is only voluntary actions for which praise and blame are given.

In this play the actions of interest are voluntary and therefore worthy of praise or blame respectively. Timon (Prodigality) and the Senators (Meanness/Avarice) are defined around the mean (average or moderate) virtue of liberality (ibid., Book IV.i.1 - 5).

Next let us speak of Liberality. This virtue seems to be the observance of the mean in relation to wealth: we praise a man as liberal...in relation to giving and getting wealth, and especially in giving; wealth meaning all those things whose value is measured by money.

Prodigality and Meanness on the other hand are both of them modes of excess and of deficiency in relation to wealth. Meanness is always applied to those who care more than is proper about wealth, but Prodigality...really it denotes the possessor of one particular vice, that of wasting one's substance; for he who is ruined by his own agency is a hopeless case indeed, and to waste one's substance seems to be in a way to ruin oneself, in as much as wealth is the means of life.

From these definitions it is clearly evident that Prodigality defines Timon's character just as Meanness defines Timon's so-called friends.

Aristotle goes on to refine his definition of both wealth and liberality which in turn helps us to understand the extremes around this mean (ibid., Book IV.i.6).

Now riches are an article of use; but articles of use can be used either well or ill.

(ibid., Book IV.i.12)

Acts of virtue are noble, and are performed for the sake of their nobility; the liberal man therefore will give for the nobility of giving. And he will give rightly, for he will give to the right people, and the right amount, and at the right time, and fulfill all the other conditions of right giving.

When we first meet Timon we could misperceive him as a Liberal man for he seems to give to people with a genuine need and he gives an appropriate amount (enough to solve the immediate problem).

An acquaintance is imprisoned for a debt of five talents. Timon immediately pays this debt (1.1.106)

I'll pay the debt and free him.

He then goes on to help one of his servants obtain a Father's consent to marry his daughter by matching the daughter's dowry (1.1.148-150)

Give him thy daughter,

What you bestow, in him I'll counterpoise

And make him weigh with her.

Both these actions are received with pledges of gratitude. Both actions, though generous, appear considered. It is only from dialogue later in the play that we learn that Timon gives to all and that in the reciprocity of gift-giving he always returns far more than he was initially gifted (1.1.283-287)

Plutus, the god of gold,

Is but his steward: no need but he repays

Sevenfold above itself, no gift to him

But breeds the giver a return exceeding

All use of quittance.

The Lords see Timon as a source of ready cash and exploit him (2.1.5-6)

If I want gold, steal but a beggar's dog

And give it to Timon, why, the dog coins gold.

It is through these and like conversations that we realize Timon is prodigal with his wealth. He does not wisely distribute it or respect his ancestors that accumulated it for his judicious use. He disrespects the past and does not understand the present. He is a victim but he is not innocent. This he makes clear in his speech (1.2.98-103)

Why, I have often wished

myself poorer that I might come nearer to you. We are

born to do benefits, and what better or properer can we

call our own than the riches of our friends? O, what

a precious comfort 'tis to have so many like brothers

commanding one another's fortunes.

Timon sees himself as leading a brotherhood that believes 'what's mine is yours and what's yours is mine'. We know by this time in the play that such a conceit is only half true. Soon Timon's 'friends' will have consumed all his wealth and left him deeply in debt (1.2.39-41)

O you gods, what a number of

men eats Timon and he sees 'em not! It grieves me to

see so many dip their meat in one man's blood.

The play through its allusions and Timon through his actions gives us the sense that he is not only prodigal but also suffers from a megalomania, where he likens himself to the bountiful sun, a giver of life and hope to all. He sees himself like a god with endless resources. His steward tries to point out to him that he does not have such bounty (2.2.152-153)

O my good lord, the world is but a word;

Were it all yours to give it in a breath,

How quickly were it gone.

The steward councils him much as Aristotle might. For example Aristotle discusses the proper use and management of wealth in his *Nicomachean Ethics* (Book IV. i.).

17 – But he will acquire wealth from the proper source, that is, from his own possessions, not because he thinks it is a noble thing to do, but because it is a necessary condition of having the means to give. He will not be careless of his property, in as much as he wishes to employ it for the assistance of others. He will not give indiscriminately, in order that he may be able to give to the right persons at the right time, and where it is noble to do so.

21 – you cannot have money…without taking pains to have it.

23 – the liberal man is one who spends in proportion to his means...while he that exceeds his means is prodigal.

29 – Prodigality exceeds in giving and is deficient in getting; Meanness falls short in giving and goes to excess in getting...

30 – Now the two forms of Prodigality are very seldom found united in the same person because it is not easy to give to everyone without receiving from anyone: the giver's means are soon exhausted...

31 – to exceed in giving without getting is foolish rather than evil or ignoble.

This is certainly in agreement with Shakespeare's take on Timon (2.2.174)

> *Unwisely, not ignobly, have I given.*

Shakespeare has in fact taken pains to align Aristotle's understanding of Prodigality to mesh with certain scenes of decadence that he has introduced. Let's first see how Aristotle's descriptions of inappropriate giving match the play (ibid., Book IV. i.).

35 – their giving is not really liberal: their gifts are not noble,...nor in the right way; on the contrary, sometimes they make men rich who ought to be poor, and will not give anything to the worthy, while heaping gifts on flatterers and others who minister to their pleasures. Hence most prodigal men are also profligate; for they spend their money freely, some of it is squandered in debauchery.

Inappropriate giving and debauchery certainly match the first banquet scene in *Timon of Athens*; the all male guests, the dancing ladies dressed as Amazons; these are signs most productions take to transform the banquet scene into a more orgiastic display of indulgence.

Timon's character is prodigal at the start of the play and remains prodigal at the end of the play. Timon's circumstances change, his relations to others change, but his core character remains prodigal. This is revealed in his dialogue with Apemantus (4.3.276-279).

Ape. *Art thou proud yet?*

Tim. *Ay, that I am not thee.*

Ape. *Ay, that I was no prodigal.*

Tim. *Ay, that I am one now.*

Timon at the end of the play is still throwing away his resources, but this time to cause harm to humanity instead of providing it with indiscriminate bounty (4.3.300-301)

> *The middle of humanity thou never knewst,*
>
> *but the extremity of both ends.*

The Senators/Lords in the play are 'entitled' characters defined by their Meanness/Avarice. They value money more than family, friends, or anyone else. They feel they are entitled to any benefits that come their way and display no gratitude, heartfelt indebtedness, to anyone. They are characters that display courtesy and engage in flattery but only as a means to an end, *"small love amongst these sweet knaves, and all this courtesy"* (1.1.255).

Aristotle elaborates a little more on the characteristics of meanness; he sees it as an overly abundant intractable trait (ibid., Book IV.i.37-38).

> *Meanness on the contrary is incurable...the mass of mankind are avaricious...Meanness is a far reaching vice...as it consists in two things, deficiency in giving and excess in getting.*

Men desire money and sex. These are the desires from which profit can be made. The usurers in the play are seen as those that provide these services for a price. Shakespeare is certainly cognizant of Aristotle's views as both assign usurers and prostitutes as exemplars of this type of meanness (ibid., Book IV.i.40).

> *The other sort of people are those who exceed in respect of getting, taking from every source and all they can; such are those who follow degrading trades, brothel-keepers and all people of that sort and petty*

usurers who lend money in small sums at a high rate of interest; all these take…more than their due.

Alcibiades represents one of the few noble characters in *Timon of Athens*. He appears untainted by money and is one of Timon's only true friends. We sense that he wishes to defend Timon but that he also defers to Timon's judgment perhaps out of respect to an elder. Consider the conversation between Timon and Alcibiades (1.2.73-75).

> Tim. *Captain Alcibiades, your heart's in the field now.*
> Alci. *My heart is ever at your service, my lord.*
> Tim. *You had rather be at a breakfast of enemies than*
>   *a dinner of friends.*

The cannibalistic imagery and Alcibiades' vow of service are very much in keeping with Alcibiades' protective nature toward Timon. Alcibiades is what Aristotle would refer to as *"the great-souled man"*. Aristotle defines this type in (ibid., Book IV. iii.).

3 – Now a person is thought to be great-souled if he claims much and deserves much...

8 – The great-souled man is an extreme, by reason of its rightness he stands at the mean point, for he claims what he deserves.

In *Timon of Athens* Alcibiades makes very few requests and is satisfied with little but he does ask for what he deserves. In Act 3 Alcibiades asks for clemency for one of his friends, he pleads for pity to be shown to a soldier who has performed great service to the State (3.6.63-64)

> *he's done fair service*
> *And slain in fight many of your enemies.*

Alcibiades believes in honour, he is motivated by honour, but not blinded by it. Honour is his internal code, he does not need it affirmed by others but he expects it to be respected by all. Aristotle elaborates (ibid., Book IV. iii.).

10-11 – the great-souled man is he who has the right disposition in relation to honours and disgraces…it is honour above all else which great men claim and deserve.

17 – Honour and dishonour then are the objects with which the great-souled man is especially concerned…He will also despise dishonour, for no dishonour can justly attach to him.

Alcibiades tries to use his honour as a type of collateral when dealing with the Senators over a matter regarding the granting of clemency for one of his soldiers. He feels the language of commerce is the only language they will understand (3.6.80-82)

I know your reverend ages love

Security, I'll pawn my victories, all

My honour, to you upon his good returns.

The Senate will not consider mercy and finds Alcibiades obtuseness worthy of contempt and banishes him (3.6.97-99).

Sen. *We banish thee forever.*

Alci. *Banish me?*

Banish your dotage, banish usury.

With this action the Senators have disgraced a man who holds honour and justice as paramount. He will do what he must to recover his lost honour. Aristotle understood this in relation to the great-souled man for he elaborates on his character and his apparent aloofness (ibid., Book IV. iii.).

18 –The great-souled man…will not rejoice overmuch in prosperity, nor grieve overmuch at adversity.

…he therefore to whom even honour is a small thing will be indifferent to other things as well. Hence great-souled men are thought to be haughty.

22 – For the great-souled man is justified in despising other people – his estimates are correct…

23 – The great-souled man does not run into danger for trifling reasons, and is not a lover of danger…but he will face danger in a great cause…

26 – It is also characteristic of the great-souled man never to ask help from others, or only with reluctance but to render aid willingly…

28 – He must be open both in love and in hate, since concealment show timidity…

30 – He is not prone to admiration, since nothing is great to him.

Aristotle's assessment of the great-souled man easily outlines Alcibiades' character explaining both his reluctance to seek help from the Senators and his willingness to go to war against them for a just cause. He sees them as corrupt and calls them corrupt; the great-souled man occupies the moral high ground and sees little need for compromise (ibid., Book IV. iii. 16).

Greatness of Soul seems therefore to be as it were a crowning ornament of the virtues.

Alcibiades and Timon have both 'gifted' the Lords/Senators and citizens of Athens with different labours but both are repaid not with gratitude or even mercy but with exile. Alcibiades has protected the city against its enemies and now finds himself exiled. Timon has certainly treated the elite of Athens as true friends offering them his fortune with open hands (1.2.19-20)

more welcome are ye to my fortunes
Than my fortunes to me

and yet he is exploited by those he trusts. No gratitude is shown and he too suffers an exile, although one that is self imposed (4.1.35-36)

Timon will to the woods, where he shall find
Th'unkindest beast more kinder than mankind.

Alcibiades and Timon deal with their exile in distinctly different ways but each has been subjected to the sin of ingratitude.

Alcibiades seeks a return of his honour through right actions. He has been dishonoured by dishonourable people, this would mean nothing more than water off a duck's back to Alcibiades, but the revelation that Athens is being administered by corrupt officials who do not understand or respect honour would cut him to the quick. Athens deserves better officials and Alcibiades deserves honour. This is reason enough for him to go to war; justice demands it.

Aristotle provides us with some understanding of justice. His definitions help us appreciate its role in Alcibiades' life and perhaps anticipate decisions he will make (ibid., Book V. i.).

15 –Justice…is perfect Virtue…it is displayed towards others. This is why Justice is often thought to be the chief of the virtues…

"In Justice is all Virtue found in sum."

And Justice is perfect Virtue because it is the practice of perfect virtue…because its possessor can practice his virtue towards others and not merely by himself…

17 – Justice alone of the virtues is 'the good of others' because it does what is for the advantage of another…

19 – Justice in this sense then is not a part of Virtue, but the whole of Virtue.

When Alcibiades lays siege to and conquers Athens, he will receive the honour he deserves, that is his due, but he will also insist that justice be done, justice to him and to Timon his friend. Athens will be reformed. Alcibiades' closing words embody Aristotle's ideas of balance and the golden mean; moderation in all things. Alcibiades does not come to defend the status quo, things will change, a Just society is going to be forced into existence. Blood will flow but to the health and benefit of the community (5.5.80-82)

I will use the olive with my sword,

Make war breed peace, make peace stint war, make

each

Prescribe to other, as each other's leech.

Timon's response to betrayal takes him from extremely generous/prodigal to extremely bitter. Aristotle describes this second personality type as well giving us a clear idea of the type of man Timon will become (ibid., Book IV. v.).

10 – The Bitter-tempered on the other hand are implacable, and remain angry a long time, because they keep their wrath in; whereas when a man retaliates there is an end of the matter: the pain of resentment is replaced by the pleasure of obtaining redress, and so his anger ceases. But if they do not retaliate, men continue to labour under a sense of resentment - for as their anger is concealed no one else tries to placate them either, and it takes a long time to digest one's wrath within one. Bitterness is the most troublesome form of bad temper both to a man himself and to his nearest friends.

The other characters in the play are again types and can be seen to embody traits that bracket the mean of friendship. Aristotle describes them and we can easily assign them to the roles of the various lords and tradesmen as well as to the character of Apemantus (ibid., Book IV. vi.).

1 – some men are considered to be obsequious; these are people who complaisantly approve of everything and never raise an objection...

2 – Those on the contrary who object to everything and do not care in the least what pain they cause are called Surly or Quarrelsome.

3 – Now it is clear that the dispositions described are blameworthy, and that the middle disposition between them is praiseworthy...

4 – But to this no special name has been assigned, though it very closely resembles friendship...

9 – The man who always joins in the pleasures of his companions, if he sets out to be pleasant for no ulterior motive, is Obsequious; if he does so for the sake of getting something by it in the shape of money or money's worth, he is a Flatterer. He that disapproves of everything is, as we said, Surly or Quarrelsome.

These characters are brought together for a purpose. Certainly one of these purposes is to demonstrate the need for moderation and to show the virtue in the mean but its other purpose is to reveal something about Gratitude and Vengeance.

Gratitude and Vengeance: Two Halves of the Same Story

Gratitude and vengeance share much in common but before we examine their relationship let's first consider the dynamics of gratitude and its ability to create social bonds.

Gratitude is a response to a freely offered gift. The gift usually provokes a series of responses in the recipient that involve reflection upon the gift, the gift-giver, and some consideration as to how they should reciprocate. Status is a factor in gift-giving. The first giver is initially of a higher status than the receiver as the receiver is indebted to the giver. This lower status remains until the receiver reciprocates.

The giver eventually gets something back. Gift giving is generally done publicly, at parties, or celebrations. This public aspect ensures that others witness the generosity and can praise the giver but also assess the response to the gift, both now and later. There are no laws surrounding the cycle of gifting but the public aspect of display and witness helps to keep the process equitable.

The gift and response are intended to be open-hearted without the desire for profit or gain. The gift should be thoughtful of the needs of the recipient and the recipient, in turn, should reflect upon the gift and the consideration shown in choosing it. It meant the recipient was 'seen' as an individual and their desires understood. It required knowledge of their uniqueness. So too does the response. The cycle of giving, getting and returning created or reinforced community relationships and knowledge of one another; it created bonds. Bonds perhaps started as bonds of obligation over time evolve into bonds of friendship.

In *Timon of Athens* gratitude, this feeling of obligation or indebtedness to another, is undermined. Citizens take Timon's generosity for granted and exploit it as any resource for their own personal benefit. By so doing they are undermining the basis of their society; they are destroying the trust in reciprocity (4.2.39-40)

> *When man's worst sin is he does too much good*
> *Who then dares to be half so kind again?*

Margaret Visser in her book *The Gift of Thanks* (Chpt. 8, The Three Graces) discusses the symbolism of The Three Graces as they relate to gift giving, receiving, and reciprocity. She highlights the harmony, openness, and community spirit they came to represent. These ideas are reflected in Aristotle as well but here they are also linked to a sense of Justice (*Nicomachean Ethics*, Book V. v).

6 – But in the interchange of services Justice in the form of Reciprocity is the bond that maintains the association...

7 – This is why we set up a shrine of the Graces in a public place, to remind men to return a kindness; for that is a special characteristic of grace, since it is a duty not only to repay a service done one, but another time to take the initiative in doing a service oneself.

Gratitude and Vengeance can be viewed as related concepts (Visser, Chpt. 25, Gratitude Instead). The Greeks lived in an honour system. This meant a person's honour could be questioned or injured by another party. The dishonoured man would then be required to recover his lost honour from the offending party. It was a primitive form of justice. Vengeance required balance and fairness; tit for tat, it required thought about what was done and how properly to redress the harm by inflicting it equally on the other party. It meant knowing your enemy. Vengeance made use of the same processes we see in gifting only now used in the service of doing harm.

With gratitude one reflected on one's indebtedness to the giver and how to reciprocate in an equal but different manner; with vengeance one reflected on the harm done or the honour taken from oneself and on how to obtain appropriate redress. With vengeance one spends time hating their enemy and plotting revenge; with gratitude one spends time appreciating the favour and planning an equally thoughtful response.

Vengeance and Gift-exchange are both social strategies and both because of their reciprocity tend to create long lasting patterns of war or peace between different groups.

In *Timon of Athens* the first half of the play exposes us to a society that no longer feels or experiences gratitude. What Timon offers they accept without any feeling of indebtedness. The labours Alcibiades has performed and the sacrifices he has made to defend Athens are also accepted but with no sense of gratitude. The Lords and Senators of Athens suffer from a sense of entitlement. They are selfish, thoughtless and forgetful of the benefits that they have received. All these characteristics undermine any feelings of gratitude, they refuse to be indebted to anyone, and have created a corrupt society of thieves or 'takers'; a society that cannot sustain itself.

Timon is an enabling character to these corrupt Lords but they have chosen to prey on his weakness. When Timon writes on his epitaph *"Here lie I, Timon, who alive all living men did hate"* (5.5.70) it contains a sad truth, for no person would take advantage of someone that they cared for. Timon's generosity is urged on by an uncaring public. Alcibiades' exile only confirms the selfish nature and the sense of superiority harbored by the Athenian Senate.

Gratitude can be described as a positive feeling towards a person; anger is a negative feeling towards another. Often expectations affect which emotion we feel. If a series of events turns out better than we expect we may feel grateful to those who assisted us. If events conspire to dash our expectations we may feel anger towards others involved. In *Timon of Athens*, Timon has expressed his hopes, his expectations, in his belief that he lives in a community of sharing brothers (1.2.101-103)

> *O, what*
>
> *a precious comfort 'tis to have so many like brothers*
>
> *commanding one another's fortunes.*

Unfortunately these expectations are dashed, his 'friends' let him down when he tests (tries) them (2.2.181-184)

> *And in some sort these wants of mine are crowned,*
>
> *...For by these*
>
> *Shall I try friends. You shall perceive how you*
>
> *Mistake my fortune: I am wealthy in my friends.*

But Timon is not wealthy in friends (3.3.6)

> *They have all been touched and found base metal*
>
> *For they have all denied him.*

Timon's dashed expectations leads to anger and his anger is displayed through flinging plates and hurling insults at the people he once trusted (3.7.80-104).

Shifting Worlds

His recognition of this betrayal marks a shift in Timon's world view. The world's soul has changed for Timon. The world's soul was understood as the all permeating soul of God that connected all creation with each other (*Aeneid*, Book VI, lines 724-732).

> *First, you must know that the heavens, the earth, the*
>
> *watery plains*

25

Of the sea, the moon's bright globe, the sun and the stars are all
Sustained by a spirit within; for immanent Mind, flowing
Through all its parts and leavening its mass, makes the universe work.
This union produced mankind, the beasts, the birds of the air,
And the strange creatures that live under the sea's smooth face.
The life-force of those seeds is fire, their source celestial,
But they are deadened and dimmed by the sinful bodies they live in –
The flesh that is laden with death, the anatomy of clay.

This spirit of interconnectedness, of brotherhood, Timon sees displaced by a malevolent spirit of Greed. In *Timon of Athens* the world's soul is now defined by this new uniting element, people's shared self-interest or flatterer's spirit (3.2.66-68)

Why this is the world's soul,
And just of the same piece is every
Flatterer's spirit.

This new world's soul 'uniting' mankind ironically does it through their shared interest in self-interest. A world where greed is king (3.4.4)

Ay, and I think
One business does command us all; for mine
Is money.

Timon's response to this epiphany is to hate all mankind. The presence of a few righteous men does not alter his decision (4.3.491-492)

I do proclaim
One honest man.

This quotation echoes *Genesis* (18.22-33) where Abraham bargained with God not to destroy Sodom and Gomorrah if as few as ten righteous people lived there.

The play's second half begins in Act 4 scene 1; we leave the city of Athens and enter into the woods. Timon who loved all now hates all. From doing everything he could to benefit mankind he now does everything he can to destroy mankind.

He sees nothing good about the world. He sees it only as a corrupt place suitable for destruction. This sentiment ties Timon to Hamlet who held an equally bleak view of Denmark. It also detaches Timon from the rest of society. He isolates himself like an island in the vast ocean of humanity.

Timon, like the Gnostic priests, has removed himself from the world and only takes from it the bare necessities to stay alive. It is apparent that he is readying himself to leave this mortal coil (4.3.371-372)

I am sick of this false world and will love naught

But even the mere necessities upon 't.

Alcibiades' response to exile is to exact justice through vengeance (3.6.109-110;112-113)

Is this the balsam that the usuring senate

Pours into captain's wounds? Banishment.

It is a cause worthy my spleen and fury,

That I may strike at Athens.

Alcibiades is a just man and when he meets with Timon in the woods he grants him the respect he always has. Alcibiades too has fallen on hard times, his men are rebelling and he is low on cash. He commiserates with Timon (4.3.90-95)

I have but little gold of late, brave Timon,

The want whereof doth daily make revolt

In my penurious band. I have heard and grieved
How cursed Athens, mindless of thy worth,
Forgetting thy great deeds when neighbour states
But for thy sword and fortune trod upon them.

Even in his depleted state he is generous to Timon and offers him financial help (4.3.99-100).

Alci. *Here is some gold for thee.*

Tim. *Keep it, I cannot eat it.*

Timon returns the generosity when he finds out Alcibiades plans to lay siege to Athens (4.3.105-107)

That by killing of villains
Thou wast born to conquer my country.
Put up thy gold. Go on, here's gold, go on.

Timon pleads with Alcibiades to unleash total destruction upon Athens (4.3.110-113)

Let not thy sword skip one:
Pity not honoured age for his white beard,
He is an usurer.

He wants the war to salt the earth and turn Athens into nothing but a memory (4.3.118-119)

spare not the babe
Whose dimpled smiles from fools exhaust mercy.

Alcibiades accepts Timon's gold and appreciates the injustices Timon has suffered but he offers him only justice and not genocide (4.3.129-130)

I'll take the gold thou givest me,
Not all thy counsel.

Alcibiades remembers for both Timon and himself. He demands both vengeance and justice. The Senators understand this (5.5.42-43)

Like a shepherd,

Approach the fold and cull th'infected forth,
But kill not all together.

Alcibiades puts the Senators in charge of selecting the offending parties. The Senators know full well that Alcibiades is acting both for himself and Timon. They know that, like gratitude, vengeance remembers. They know they must get their choices right for to deny justice would bring on far greater wrath. They recognize justice when they see it and will not deny it particularly in this case for their own sakes depend upon it (5.5.56-58)

Those enemies of Timon's and mine own
Whom you yourselves shall set out for reproof
Fall, and no more.

Alcibiades is not to be crossed or denied (5.5.64)

Descend, and keep your words.

Ingratitude: The Oldest Social Disease

In *Timon of Athens*, Athens has become a shameless society. It is an ungrateful society. Timon's generosity is not met with gratitude but rather the shameless exploitation of his generosity. The people of Athens care nothing of the rules of honour and are resistant to the pressures of shame. Alcibiades tries to shame the senate only to be met with banishment. Strangers gossip at what they see and conclude that Athens is an ungrateful place (3.2.75-76)

O, see the monstrousness of man
When he looks out in an ungrateful shape.

They see that calculation and self-interest now controls most Athenians (3.2.88-90)

But I perceive
Men must learn now with pity to dispense,
For policy sits above conscience.

Honour and shame are really the only two forces a culture can use to regulate moral matters, i.e., matters that lie outside the law but which still affect the smooth operation of society.

Seneca felt that ingratitude was a part of every sin, for every sin was the result of a breaking away from society (Seneca, *Moral Essays*, Vol. III, On Benefits, I.x.3-4).

Homicides, tyrants, thieves, adulterers, robbers, sacrilegious men, and traitors there always will be; but worse than all these is the crime of ingratitude, unless it be that all these spring from ingratitude, without which hardly any sin has grown to great size.

Gratitude enhanced social cohesion and harmony while ingratitude threatened both. Cicero felt that gratitude was the foundation of Natural law (*The Gift of Thanks*, Visser, Chpt. 12, Unpacking Gratitude, note 21, p.408). Gratitude grew out of love, but love had to be there first and had to be offered freely. A caring society can only develop if caring happens. The caring and love we offer our kin must somehow be extended to the larger group; our natural feelings of love for our families becomes the basis of Natural law which we project onto a larger social structure (Seneca, *Moral Essays*, Vol. III, On Benefits, IV.xviii.1).

To prove to you that the sentiment of gratitude is something to be desired in itself, ingratitude is something to be avoided in itself because there is nothing that so effectually disrupts and destroys the harmony of the human race as this vice. For how else do we live in security if it is not that we help each other by an exchange of good offices? It is only through the interchange of benefits that life becomes in some measure equipped and fortified against sudden disasters. Take us singly, and what are we? The prey of all creatures, their victims, whose blood is most delectable and most easily secured.

Socrates, in his *Crito*, (*The Gift of Thanks*, Visser, p. 91) posits that it is a citizen's obligation to obey the laws of the city. They do this out of gratitude for the benefits they have received over the course of their lives. For they have been afforded the opportunities provided to them through peace, order and good governance. If the feeling of gratitude for benefits received is undermined then so too is the very foundation of the law.

Timon delivers a prayer in (4.1) as he leaves Athens. In it he encourages everyone to turn against moral behaviour and even commit crime. He encourages lawlessness. He curses Athens with plagues and strips himself of any connection he has to the city. For all he cares Athens can sink beneath the sea. Timon is delivering a prophecy of where Athens is headed if it continues on its path of ingratitude. Timon sees what Socrates sees, ingratitude undermining and destroying all the institutions of society. Timon, unlike Socrates, just wishes to speed up the process of decay rather than make any attempt to stop it.

Imagery in Timon

In *Timon of Athens* we are metaphorically exposed to the monstrous beast Athens has become through the constant use of cannibalistic imagery. This undercurrent of imagery tells us that the society is consuming itself, destroying its own chances of survival. The imagery is generously sprinkled throughout the play. I will list a few example of this cannibalistic imagery below:

No, I eat not lords. (1.1.207)

I feed

Most hungrily on your sight. (1.1.258-9)

O you gods, what a number of

men eat Timon and he sees 'em not!

It grieves me to see so many

dip their meat in one man's blood. (1.2.39-41)

I never tasted Timon in my life. (3.2.80)

Cut my heart in sums. (3.4.90)

Tell out my blood. (3.4.92)

Tear me, take me, and the gods fall upon you. (3.4.97)

That the whole life of Athens were in this!

Thus would I eat it. [Eats a root.] (4.3.281-282)

You must eat men. (4.3.420)

Along with the idea of cannibalism is the concept of corruption both in the legal sense and biological sense. Corruption means the breakdown of either morals or of a physical body. In *Timon of Athens* it refers to both. The play is pocked with references to disease corrupting the body and compromising the morals of its citizens. Corruption defines Athens turning rotten; again this is a process that takes place from the inside–out.

(3.1.52-53)

> *Has friendship such a faint and milky heart*
> *It turns in less that two nights?*

(3.1.54-61)

> *This slave*
> *Unto his hour has my lord's meat in him:*
> *Why should it thrive and turn to nutriment,*
> *When he is turned to poison?*
> *O, may diseases only work upon't,*
> *And when he's sick to death, let not that part of nature*
> *Which my lord paid for be of any power*
> *To expel sickness, but prolong his hour!*

(4.1.21-23)

> *Plagues incident to men,*
> *Your potent and infectious fevers heap*

On Athens.

Women, or more precisely prostitutes (as there are no other type of women represented in the play), are seen as a source of disease and corruption again both of morals and the body

(4.3.63-64)

This fell whore of thine

Hath in her more destruction than thy sword

(4.3.83-86)

Be a whore…

Give them diseases…

bring down rose-cheeked youth

(4.3.141)

Be strong in whore, allure him, burn him up.

Timon wishes Athens destroyed and employs all means possible to achieve this goal. His restored wealth buys him the means of vengeance. It secures Alcibiades troops, whores, and numerous thieves. Gold also affords him the chance to meet with and rebuff the Senators. His gold buys him the last word.

These images of corruption and self-destruction go hand-in-hand with the central concept of ingratitude. Ingratitude is a disease that operates from within a society, it slowly destroys the trust one citizen places in another, it leads to the corruption of the whole as the social bonds are broken. Trust evaporates. The healthy community increasingly becomes a loose collection of isolated individuals looking after their own self-interests. Finally the social contract lies in tatters and it's everyman for himself. It marks a return to a type of barbarianism that destroys what little civilization has been created. It truly is a disease that iterate through a community rotting the bonds that hold individuals together.

Timon a god Among Men

Timon can be understood as prodigal in nature but we can also understand much more about him from the play. In *Timon of Athens* we are presented with a very abstract slice of life. This is essentially an all male play except for the presence of a few women who are prostitutes. The meaning is clear; there is no reproduction in this sterile world at least in the biological sense. Nature is sidelined. The only thing that reproduces itself is money. Usury can be said to give birth to money because the lending of money births more money that resembles the parent (*Timon of Athens*, The Arden Shakespeare, 3rd Series, Introduction, p. 80-81). The selling of money and sex were both considered types of usury so it is not surprising that these are the kinds of individuals that populate the play.

In this sterile world Timon is a veritable god, dolling out his bounty on the willing public. He is indiscriminate, like the sun, in his giving. For the sun shines on the just and unjust alike (Matthew 5:45). Timon is imitating God in this aspect. He is operating under the illusion that he is the ultimate source of prosperity in Athens. Timon is not just prodigal he exults in his pride.

These two qualities, pride and prodigality, make him subject to abuse by the citizens of Athens. Gift giving, receiving and reciprocity if balanced and fair, can create bonds but if unfair can create feelings of inferiority and engender hate (*The Gift of Thanks*, Visser, Chpt. 16, Freedom and Equality). In gifting status is involved. The one who gives first puts the receiver under an obligation and temporarily in his debt. This places the receiver is a position of lower status. When the receiver returns the gift he may do so with a gift of equal or slightly greater value, restoring his status and then some. Timon when gifting or reciprocating, consciously or unconsciously, does not allow for equity. He keeps the other in a state of perpetual obligation. This enforced position of lower status can lead to resentment and hate. Consider the case of Ventidius (1.2.6-11).

> Ven. *I do return those talents,*
>
> > *Doubled with thanks and service, from whose help*
> >
> > *I derived liberty.*
>
> Tim. *O, by no means,*
>
> > *Honest Ventidius, you mistake my love:*
> >
> > *I gave it freely ever, and there's none*
> >
> > *Can truly say he gives if he receives.*

Timon has undone reciprocity. People wish to return a favour. By holding them in perpetual obligation you can harm social relations.

Timon's pride certainly feeds his denial that he has any monetary problems but it also gets in the way of his humility or lack thereof. In order to accept a gift one must accept a lower status, allow praise to be given to another. This Timon will not do. He denies reciprocity and always maintains his position by giving first or responding in an incommensurate way (1.1.285-287)

> *no gift to him*
>
> *But breeds the giver a return exceeding*
>
> *All use of quittance.*

This pride also interferes with Timon's sense of awe. In order to experience awe one must experience deep felt gratitude. Experience one's smallness before the grandeur of the universe (*The Gift of Thanks*, Visser, Chpt. 27, Recognition). The people of Athens are not grateful to Timon but neither is Timon grateful to his ancestors or to the world for his blessings. He, like his fellow Athenians, is proud and self-centered. He is just a different symptom of the disease of ingratitude.

Timon is always an outsider in the play. In the first half of the play he acts as the benefactor to all; associating with everyone but maintaining a status higher than the rest (1.2.98-99)

Why, I have often wished

myself poorer that I might come nearer to you.

In the second half of the play he separates himself from everyone through his contempt for all humans. Even Apemantus, a fellow cynic, is rejected by Timon when he comes to provide him with some relief. Timon will not permit himself any fellowship even with another cynic. Timon perceives no kinship with Apemantus. Timon sees Apemantus as a social reformer whose wry comments are intended to shame the shameless. Timon despises the world completely and only wishes its destruction and not its re-education. Timon's prodigality and pride still define him, still isolate him. Apemantus recognizes this for he sees Timon has not checked his pride (4.3.238-240)

If thou didst put this sour cold habit on

To castigate thy pride, t'were well; but thou

Dost it enforcedly.

Prodigality and pride still define Timon (4.3.276-278).

Ape. *Art thou proud yet?*

Tim. *Ay, that I am not thee.*

Ape. *Ay, that I was no prodigal.*

Tim. *Ay, that I am one now.*

Timon's Furies

Timon's pride and prodigality made him think of himself like a god. It is from this conceptual height that Timon's behaviour becomes understandable. It explains his isolation from others. There is something god-like in this separation. The bountiful giving of the first half of the play and violent fury expressed in the second half of the play are reminiscent of the behaviour of the ancient Greek gods. In fact the play's structure is very reminiscent of Aeschylus's drama *The Eumenides*.

In *The Eumenides* we are shown how the Furies bring destruction upon those who are guilty of certain crimes, patricide being one of them (murdering one's parent being the ultimate expression of ingratitude). In *The Eumenides*, Vengeance gives way to Blessings. The Furies, goddesses of vengeance are turned into Eumenides, responsible for bringing blessings to mankind (*The Gift of Thanks*, Visser, Chpt. 25, Gratitude Instead). Aeschylus's play shows the evolution of the Furies from being the deliverers of perpetual rage and blight to their becoming deities that are honoured for bringing blessings (*Greek Tragedies*, Vol.3, *The Eumenides*, Aeschylus, translated by Richard Lattimore, p. 1 - 41). This changing of the Furies to the Eumenides happens all at once. They go from being vengeance fiends to promoters of peace in response to a gift from the Athenians. They promise in return to prevent civil war (*The Eumenides*, line 976-977)

> *Civil war*
> *Fattening on men's ruin shall*
> *Not thunder in our city.*

They change the colour of their robes from black to red and promise to remain Eumenides doling out blessings as long as the citizens of Athens do not betray their benevolence towards one another (*The Eumenides*, line 984-985)

> *Let them render grace for grace.*
> *Let love be their common will.*

The Eumenides retain the possibility, however, of changing back into the bat-winged, iron-footed Furies should the citizens of Athens betray this benevolence they afford one another. For *"What man who fears nothing at all is ever righteous?"* (*The Eumenides*, line 699).

Timon of Athens can be conceived of as a continuation of Aeschylus's tale. The Athenians have betrayed the benevolence they have received from their fellow Athenians, Timon and Alcibiades. The

Eumenides are free to become the Furies once more, to punish this ingratitude. They accomplish this by harnessing Alcibiades' sense of justice with Timon's fury. Timon's rage and his new found wealth are now released to deliver great harm rather than great benefit. Blessing has become Fury. The civil war Athens avoided in *The Eumenides* now becomes a reality as Alcibiades conquers the city. Sacrifices will have to be made and gifts offered if the Furies are to become the Eumenides once more. Athens will not receive benefits until social order can be restored. This can only happen if gifts of thankfulness and a sense of gratitude returns to its citizens for this is the very basis of all law and order (3.7.68-70).

> *The gods require our thanks:*
> *You great benefactors, sprinkle our society with*
> *thankfulness.*

There are several aspects in *Timon of Athens* that tie into Aeschylus's drama. First is the continuation of the dog imagery. The Furies were regarded as the 'dogs of Hades'. The Furies also share Alcibiades' sense of justice, that same sense of justice that the Senators appealed to in (5.5.42-43). Aeschylus expresses their blameless justice in *The Eumenides* (line 312-315).

> *We hold we are straight and just. If a man*
> *can spread his hands and show they are clean,*
> *no wrath of ours shall lurk for him.*
> *Unscathed he walks through his life time.*

Their similarity to Alcibiades is also found in line 383.

> *For we are strong and skilled;*
> *we have authority; we hold*
> *memory of evil.*

Alcibiades wants justice both for himself and Timon; memory plays a key role in both gratitude and revenge.

Timon's rage (4.1.1- 41) is very similar to the rage expressed by one of the Furies when their traditional laws were set aside in the special case made for Orestes, (*The Eumenides*, line 778-787).

> *Gods of the younger generation, you have ridden down*
>
> *the laws of the elder time, torn them out of my hands.*
>
> *I, disinherited, suffering, heavy with anger*
>
> *shall let loose on the land*
>
> *the vindictive poison*
>
> *dripping deadly out of my heart upon the ground;*
>
> *this from itself shall breed*
>
> *cancer, the leafless, the barren*
>
> *to strike, for the right, their low lands*
>
> *and drag its smear of mortal infection on the ground.*

Timon expresses the self same wish, that the Athenian society will become a poison to itself.

The Furies/Eumenides are gods (*The Eumenides*, line 929-930)

> *To them is given the handling entire*
>
> *of men's lives.*

When the Athenian society was just they were given the right to dole out benefits (*The Eumenides*, line 895)

> *No household shall be prosperous without your will.*

Timon mimics the Eumenides; he distributes his bounty for other's prosperity. He expects benevolence and gratitude in return but instead receives only shameless indifference. This lack of gratitude drives him to mimic the Furies in his rage against mankind. He flees the city he hates and chooses to live in a cave. This too echoes *The Eumenides* for they are an underground divinity born from Uranus' blood that fell on Gaea, the earth. They are the 'Daughters of the Earth and Shadow' (*The Eumenides*, line 1022-1023)

> *and by the light of flaring torches now attend*

your passage to the deep and subterranean hold.

The Eumenides were also capable of bestowing the earth's wealth on whomever they choose (*The Eumenides*, line 944-947).

Earth be kind
to them...Secret child
of earth, her hidden wealth, bestow
blessing and surprise of gods.

It can be argued that the Eumenides conferred the gold upon Timon. The earth's treasure became Timon's treasure to exact the appropriate revenge on an ungrateful Athens. But Timon is not a god, not a Fury, he is only a reflection of these. Soon after the Eumenides have rewarded him with gold he prays to the Furies to once more make the earth dry and sterile (4.3.186-187)

Ensear thy fertile and conceptious womb,
Let it no more bring out ungrateful man.

Timon's pride and fury have undone him. His pride has isolated him and his fury has been turned on even himself. He has become the unicorn he describes (4.3.334-336)

Wert thou the
unicorn, pride and wrath would confound thee and
make thine own self the conquest of thy fury.

Gnostic Timon?

Timon's pride and fury, his extremity, makes him more like a demon or an angel than a human. Timon, like the rest of Athens, is ungrateful; he is ungrateful for his life, and for the blessings he has received. He plans his own death (5.2.70-73)

Why, I was writing of my epitaph
It will be seen tomorrow. My long sickness
of health and living now begins to mend

and nothing brings me all things.

The gnostic spirit is evoked by these lines. The very unchristian idea that the world was created by Satan and only the Heavens by God. The gnostic philosophy survived into the middle ages as the Cathar religion. To elaborate slightly, the Cathar's felt that the world was the handiwork of Satan; that all matter was corrupt. The god deserving of worship was not the god of this world but rather the god of Light who ruled the ethereal, invisible, spiritual domain in heaven. To find salvation was to renounce a material life and choose a life of self-denial. If one did not do this they would keep returning to this world, i.e., be reincarnated until such time as they were ready to embrace a life of material and physical denial. Once this spotless state was achieved the soul would ascend back to its home in heaven. The Cathars believed we created our own hell on earth and our punishment was in our continuous reincarnation in this plane of existence.

The Cathars were referred to as dualists because they believed in two principles of creation; Evil created the visible world and Good created the invisible world. Within every human was a divine spark that belonged to heaven (*Aeneid*, Book VI, lines 724-732, quoted earlier). This remnant of god was waiting in us patiently to be freed from the cycle of reincarnation to find its way back to heaven.

When one reads the quotation from the *Aeneid* and considers Timon's final resting place, the imagery in both converges. Timon's grave is to be where the heavens meet the earth and the sea (5.2.100-103)

Timon hath made his everlasting mansion
Upon the beached verge of the salt flood,
Who once a day with his embossed froth
The turbulent surge shall cover.

The Cathars were pious and believed in the Bible but they interpreted it in a uniquely gnostic way. Their point of view was informed by both Greek philosophy and Hermetic wisdom. Their material divorce from this world was certainly supported by Biblical texts such as:

> (John 18:36) *My kingdom is not of this world...*
>
> (Matt.6:24) *No man can serve two masters...*
>
> *Ye cannot serve God and money.*

Timon despairs of living and he despairs of all life. He only sees corruption. He wishes to speed both his end and the end of the world. When one reflects on the conversation of the strangers (3.2.66-68) you can see how Timon's world view could have radically changed, that it could have undergone an epiphany. If the World Soul was no longer one interconnected by love, sharing and harmony and if in fact the World Soul was like the strangers perceived, one of greed and doing things only for personal gain, then it is easy to imagine Timon adopting the dualist view; that the world was the creation of Satan, and if so then damn it all.

Commerce vs. Gifting

Timon of Athens deals mainly with the consequence of ingratitude but part of Timon's downfall comes about because of his venturing into the market economy. He borrows money with which he buys gifts. The borrowing of money is regulated by the legal system but gift giving and reciprocity is only regulated by the recipient's sense of morality (2.2.230-231)

> *Ne'er speak, or think,*
>
> *That Timon's fortunes 'mong his friends can sink.*

The market economy is about profit, the gift economy about building relationships. The market economy relies on a universal currency, traditionally gold. The gift economy profits through unique gifts matched to the needs or desires of the recipient. It thrives on surprise. The market economy remembers dates, amounts, and when debts are due. Contracts guarantee memory. In the gift economy, gifts are freely given without expectation of return. When and if reciprocity occurs is solely dependent on the recipient who will choose when and how to express their gratitude for the gift received. The response even if not equitable may be deeply moving. The gift and response are within each person's means. The market economy avoids emotional entanglements and may or may not develop long term relationships. The gift economy's whole point is to create long lasting relationships that emotionally tie together the groups or individuals.

Timon has given freely to Athens. He expects gratitude. He expects help in his time of need. What he meets up with is the market economy, a soulless entity which cares not who he is nor what favours he has done in the past. All that matters is how much he owes and when he must pay (2.2.38-41)

> *How goes the world, that I am thus encountered*
> *With clamourous demands of broken bonds*
> *And the detention of long-since-due debts*
> *Against my honour?*

This growing market economy threatens the ties that bind society together. It isolates individuals and makes their relations with others colder. The market economy specializes in faceless, emotionless transactions. There is little room for friendship in business relationships (3.1.41-43)

> *this is no time*
> *to lend money, especially upon bare friendship without*
> *security.*

God is Gold

Gold is the universal currency for trade. With it one can buy whatever they desire (4.3.149)

Believe't that we'll do anything for gold.

In Timon's world it is also the universal god (5.1.46-47)

What a god's gold, that he is worshipped

In a baser temple than where swine feed!

The desire for gold is the madness that corrupts Timon's world. Timon, like the sun, distributes his bounty on everyone but his recipients horde the blessings like thieves. They take what they can from Timon and return nothing to anyone without charging interest. It is a greed not just for money but also for benefit (as shown by the Alcibiades subplot) that has corrupted the Athenians. They have become shameless in their taking.

This is why the strangers have perceived a shift in the world soul. This is why Timon sees everything in his world, even nature, as a thief (4.3.430-437)

I'll example you with thievery:

The sun's a thief and with his great attraction

Robs the vast sea; the moon's an arrant thief

And her pale fire she snatches from the sun;

The sea's a thief whose liquid surge resolves

The moon into salt tears; the earth's a thief

That feeds and breeds by a composture stol'n

From general excrement. Each things' a thief.

The world soul has changed for Timon from the world that was interconnected and interdependent, joined together by God's soul; a soul of love and sharing. This world view was reflected in his earlier speech (1.2.99-103) and refrained here in (2.2.177-179)

If I would broach the vessels of my love

And try the argument of hearts by borrowing,

Men and men's fortunes could I frankly use

As I can bid thee speak.

Timon has come from seeing the world as a loving God's creation to seeing it as the creation of a Thief. Gnosticism is reflected in this changing view. It explains Timon's lack of 'awe' in the world; he can hate everything because nothing reflects God. Leaving this world is Timon's only way to find his way back to a world he has lost, a world of fellowship and sharing. Gold can't take him back to his old life; his blinders have been removed. His innocence is lost. He has discovered that he has no friends and gold cannot buy him any. It cannot buy him the love he seeks. It cannot buy him gratitude. He does not desire to live in a corrupt world. All the things he desires gold cannot buy. At best gold can remain asleep (4.3.288-290).

Ape. *Here is no use for gold.*

Tim. *The best and truest,*

   For here it sleeps and does no hired harm.

At worst gold corrupts everything. Taints all relationships. Confounds the truth (4.3.25-26; 28-30)

What is here?

Gold? Yellow, glittering, precious gold?

Thus much of this will make

Black white, foul fair, wrong right,

Base noble, old young, coward valiant.

Timon, like the Cathar priests, can only find happiness in death (*nothing brings me all things*). His return to a loving God. Timon's only use for gold is to destroy the world; his altered world view allows him to see no possible good for the world for the world itself is evil. The quicker it goes into oblivion the better. The sooner he leaves the better.

Conclusion

Part of Timon's tragedy is that he never knew moderation, never knew the mean. His character always occupied the extreme margins of behaviour. Always proud, always wasteful, always driven by slim purpose. He was a character hungry for the affection of the masses (4.3.258-263)

> *But myself –*
> *Who had the world as my confectionary,*
> *The mouths, the tongues, the eyes and hearts of men*
> *At duty more than I could frame employment,*
> *That numberless upon me stuck as leaves*
> *Do on the oak.*

He adored being doted on until he discovered he had not earned their love but rather purchased it. When gratitude was not returned, fury over took him. His gold did not buy him friendship but it could purchase destruction (4.3.110)

> *Let not thy sword skip one.*

The Furies and Eumenides inform Timon's character and a gnostic cynicism infects his consciousness but the trigger that sets off the tragedy is Ingratitude.

The Athens we see destroyed is not the Athens that will replace it. Alcibiades' character threatens to ensure balance (5.5.80-82). The all male cabal of usurers that exploited Timon will meet with justice. Gratitude will be enforced until true bonds of friendship are restored. Exploitation of others will be a thing of the past, the people of Athens will be the witnesses to ensure that favours granted will be remembered and returned. Shame will replace shamelessness. They will become a Thankful people; if not Fury will return.

Seneca (*Moral Essays*, Vol. III, I.3.4) on The Graces:

Why do the sisters hand in hand dance in a ring which returns upon itself? For the reason that a benefit passing in its course from hand to hand returns nevertheless to the giver; the beauty of the whole is destroyed if the course is anywhere broken, and it has most beauty if it is continuous and maintains an uninterrupted succession.

It is the constant flow, the uninterrupted succession of favours granted, remembered and returned that guarantee society's growth and sustenance. This endless exchange, this harmony, provides the fruitful ground for the imagery that describes the gift of thankfulness.

Bibliography

1) *Timon of Athens*, W. Shakespeare and T. Middleton, edited by Anthony B. Dawson and Gretchen Minton, The Arden Shakespeare, 3rd Series, Cengage Learning, 2008.

2) *The Nicomachean Ethics*, Aristotle, translation by H. Rackham, The Loeb Classical Library, Harvard University Press, 1956.

3) *The Gift of Thanks; The Roots, Persistence, and Paradoxical Meanings of a Social Ritual*, Margaret Visser, Harper Collins Publ. Ltd., 2008.

4) *The Eclogues, Georgics, and Aeneid of Virgil*, translation by C. Day Lewis, Oxford University Press, 1974.

5) *Greek Tragedies*, Vol. 3, Aeschylus, Sophocles, Euripides, edited by David Grene and Richard Lattimore, University of Chicago Press, 1972.

6) *The Perfect Heresy*, The Life and Death of the Cathars, Stephen O'Shea, Profile Books Ltd., 2001.

7) *Moral Essays*, Seneca, vol.3, transl. by John Basore, The Loeb Classical Library, Harvard University Press, 2006.

8) *Timon of Athens and the Morality Tradition*, L. Walker, Shakespeare Studies, 12, 1979, p. 159-177.

Abstract for *Troilus and Cressida*
Combinatorics in *Troilus and Cressida*

Combinatorics is a simple science; it is the study of combinations. What I suggest in this essay is that *Troilus and Cressida* can be understood in this way. The major concepts in the play – war and love, the interests of the community and the individual, the noble and the base – combine in so many and in such varied ways as to produce a highly interlaced drama that champions moral ambiguity as a form of hope.

Combinatorics in *Troilus and Cressida*

Introduction

Troilus and Cressida is a tightly woven work exploring the relationship between 'the one' and 'the many', between order and chaos, and between love and war. It is written in a series of parallel texts; one taking place on the Martian battlefield the other on the Venerean battlefield. These texts mimic and echo each other – each manifesting a different conflict in our divided nature. The texts pertaining to honour in the Greek camp apply to considerations of love in the Trojan city. War affects love and love is seen in the acts of war. The concepts penetrate and inform each other. War and love, honour and desire, become inseparable in the text of *Troilus and Cressida*.

In terms of plot we are dropped into the middle of the Trojan War. The past is set in the war and the future will take place in the war. The war neither begins nor ends in the slice of time that makes up the background to this play. The time frame is set by one love affair which we see blossom and die. The war that occurs around this affair helps to explain and inform our understanding of it. The affair, in turn, helps to explain and inform our perception of the war.

Troilus and Cressida can be regarded more than any of Shakespeare's plays as a 'relativistic drama'. Point of View is everything. Moral judgments are difficult to make because they depend on whose point of view you accept to define the situation. It is a play that highlights the relative nature of ethics. There is no moral center in this play. When one considers the other plays written around this time (1603) like *Hamlet* and *Othello* one discovers a distinctly different kind of morality. You may sympathize with Othello but you never think he is morally justified in his action. There is a clear morality in *Othello*. The same can be said of *Hamlet*. We understand, we empathize but we never lose sight of the fact that Hamlet is committing grievous errors in his quest for revenge. In *Troilus and Cressida* the morality is ambiguous; no one is clearly a villain or a hero. Everybody is morally compromised. The moral scale becomes a grey scale, nothing is black or white, some actions are a little worse than others and some a little better.

Because of the integrated nature of the work, because events discussed in the Greek camp apply to situations in the Trojan world and vise versa I feel the play may best be discussed in a chronological order, following Time's lead. This way we can maintain some sense of orientation in a play that is designed like a hall of mirrors. What I will try to do is to refer to a specific scene, discuss concepts that the scene introduces, show how these concepts find resonance in other sections of the play and then progress on to the next scene. This way we will ratchet our way back and forth through the play but all the time letting the play's basic structure guide us; but first some background.

Time and Fate

Time can be thought of as a character in *Troilus and Cressida* because it participates in the action of the play. Time allows for events to unfold but it also allows for accidents to happen and the unforeseen to take place. Time and Fate are related and connected concepts.

Fate is from the Latin *fatum*, which means, "a thing said" (*Beyond Fate*, M. Visser, p. 21). A curse is a *fatum*; it is a thing said that must come to pass. The prophecies of Cassandra also qualify as these too must come to pass. A curse and a prophecy can be viewed as creatures of time just as we are. We all are relevant for only a span of time.

Troilus and Cressida is a play that uses time, not in a dramatic way, like *Romeo and Juliet*, where timing (not time) is of the essence. In *Troilus and Cressida* time is an inevitability, it is fate. Troy will fall, love will pass, and all will become dust, inevitably. There will be no survivors in the end. It is tragic and sounds cynical but it is only factual. We, as the audience, know this more than anybody; the story of the fall of Troy is common knowledge, the acceptance of our own passing less so.

Time encompasses us as individuals. It binds us. It is a part of our 'to be'. Our actions depend on it until we act no more, until we 'be' no more. Time encircles us like an imprisoning wall, we cannot escape our time.

Fate can also be seen as encircling especially when force, oppression by power, personifies Fate. In *Troilus and Cressida* the Greek army, for seven years, has been an ever present force testing the walls of Troy. The lives of the people within Troy have become a little smaller because of this. Fate, in the shape of the Greek forces, has diminished each of them and restricted their options. Boundaries place limits on us; boundaries limit our growth.

The Greeks believed that the universe came out of boundlessness (*Beyond Fate*, M. Visser, Chapter IV, Transgression) but once it was defined, boundaries arose as a consequence of the limits placed on it. In ancient Greece the word for fate is *moira* derived from the verb meaning both to receive one's portion and to be divided from (*Beyond Fate*, Visser, p.35). In a limited world everyone received their portion but since life was movement it meant boundaries would be crossed. *Hybris* was a term the Greeks used for the crossing of boundaries; this was seen as a transgression, the consequence of which was disorder, chaos. When boundaries were crossed another person's portion or *moira* was threatened. The act of transgression may require an act of revenge both as a form of justice and to re-establish balance.

The Trojan War was the consequence of crossing boundaries. Hesione, Priam's sister, was abducted by the Greeks for a grievance against Priam's father, Laomedon. Priam, in retribution for this, ordered the abduction of Helen from the Greeks. Menelaus, Helen's husband, responding to this action launched the invasion of Troy, Priam's city. Women were considered 'property'; they were personified versions of honour. To take a woman was to take property, to cross boundaries, to steal another's honour; it required an appropriate response. This world view by its very nature creates a series of 'tit for tat' reprisals as a primitive form of justice. Such a system is by necessity ongoing, self perpetuating, and often generational. It is why the Greeks viewed all creation as a battleground where boundaries were constantly tested and often crossed.

In *Troilus and Cressida* we are looking at a world of walled cities and bounded individuals. They are bounded physically, by their circumstances and by the expectations placed on them.

Boundaries

Birth is our beginning and death our end. Life is like a line and time connects the points of our existence (*Beyond Fate*, Visser, Chapter I, Drawing a Line). The individual life – the selfish life – is focused on oneself. It is a life of limitation and inward contemplation. We are bounded, limited, and walled in by our physical selves. It is the physical that gives us shape and partly defines who we are, keep in mind Cressida's plea (3.2.123-124)

> *And yet, good faith, I wished myself a man,*
> *Or that we women had men's privilege.*

Her life, her fate, is partly in the hands of others just because of her sex, her physical outline. This physical aspect partly defines who we are; the other part is defined by circumstances – the word literally means "things standing in a ring around" (Visser, p.34). These events that take place around our lives enclose us and create us. They are the events that 'define us' for they are the events that we react to and sometimes they are the events that we create.

In *Troilus and Cressida* we encounter different examples of this idea of enclosure. In the Prologue, we are told that the Greeks have come to ransack the enclosed city of Troy (Prologue 7-10)

> *...and their vow is made*
>
> *To ransack Troy, within whose strong immures*
>
> *The ravished Helen, Menelaus' queen,*
>
> *With wanton Paris sleeps.*

This prologue further introduces us to other strong themes that will reoccur throughout the play – the idea of enclosure both communal and individual, and ideas associating war and love. For instance, the Greeks lie outside Troy waiting for their opportunity to penetrate her strong walls – an example of war filled with sexual innuendo. This image from the macrocosm is immediately related to a more intimate example from the microcosm: Helen's personal boundaries have been violated; she is the ravished queen. The prologue alerts us to the fact that boundaries that define the community and the individual are going to be explored in the play and that individual boundaries are going to invade community boundaries.

When considering the idea of boundaries, the play explores physical boundaries and psychological boundaries. The most visceral example is that concerning Hector. Hector's suit of armor protects his person much like the city walls protect Troy. Both are physical barriers against intrusion. Late in the play Hector sees a suit of armor he wishes to take from its owner as a spoil of war. His pursuit of this armour meshes ideas of war and rape much as the prologue did (5.6.29-33)

> *I like thy armour well;*
>
> *I'll frush it and unlock the rivets all,*
>
> *But I'll be master of it.*

[Exit one in armour.]

Wilt thou not, beast, abide?

Why then, fly on. I'll hunt thee for thy hide.

[Exit in pursuit].

Desire drives Hector in pursuit of a suit of armour, a very similar word to the French, 'amour', for love. Hector pursues, assaults, and strips his victim (5.9.1-2)

[Enter Hector dragging the Greek in armour].

Most putrefied core, so fair without,

Thy goodly armour thus hath cost thy life.

Hector's words are ironic for as he strips off his own armour

(5.9.4.1)[He starts to disarm]

he is set upon by Achilles and his Myrmidons. This time it's Hector's armour that will cost a life, his own (5.9.9-10.1)

I am unarmed. Forgo this vantage, Greek

[They fall upon Hector and kill him].

Stabbing Hector with long phallic swords, the swords repeatedly entering his body, is just one more image of rape and the violation of individuals' boundaries. This scene graphically illustrates the violence that can be associated with violating another's physical boundaries; it is a foreshadowing of the fall of Troy.

Cressida's story parallels Hector's but instead of physical boundaries it gives us some insight into the nature of psychological boundaries. She fears that if she opens up to Troilus, drops her defenses, that he will see himself as her conqueror and master (1.2.280; 284)

Men prize the thing ungained more than it is.

'Achievement is command; ungained, beseech!

Cressida is not in mortal danger if she drops her psychological defenses but she is putting herself in an emotionally vulnerable position. The death that Cressida fears is the death of the self, her individuality.

She knows how to protect her person, Pandarus teases her about this when he points out that no one can know what defense she will employ in any given situation (*at what ward you lie*). She responds (1.2.251-255)

> *Upon my back to defend my belly, upon my*
> *wit to defend my wiles, upon my secrecy to defend*
> *mine honesty, my mask to defend my beauty, and you*
> *to defend all these; and at all these wards I lie, at a*
> *thousand watches.*

Cressida defends herself and expects her guardian to defend her as well. She hopes that she has put up double walls. Pandarus, however, seems to be taken with Troilus and attempts to sing his praises to Cressida (1.2.243-246)

> *Do you know what a man is? Is not*
> *birth, beauty, good shape, discourse, manhood,*
> *learning, gentleness, virtue, youth, liberality and so*
> *forth the spice and salt that season a man?*

To this Cressida responds (1.2.247-248)

> *Ay, a minced man; and then to be baked with*
> *no date in the pie, for then the man's date is out.*

This cryptic remark means: where's the place for a woman (sweetness) in his life? Where's the place for her? She has some doubt about Troilus' ability to commit and harbours the same doubts within herself. She also fears for her independence, not sure she wants to be part of 'the one pie'. Cressida expresses these concerns in her soliloquy (1.2.273-286) and plans to delay Troilus as much as possible for as she expresses "*Yet hold I off. Women are angels, wooing; Things won are done*". She fears that only lust fuels his passion for her, that Troilus has only a limited attention span.

When she finally confesses that she has loved him from the start, she is taking off her armour (3.2.112-114),

> Tro. *Why was my Cressid then so hard to win?*
>
> Cres. *Hard to seem won; but I was won, my lord,*
>
> *With the first glance*

she is shocked by her own honesty. She feels this confession gives Troilus too much power in their relationship, that she has exposed too much of her 'real' self to him (3.2.115)

> *If I confess much, you will play the tyrant.*

She is at once wanting to trust, to join with him and at the same time wanting to keep another self in reserve. A self not bound to him. A self not lost in their relationship, in their 'coupledom'. A self capable of escape, of looking after the 'Cressida' she loves (3.2.143-145)

> *I have a kind of self resides with you,*
>
> *But an unkind self that itself will leave*
>
> *To be another's fool.*

She is clearly of two minds over the prospect; she expresses the uncommitted fearfulness of doubt. One part loves Troilus but another part wants to protect herself. It is an issue of trust. She attempts to be both committed and non-committed. It is a military strategy of always leaving yourself a way of escape, a chance at retreat. She loves Troilus but she does not yet trust Troilus. Love can happen at first glance but trust can only be gained over time.

Cressida tries to get Troilus to reveal something of himself, she angles for his thoughts, essentially she is trying to get Troilus to admit that he loves her too now that she has 'put it out there' so to speak. She admits to her verbal clumsiness (3.2.148)

> *I show more craft than love.*

This comment reveals something Cressida believes about love, she believes that it is unconditional, she knows she should not be seeking reassurance, she acknowledges this weakness in herself but she does not wish to be alone in her feeling.

Hector's war story and Cressida's love story echo each other and provide visual metaphors for the fears felt and dangers faced. How terrible the consequences for both should the walls be breached, the armour pierced, and the person be dismembered. The love story and the war story both carry extreme consequences for missteps taken.

Passions and Desires

We know that war (blood lust) and love (lust of the flesh) both assail, both conquer and both enslave; we also know that war and love fully engage the passions or one's desires. This assumption is confirmed in Troilus' first few lines of dialogue: his heart is under siege (1.1.1-5)

> *Call here my varlet; I'll unarm again.*
> *Why should I war without the walls of Troy,*
> *That find such cruel battle here within?*
> *Each Trojan that is master of his heart,*
> *Let him to field; Troilus, alas, hath none.*

We also discover that Troilus is leaving the battlefield because he is too distracted by his feelings of love. Just as Troilus is engaged in a battle to win Cressida so is Agamemnon engaged in a battle to win Troy. The language of warfare and love are very similar and this leads to an easy crossover and intermingling of their imagery. This is partly what creates a unity to the play.

As Troilus is engaged in an emotional battle to win Cressida, Agamemnon is engaged in a physical battle to win Troy. Neither has achieved their goal and both the warrior and the lover speak of the need for patience (1.3.12)

> *That after seven years' siege yet Troy walls stand*

versus (3.2.110-111)

> *I have loved you night and day*
>
> *For many weary months.*

Both individuals are being tested, Agamemnon with Jove's trials (1.3.18-21)

> *Do you with cheeks abashed behold our works*
>
> *And think them shames, which are indeed naught else*
>
> *But the protractive trials of great Jove*
>
> *To find persistive constancy in men?*

and Troilus with Cressida's indifference and Pandarus' speeches (1.1.14-24).

> *Pan. He that will*
>
> > *have a cake out of the wheat must tarry the grinding.*
>
> *Tro. Have I not tarried?*
>
> *Pan. Ay, the grinding; but you must tarry the bolting.*
>
> *Tro. Have I not tarried?*
>
> *Pan. Ay, the bolting; but you must tarry the leavening.*
>
> *Tro. Still have I tarried.*
>
> *Pan. Ay, to the leavening; but here's yet in the word*
>
> > *hereafter the kneading, the making of the cake, the*
> >
> > *heating the oven, and the baking. Nay, you must stay*
> >
> > *the cooling too, or ye may chance burn your lip.*

As long-winded as Pandarus' speech is it is comparable to the speeches of Agamemnon and Nestor concerning the trials placed before the Greeks and how it is testing their determination (1.3.1-54) – the argument of which can virtually be summarized in one line (1.3.33-34)

> *In the reproof of chance*
>
> *Lies the true proof of men.*

Both Nestor and Agamemnon blame unforeseen circumstances for their failures; this is something we will see Troilus do as well (4.4.54) *"No remedy"*. None of these characters attempts to change the nature of those circumstances. This is where Ulysses steps in – he does not agree with Agamemnon and Nestor that they must just keep trying and endure – he feels that the problem lies in insubordination and he focuses his reproof on one man, Achilles. He feels that pride has made Achilles ungovernable (1.3.144-146)

> *Having his ear full of his airy fame,*
> *Grows dainty of his worth and in his tent*
> *Lies mocking our designs.*

Achilles only does what he wishes to; he is a physical, sensual character who sees little merit in the thinking or planning done by the other generals (1.3.198-200). He counts *"wisdom as no member of the war"* and esteems *"no act / But that of the hand"*.

Because of Achilles' selfishness he breeds a selfishness in others, like Ajax. Everyman is beginning to feed their own pride and look after their own interests. This breakdown of the community and community goals is driven by the individuals' selfish desires and is fueled by their passions. Ulysses believes that it is not circumstances that are defeating their efforts but themselves (1.3.137)

> *Troy in our weakness lives, not in her strength.*

Ulysses sees this 'everyman for himself' policy embodied in Achilles as destructive to both order and community. Ulysses sees it as a revolt of passion (human hunger or desire) over reason; he believes the consequence of such a revolt is the destruction of community and civilization. Ulysses fears a 'might is right' policy if everyone follows Achilles' lead (1.3.114-116)

> *Strength should be lord of imbecility,*
> *And the rude son should strike his father dead;*
> *Force should be right.*

Ulysses fears a future where power is controlled only by the appetite and since desire can never be satisfied he sees a world that inevitably must consume itself (1.3.119-124)

> *Then everything includes itself in power,*
> *Power into will, will into appetite;*
> *And appetite, an universal wolf,*
> *So doubly seconded with will and power*
> *Must make perforce an universal prey*
> *And last eat up himself.*

The resulting chaos is to no one's advantage. This idea of the dangers presented when 'desire runs the show' is understood and echoed by Cressida near the end of the play. Shakespeare has taken his earlier idea voiced by Ulysses about the macrocosm and made it intimate and personal; Cressida speaks of moral compromise rather than universal destruction (5.2.115-118)

> *Ah, poor our sex! This fault in us I find:*
> *The error of our eye directs our mind.*
> *What error leads must err. O, then conclude:*
> *Minds swayed by eyes are full of turpitude* (baseness).

Cressida is saying that when our decisions are made only based on worldly desires that they must, by necessity, be in error and result in moral compromise. Her conclusions are not as far reaching as Ulysses' apocalypse, they speak more about feelings of personal failure, the fact that life forces us to compromise our ideals.

The One and The Many

As individuals we yearn for freedom to do and be what we please, but we are not totally self-sufficient; we depend on others, our family, friends, and community. These others detract from our personal freedom, make demands, reduce possibilities and assign us roles. Living in communities involves obeying rules otherwise the order, safety, and structure it provides is lost. This is why Achilles must be brought into line; he has transgressed too many social boundaries, become 'too big for his britches', he has asserted too much of his individual power, become too obsessed with his own concerns. Achilles has broken away from his social group and must be brought back under its control before others follow his example and assert their own individuality. Self-involved renegades do not make a good army. This is why Ulysses defends the rights of the community, 'the many', over the rights of the individual, 'the one'. Ulysses' speech points out how social order is the basis of society and how without it social harmony breaks down (1.3.101-110)

> *O, when degree is shaked,*
> *Which is the ladder to all high designs,*
> *The enterprise is sick. How could communities,*
> *Degrees in schools and brotherhoods in cities,*
> *Peaceful commerce from dividable shores,*
> *The primogeneity and due of birth,*
> *Prerogative of age, crowns, scepters, laurels,*
> *But by degree stand in authentic place?*
> *Take but degree away, untune that string,*
> *And hark what discord follows.*

Ulysses sees Achilles as the beginning of this untuning of the Greek camp; Achilles is not respecting his superiors, not accepting his place in the hierarchy. Ulysses blames Achilles and to a lesser extent Achilles' friends, Patroclus and Thersites, for demoralizing the camp (1.3.197-199)

> *They tax our policy and call it cowardice,*
> *Count wisdom as no member of the war,*
> *Forestall prescience, and esteem no act*

> *But that of hand*

by undermining the decisions of the other generals. Ulysses fears Achilles' insolence is infecting others (1.3.187-188)

> *Many are infect.*
>
> *Ajax is gown self-willed.*

Ulysses further hopes that by bringing Achilles back into compliance with the group he will end this insurrection. For Ulysses the needs of the many outweigh the rights of the few.

Cressida's story is a mirror image of this; it picks up on the same themes but views them from the individual's point of view. Cressida, in a prior scene, has argued that the individual must protect themselves and that their guardian's job is also to protect those under their care. Again Cressida's example is personal and intimate; she feels that the community has a responsibility to protect the individual and failing this then the individual must protect themselves. Achilles' actions represent the insurrection by an individual that undermines communal interests. The Cressida plot line shows what happens when an individual is abandoned by her community. Cressida's situation is the opposite of Helen's who is protected by the might of the whole community.

In Cressida's case the community, ignoring the wishes of the individual, has decided to trade her for the warrior Antenor (4.2.67-70)

> Aen. *We must give up to Diomedes' hand*
>
>   *The Lady Cressida.*
>
> Tro. *Is it concluded so?*
>
> Aen. *By Priam and the general state of Troy.*

This is expressly against her will; three times Cressida says she will not go (4.2.95; 97; 110)

> *I will not go*
>
> *I will not, uncle*
>
> *I will not go from Troy*

but no one intercedes, no one come to her defense, not her uncle, not Troilus (4.4.53-54)

> Cres. *I must, then, to the Grecians?*
>
> Tro. *No remedy.*

In *Troilus and Cressida* we are presented with two individuals, Achilles and Cressida, who find themselves at odds with the wishes of their societies. Achilles' actions or really lack of action can be seen as selfish, a result of his own hubris and seeing himself as not needing the community. Cressida's actions are not selfish but rather defensive, taken in response to the actions of her community; Cressida is forced into certain behaviours because she is abandoned by all those she loved. No one champions her case, she has no defenders; not even Troilus – he makes no effort to prevent her exchange. Troilus, like Ulysses, chooses instead to support and defend the majority. This is made clear, ironically, in his defense of the policy to keep Helen.

The Defense of Helen

Troilus' argument to keep and defend Helen is not based on logic; it is, rather, based on consensus. Nestor has made an offer to the Trojans that if they return Helen (the one) the war will be ended (2.2.3; 7)

> *Deliver Helen, and all damage else –*
>
> *Shall be struck off!*

Hector feels that Helen is not special and that Helen, the individual, is of no more worth than any one Trojan lost in her defense (2.2.21-23)

> *If we have lost so many tenths of ours*
>
> *To guard a thing not ours, nor worth to us*
>
> *(Had it our name) the value of one ten.*

Troilus replies to this argument by asserting that Helen's worth is what 'the many' deem it to be (2.2.81-82)

> *Why, she is a pearl*
>
> *Whose price hath launched above a thousand ships.*

Troilus also argues that the plan to abduct Helen was conceived and agreed upon by council (the many) (2.2.72-74)

> *It was thought meet*
>
> *Paris should do some vengeance on the Greeks.*
>
> *Your breath of full consent bellied his sails*

also (2.2.84-85)

> *If you'll avouch 'twas wisdom Paris went—*
>
> *As you must need, for you all cried 'Go, go!'*

Troilus challenges the council to live up to the consensus they entered into with cool minds.

At this point Cassandra (an individual voice) warns council that they should return Helen (2.2.112)

> *Troy burns, or else let Helen go.*

Hector supports Cassandra saying her fear and his logic should be enough to change Troilus' mind and council's (2.2.115-118).

> *Or is your blood*
>
> *So madly hot that no discourse of reason,*
>
> *Nor fear of bad success in a bad cause,*
>
> *Can qualify the same?*

Hector believes they should return Helen but understands the collective nature of the decision and so is willing to relent to the majority opinion (2.2.188-193)

> *Hector's opinion*
>
> *Is this in way of truth; yet ne'ertheless,*
>
> *My sprightly brethren, I propend to you*
>
> *In resolution to keep Helen still;*
>
> *For 'tis a cause that hath no mean dependence*
>
> *Upon our joint and several dignities.*

Hector, in this sense, believes in the same principles as Ulysses. He will support the decision of the generals over his own opinion. Hector will do what Achilles will not: respect 'the many' over 'the one'. Troilus doesn't even question this. This is why Troilus doesn't make any effort to help Cressida. 'The many' have decided she should be exchanged; case closed. Troilus cannot break from corporate control – even in his courting it is Pandarus who must lead him. Troilus functions only as a member of a pack.

The Restrained and Unrestrained Man

When Hector engages in debate with Troilus over the topic of 'the return of Helen' he points out that Troilus thinks like a young man (2.2.163-167)

> *Paris and Troilus, you have both said well*
>
> *And on the cause and question now in hand*
>
> *Have glozed – but superficially, not much*
>
> *Unlike young men, who Aristotle thought*
>
> *Unfit to hear moral philosophy.*

This reference to Aristotle was to his *Nicomachean Ethics* (Book I.iii.5-7).

"Again, each man judges correctly those matters with which he is acquainted; it is of these that he is a competent critic...to be a good critic generally, he must have had an all-round education. Hence the young are not fit to be students of Political Science. For they have no experience of life and conduct, and it is these that supply the premises and subject matter of this branch of philosophy. And moreover they are lead by their feelings; so that they will study the subject to no purpose or advantage, since the end of this science is not knowledge but action. And it makes no difference whether they are young in years or immature in character: the defect is not a question of time, it is because their life

and its various aims are guided by feeling; for to such persons their knowledge is of no use, any more than it is to the person of defective self-restraint. But Moral Science may be of great value to those who guide their desires and actions by principle" [1].

Ethics was seen as a practical pragmatic science of cool deliberation based on worldly experience and the setting of principled end-goals. Hector and Ulysses both provide speeches that are examples of this type of 'big picture' thinking. Troilus and Achilles are examples of persons guided by feelings (love/revenge), they are impulsive characters.

Understanding Aristotle can help us understand the characters in the play. Aristotle expands on these ideas further on in his book when he writes on Prudence (practical wisdom) (ibid., Book VI.vii.6)

"Prudence...is concerned with the affairs of men, and with things that can be the object of deliberation"
also (ibid., Book VI.viii.1)

"Prudence is indeed the same quality of mind as Political Science".

Political wisdom was an application of Prudence, an extension of it from one's private life into that of the life of the community. This Political form of Prudence was then employed not just to understand issues but to do something about them (ibid., Book VI.x.2)

"Understanding is not however the same thing as Prudence; for Prudence issues commands, since its end is a statement of what we ought to do or not to do, whereas Understanding merely makes judgments".

From this background material one can begin to understand Hector and Troilus. Hector acts; Troilus feels. Both possess understanding but Hector's experience allows for action; Troilus feels, he makes judgments but he doesn't act on them in a political sense. Troilus will judge Cressida's actions in the Greek camp but he was not equipped to stop her being exchanged for Antenor in the first instance. Troilus acts on his feelings of love and vengeance but he does not have the cognitive skills to plan or to prevent Cressida from being traded away; he lacks political acuity. In many ways Troilus lives in the present, he is a little instinctual, like an animal, he can react to feelings of love and of revenge but has trouble generating planned responses to problems that arise.

Troilus confesses to this 'immature trait' of thinking with his passions when debating Hector. Troilus feels that <u>the senses</u> (eyes, ears) rather than <u>reason</u> are the mediators between judgment and the will (2.2.63-65)

> *My will enkindled* (enflamed) *by mine eyes and ears,*
> *Two traded pilots 'twixt the dangerous shores*
> *Of will and judgment.*

Tradition held that the lowest form of judgment concerned our basic needs and desires (hunger, thirst, sex). This form of judgment was physical and sensual and was shared with the animals. Humans were capable of enriching their judgment by training it through education. We could come to know ourselves – something the animals could not do. To know yourself was the gateway to virtue because you could embrace your best qualities to do good and also avoid your worst qualities. To act without this knowledge was to be instinctive; it denied your humanity – your opportunity to be more than an animal. Hector points out this mistake in logic that Troilus has made (2.2.168-173)

> *The reasons you allege do more conduce*
> *To the hot passion of distempered blood*
> *Than to make up a free determination*
> *'Twixt right and wrong; for pleasure and revenge*
> *Have ears more deaf than adders to the voice*

Of any true decision.

Hector sees Troilus arguing for a passionate response and not a reasoned response.

A similar situation exists in the Greek camp. Ulysses possesses political wisdom, he figures out the problem with the Greek army, he formulates a solution and sets it in motion. Achilles is his problem but despite Ulysses' planning, Achilles' actions are beyond his control. Achilles' actions are determined by his feelings; he too lives in the present. Only Patroclus' death brings him back to the battlefield, an emotional trigger, not Ulysses' scheme of withholding honour.

Ulysses is often accompanied by Nestor, the oldest Greek in the camp and the most experienced. Aristotle considers experience to be as important as prudence in decision making (ibid., Book VI.xi.6)

"Consequently the unproved assertions and opinions of experienced and elderly people, or of prudent men, are as much deserving of attention as those which they support by proof; for experience has given them an eye for things, and so they see correctly".

So experience combined with realistic, achievable and wise goals are the hallmarks of political science.

Honour, Shame and Control

Everyone is born with a 'portion' of life, their inviolable limits. In an Honour/Shame culture other people's ideas of honour or shame circumscribe this portion or lot of one's life (*Beyond Fate*, Visser, Chapter I, Drawing a Line). In such a world everyone is expected to try to be as 'big' as possible, obtain as much honour as possible. Honour is assigned by other people as is shame. *Troilus and Cressida* begins with two clear examples of honour/shame. Hector's plot line is determined by these twinned motivators, shame and honour; this plot line begins with Hector being struck down by Ajax (1.2.33-35)

They say he yesterday coped Hector in the

battle and struck him down, the disdain and shame

whereof hath ever since kept Hector fasting and waking.

Hector's shame leads him to issue a challenge for one-on-one combat with the Greeks; this engages Ulysses' subplot to control Achilles using honour and shame. Initially Nestor and Ulysses decide that rather than 'enlard' Achilles' 'fat-already pride', they will arrange for Ajax to battle Hector. If Ajax loses, the Greeks will not be disheartened because he was not their best warrior and if he wins, all the better. Ulysses and Nestor, acting for the community, have chosen to send Ajax into a battle that he may not be ready for, all in the hope of lessening Achilles' pride (1.3.387)

Ajax employed plucks down Achilles' plumes.

Nestor and Ulysses represent the 'political machinations' that go on behind the scenes that make decisions over individuals' lives without taking into consideration the interests of those individuals involved. They are the 'big picture' planners yoking others' efforts (Ajax's and Achilles') to their schemes (2.1.101;103-104)

There's Ulysses and old Nestor –

yoke you like draught-oxen and make you plough up

the war.

Ulysses expands on this scheme by enlisting the help of the other generals; he hopes to have them ignore Achilles, not give him the respect he deserves. This way Ulysses can undercut Achilles' pride and make him more malleable to his suggestions (3.3.38-41)

Achilles stands i'th'entrance of his tent.

Pleas it our general pass strangely by him,

As if he were forgot; and, princes all,

Lay negligent and loose regard upon him.

Ulysses wishes to make Achilles hunger for honour, he wishes to make Achilles once more receptive to community pressure. Ulysses' advice is not to Achilles' advantage but it is to the community's advantage. Sadly, Ulysses is trying to encourage a type of 'unrestraint' in Achilles. Aristotle wrote of this quality (*Nicomachean Ethics*, VII.iv.2)

"The other sources of pleasure are not necessary, but are desirable in themselves: I mean for example victory, honour, wealth, and the other good and pleasant things of the same sort. Now those who against the right principle within them (moderation) exceed in regard to the latter class of pleasant things, we do not call unrestrained simply, but with a qualification – unrestrained as to money, gain, honour, or anger – not merely 'unrestrained'".

Ulysses tries to goad Achilles into action by discussing the fleeting nature of fame and honour (3.3.146-191). Ulysses is encouraging Achilles to sin against moderation, he is encouraging excess, he does this with the 'greater good' of the community in mind.

This sin of unrestraint is not dismissed by Aristotle (*Nicomachean Ethics*, Book VII.iv.5)

"...for instance money, gain, victory, honour: and inasmuch as in relation to all these naturally desirable things, as well as to the neutral ones, men are not blamed merely for regarding or desiring or liking them, but for doing so in a certain way, namely to excess...excessive devotion to them is bad and to be avoided".

This warning by Aristotle, common knowledge to both Greeks and Shakespeare, is ignored by Hector who already suffers from this sin of unrestraint when it comes to honour. Hector wishes to be seen on the battlefield, he wishes to be admired, but he wants it to excess. He wants it to the point that he ignores the pleas of his wife, Andromache; his sister, Cassandra; and his father, Priam (5.3.1-94). Hector imposes his will, the reasonable man will not be reasoned with on this point (5.3.27-28)

> *Life every man holds dear, but the dear man*
> *Holds honour far more precious–dear than life.*

It is this sin of excess, of choosing honour over love of family, that gets Hector killed. Paris under similar circumstances acquiesces to the will of his lover, Helen (3.1.130-131)

> *I would fain have armed today, but*
> *my Nell would not have it so.*

The play shows us that Ulysses is a clever man and that he carries with him the whiff of authority. His certainty implies that he knows what's best for everyone. Arrogance, however, should not be misinterpreted as authority; Aristotle draws a line between Prudence (practical wisdom aimed at a virtuous end) and cleverness (*Nicomachean Ethics*, Book VI.xiii.1)

> *"Prudence and Cleverness are not the same, but they are similar"*
(ibid., Book VI.xii.6)

> *"Virtue ensures the rightness of the end we aim at, Prudence*
> *ensures the rightness of the means we adopt to gain that end"*
(ibid., Book VI.xii.9)

> *"There is a certain faculty called Cleverness, which is the capacity*
> *for doing the things aforesaid that conduce to the aim we propose, and*
> *so attaining that aim. If the aim is noble, this is a praiseworthy faculty:*
> *if base, it is mere knavery".*

In Ulysses' case we have a man counseling Achilles against the precepts of self knowledge; because of this Ulysses is not virtuous but he is clever. Despite being clever Ulysses, in the end, does not manage to control Achilles' behaviour. Achilles, surprisingly, seems to act out of love. Two separate reasons are given for Achilles' behaviour of withdrawing from the battlefield and both have to do with love. Ulysses believes Achilles is in love with Priam's daughter, Polyxena, and has withdrawn from the fighting for this reason (3.3.194-195)

> *'Tis known, Achilles, that you are in love*
> *With one of Priam's daughters.*

Patroclus sees himself as the reason Achilles will not fight (3.3.221-222)

> *They think my little stomach to the war,*
> *And your great love to me, restrains you thus.*

Either way, Achilles responds to the wishes or needs of another individual to affect his actions. Achilles does what Achilles wishes to do; he does not do what the collective Greek army wishes of him. Even when Achilles goes back into the fighting it is not because of Ulysses' schemes, or the generals' wishes, or to grab more honour, it is because Patroclus is killed. A single death brings Achilles back into the fray; the power of 'the one' is his only motivation (5.5.17)

> *Go, bear Patroclus' body to Achilles*

also (5.5.30-32)

> *Great Achilles*
> *Is arming, weeping, cursing, vowing vengeance.*
> *Patroclus' wounds have roused his drowsy blood.*

So Hector, rejecting the love of family, goes to war for honour and Achilles, rejecting honour, goes to war for the love of Patroclus.

Scheming and planning to use individuals for the greater good of your society are not limited to the Grecian camp – similar machinations are also occurring in Troy. The Trojans have decided to trade Cressida for Antenor. Individuals, like Cressida and Achilles, do not matter in these greater schemes – if anyone is going to look after their interests it is only going to be themselves.

Intrinsic Value vs Conferred Value

The question of a person's value has come up in Hector's debate with Troilus over Helen's value (2.2) but it also applies to Ulysses' assessment of Achilles' value. What is up for debate is the question of whether one's value is assigned to us by our community or whether it is an intrinsic part of our individuality.

Troilus argues that Helen's value lies in her conferred worth. The Greeks have launched a thousand ships and started a war in order to recover her. Her value is therefore inestimable, she is of great worth. Helen, in fact, bathes in this conferred value and behaves like a queen. She accepts this high estimation of herself and we never see her question her value in this play.

Hector argues that only Helen's intrinsic worth should be taken into consideration and that she should therefore not be regarded as worth more than any other Trojan. This low estimation of her intrinsic worth is also held by Diomedes, a Greek, who sees her only as a whore and not worth the battle required to recover her (4.1.57-76).

The ideas of conferred and intrinsic values are also echoed in the concept of regard – how the community regards you and how you regard yourself. Ulysses' speech to Achilles is the best source for this related debate (3.3.93-217). In the speech Ulysses does an unusual thing: he argues against self-knowledge. This is significant because one of the commandments of Apollo was "to know yourself". Ulysses is in this instance putting society's interests ahead of those of an individual's. Ulysses is trying to convince Achilles that he is only as others perceive him (3.3.116; 118-120)

> *That no man is lord of anything,*
> *Till he communicate his parts to others;*
> *Nor doth he of himself know them for aught*
> *Till he behold them formed in th'applause.*

Ulysses is trying to manipulate Achilles. Ulysses wants him to go back to the battlefield so he tells Achilles that he is only as good as his last brave deed and that nobody remembers his past accomplishments (3.3.149-153). Ulysses is trying to attack Achilles' sense of self-worth by implying that the community sets this value. Ulysses is arguing that all values are 'relative' and are set by the community.

Cressida provides us with another aspect of this dialogue. She is an example of a character possessing 'self-knowledge' (1.2.249-255) (3.2.109-152). In her discussions with others she reveals how she protects herself, how she fears the loss of her self-identity, and finally through her honesty she reveals truths to others that may use that information to harm her (3.2.120).

Why have I blabbed?

She knows her strengths and vulnerabilities. This was the goal of the commandment 'to know yourself'. It was to give yourself the conscious ability to build on your strengths and avoid your weaknesses.

In *Troilus and Cressida* we discover that Achilles is unaffected by society's judgments; he simply doesn't care – his sense of self-worth is unassailable. Cressida will, however, be challenged by community expectations and judgments; she will be seen by some as a whore. Cressida must find a way to rise above their judgments. There is some hope we are afforded by Shakespeare; Diomedes promises to treat her as an individual (4.4.132-133)

To her own worth

She shall be prized.

Despite Thersites' assessment of Diomedes' character there is nothing in Diomedes' dialogue and actions that show him to be any less honourable than any other character in the play. Cressida's fight with community expectations has been ongoing. In her dialogue she twice laments the limitations placed on her sex (3.2.123-124)

And yet, good faith, I wished myself a man,

Or that we women had men's privilege

also (5.2.115)

Ah, poor our sex!

Cressida is an intelligent character, *"a woman of quick sense"* (4.5.55), she understands her situation (5.2.118)

Minds swayed by eyes are full of turpitude.

She understands that decisions made that take into account worldly concerns always involve some moral compromise and uncertainty. She is not self-willed like Achilles, not quite so oblivious to the world around her, she knows what she must do in order to survive in this physical world and she knows it will compromise her values. She is Ulysses' equal, clever enough not to be always prudent.

Anticipation and the Fleeting Nature of Time

Troilus has complained to Pandarus of the turmoil he is in, waiting for Cressida to agree to meet with him (1.1.14-24). Ulysses has explained the fleeting nature of fame to Achilles (3.3.146-191). Both these ideas, anticipation and impermanence, come together in Cressida's mind as she too awaits Troilus and tries to determine what strategy she should adopt with him (1.2.277-278; 280)

Yet hold I off. Women are angels, wooing;

Things won are done

Men prize the thing ungained more than it is.

Cressida believes that men only love women when courting, wooing, or trying to conquer them; once bedded they would be on to their next conquest. Love for men, she believed, was only in the pursuit.

Ulysses makes comparable arguments to Achilles pointing out that people are fickle and that you're only as good as your last great feat; once it is done, it is in the past, it's forgotten. The next in line to do a significant act is the next hero to be praised. Ulysses points out that honour lies in persistence, in the present, once it is past it is soon forgotten (3.3.151-153)

> *Perseverance, dear my lord,*
> *Keeps honour bright; to have done is to hang*
> *Quite out of fashion*

also (3.3.181)

> *The present eye praises the present object.*

Cressida fears once she has been conquered she will be forgotten. She feels that love like honour requires perseverance to keep it bright.

Cressida is a character that can be defined by her preparedness. She has explained to Pandarus how she protects herself. She has also explained that she expects her guardian to protect her as well. She has also revealed to Troilus that she prepares for her worst fears; that she lives in expectation of evil and not good (3.2.68-70)

> *Blind fear, that seeing reason leads, finds safer*
> *footing than blind reason, stumbling without fear. To*
> *fear the worst oft cures the worse.*

Cressida's clear sighted reason prepares her to face her worst fears; fears of uncommitted lovers. These are the monsters that haunt Cressida *"They / that have the voice of lions and the act of hares, are they / not monsters?"* (3.2.84-86).

Cressida's fears are in fact realized in the play. Cressida, once traded, engages in several defensive measures to both protect herself and raise her conferred value. She greets the Greek generals with pleasantness and an easy flirtation. She knows she must be desired by them in order to become a commodity to be fought over. Women are 'symbols of honour', honour personified, to be taken, traded and fought over. It is the duty of men to guard their honour. Just as Troilus felt Helen's value could be measured by what the Greeks were willing to expend in her recovery, so too Cressida understands her value is going to be determined by desire and competition. She employs this strategy on Diomed. He finds he is competing for her love against some unknown suitor whose sleeve Cressida still adores (5.2.96-99).

> Cres. *'Twas one's that loved me better than you will.*
>
>   *But now you have it, take it.*
>
> Dio. *Whose was it?*
>
> Cres. *By all Diana's waiting-women yond,*
>
>   *And by herself, I will not tell you whose.*

Cressida has realized that we only want people because others want them too. She is new to the Grecian camp but she understands that she must still create the illusion that there is a competition for her affection, even if it is with someone who is not present. She cannot risk being easily won, she does not wish to be taken for granted, he must earn her love, he must demonstrate his devotion, he must outcompete the competition. If Cressida has learned anything it is that her love must be continuously and persistently earned.

Cressida has shown herself in this drama to be Ulysses' equal. This is why Ulysses is disgusted with her (4.5.55-64). Cressida does not know her place. Nestor has praised her as "*a woman of quick sense*". All the other generals are smitten with her, but to Ulysses she represents the same danger that Achilles does, neither knows their place. Ulysses sees Cressida as potentially divisive and disruptive to the community because she encourages competition (actively or passively) amongst the generals. For Cressida this is a survival tactic, it encourages acts that prove love over idle talk of love. She knows she must be prudent by applying a practical wisdom to her new situation. Prudence is the correct word because her goal is virtuous, she wishes to be the object of true love; she does not want to be exploited.

Ulysses, however, only sees a scheming individual. When Ulysses "*begs*" for a kiss (4.5.48) Cressida asks him to humble himself "*Why, beg too.*" It is innocent word play but it is also a request that he do more than just ask. This he will not do. Ulysses' clear view of the order of the universe and his understanding of rank and degree will not permit him to humble himself in any way before a woman. Ulysses and Cressida are intellectual equals but they are at opposite ends of the status system. They are also at opposite ends when one considers their goals; Ulysses believes in defending the community and the status quo, Cressida is engaged in the active defense of the individual who has been abandoned by the community. Society's rights against individual rights. They are worlds apart.

Marriage in Troilus and Cressida

Until the 13th century marriage was considered primarily a private contract between two families concerning property exchange; it was a property contract. This idea is certainly found in *Troilus and Cressida* where the language of contract law is used by Pandarus, acting as Cressida's guardian, as he passes her over to Troilus' care. The scene is meant to read like a wedding.

> [to Troilus]
> *Here she is now. Swear the oaths now*
> *to her that you have sworn to me.* (3.2.39-40)
> *Come, draw this curtain, and let's see your picture.*
> [She is unveiled.] (3.2.45)
> [to Troilus]
> *So, so, rub on, and kiss the mistress.*
> [They kiss.] (3.2.48)
> *Here's 'In*
> *witness whereof the parties interchangeably'.* (3.2.56-57)

The parties are brought together, oaths are sworn, the bride's veil is lifted, they kiss, and are sworn using a legal formula that was used in indentures (*Troilus and Cressida*, Arden Shakespeare, 3rd series, edited by D. Bevington, note 3.2.56-7). This pattern of events recalls the betrothal ceremony in the Book of Common Prayer. Once the legalities are out of the way (3.2.192-193)

> Go to, a bargain made. Seal it, seal it; I'll be
> The witness

the marriage is consummated.

This should make Troilus Cressida's husband. He should now be more protective of her life than of his own. This is what love and chivalry demanded of the husband. The understanding of chivalry, *discordia concors* (loving strife), was that the beautiful female inspires the male to acts of heroism and that the male protects and adores the female. This is what we expect of Troilus but this is not what the play delivers. Troilus' actions do not live up to his commitment. When council decides to agree to the trade of Cressida for Antenor, Troilus acquiesces. He does not question their action, he is not Cressida's protector, he does not act as Cressida's husband. When the time for the exchange occurs Troilus rather takes up the role of the celibate church acting instead as Cressida's caretaker. He then hands her over to Diomed. The marriage ceremony is once again evoked in the scene (4.3.6-10)

> I'll bring her to the Grecian presently;
> And to his hand when I deliver her,
> Think it an altar and thy brother Troilus
> A priest, there off'ring to it his own heart.

If anyone is to be blamed for breaking the matrimonial bonds it is Troilus as he gives up his claim to Cressida without protest and, in fact, facilitating the exchange (4.4.108-110). What is a girl to think?

Welcome, Sir Diomed. Here is the lady
Which for Antenor we deliver you.
At the port, lord, I'll give her to thy hand.

In the marriage ceremony the father or guardian would deliver his daughter to the altar. The priest would ask the question "Who giveth this woman to be married unto this man?" The father would physically relinquish his daughter to the priest. At this point the father's role in his daughter's life is ended. The bride then stands at the altar between the father and the husband-to-be. By transferring his daughter to the priest the father is acknowledging that there is no impediment to the marriage (she is intact). The ritual of marriage transfers the daughter's loyalties from one family to another. In this case Cressida is being tranferred from the Trojans to the Greeks.

In *Troilus and Cressida* there have been two 'mock-marriage' ceremonies, one to Troilus and one to Diomed. Cressida's reception into the Greek court can be viewed as a receiving line where the new family kisses the bride and welcomes her into their family. The marriage metaphor certainly supports this reading. Cressida has been transferred from one male domain into another and Troilus has been forced to pay the 'bride price' with his own heart. This welcome into a new community is reinforced by Ulysses' comment (4.5.21-22)

Yet is the kindness but particular;
'Twere better she were kissed in general.

In this comment Ulysses is asking Agamemnon if he is taking a private interest in kissing Cressida or whether it is a welcoming kiss whereby it would be better if everyone welcomed her.

Troilus views Cressida's expulsion from Troy as a kind of banishment from paradise; he thinks of her as leaving her spiritual home and descending to an earthly camp. After he has spied on her activity with the Grecians he feels he is no longer spiritually married to her (5.2.161-167)

> *Cressid is mine, tied with the bonds of heaven;*
>
> *Instance, O instance, strong as heaven itself,*
>
> *The bonds of heaven are slipped, dissolved and*
>
> *loosed,*
>
> *And with another knot, five-finger-tied*
>
> *The fractions of her faith, orts of her love,*
>
> *The fragments, scraps, the bits and the greasy relics*
>
> *Of her o'ereaten faith, are bound to Diomed.*

Troilus sees his spiritual ties to Cressida dissolve, essentially he feels they are now divorced in heaven. She is free, in his mind, to create base earthly ties in sinful flesh to another. He no longer recognizes her earthly self as being the woman he loved.

Love and War

A theme that is never far below the surface in *Troilus and Cressida* is the similarity between love and war in respect to their domination over our reasonable selves (3.2.151-152)

> *To be wise and love*
>
> *Exceeds man's might.*

Both love and war are forms of madness (a type of lust) that for a time take precedence over reason. Troilus is tossed between these extremes. As a man driven by his passions he finds himself unable to fight, at the beginning of the play, because he is too distracted by thoughts of love. At the end of the play he is no longer in love and so his passions can once more be directed back to vengeance and the battlefield. Both war and love fully engage the passions and because of this seem to be mutually exclusive within the human heart.

Although mutually exclusive they still feed one another. Achilles is happy to wile away his time with Patroclus but once Patroclus is killed, once Achilles loses his 'loved one', the emptiness, the loss releases the floodgates of his rage.

Love is required in the 'tit for tat' exchanges that keep wars going. If you didn't love something you wouldn't be willing to fight for it. Linked opposites.

This idea is certainly recognized by Thersites, he plays the role of the fool in the Grecian camp. In the play he is the cynic that shines the light of honesty on the art of war. Thersites sees no heroes only politics and individuals used and abused for other's interests (2.3.17-19)

> *Vengeance on the whole camp! Or rather, the Neapolitan*
> *Bone-ache! For that, methinks, is the curse dependent on*
> *Those that war for a placket.*

In this soliloquy Thersites would like to see the whole Greek army cursed with venereal disease, an appropriate affliction for going to war over a woman's (Helen's) petticoat (placket).

The themes of love/sex and war/death are intertwined throughout the play. This becomes very apparent when Pandarus performs for Helen and Paris in a subsequent scene. Helen requests a love song, a song with the sadly prophetic title (3.1.104)

> *Let thy song be love. 'This love will undo us all'.*

Pandarus sings a song full of innuendos in which arrow shafts stand in for phallic shafts and death and dying describe sexual orgasm (3.1.109-121):

> *Love, love, nothing but love, still love, still more!*
> *For, O, love's bow*
> *Shoots buck and doe.*
> *The shaft confounds*
> *Not that it wounds*

But tickles still the sore.

These lovers cry, 'O!O!', they die!

Yet that which seems the wound to kill

Doth turn 'O!O!' to 'Ha, ha, he!'

So dying love lives still.

'O!O!' a while, but 'Ha, ha, ha!'

'O!O!' groans out for 'Ha, ha, ha!' –

Heigh – ho!

Pandarus (3.1.126-8) then reiterates what Hector said earlier about vipers being deaf to reason (2.2.171-173). Pandarus conflates all three: love and war and lack of reason

Is this the generation of love? Hot blood, hot

Thoughts and hot deeds? Why they are vipers. Is love a

Generation of vipers? – Sweet lord, who's afield today?

Troilus, in the thralls of anticipation, adds to this connection of sex with death (3.2.8-12)

Like a strange soul upon the Stygian banks

Staying for waftage. O, be thou my Charon,

And give me swift transport to those fields

Where I may wallow in the lily-beds

Proposed for the deserver!

Here Troilus likens Pandarus to Charon because Pandarus is going to take him to the Elysian fields (heaven for dead heroes), in this case, Cressida. Troilus' overblown imagery is quickly deflated by Pandarus' response (3.2.15)

Walk here i'th'orchard. I'll bring her straight.

Pandarus does for Love what Thersites does for War. He demythologizes it. Brings it down to earth. He removes the romance from it. Pandarus is the 'Thersites of love', the jaded cynic and commentator. His nature is sweeter than Thersites but his job is the same. Both Pandarus and Thersites are beyond the thrall of the passions, this is why they are cynical and removed and capable of judgment.

Uncommitted and Inconstant Lovers

When Pandarus delivers Cressida to Troilus (3.2) her worries intensify. The normally confident Cressida is hesitant, she has trouble trusting Troilus. She mentions her fears, that lovers swear more performance than they are able; she is concerned not about sexual performance but about what they promise in the role of protector. All her discussions up to this point have been about protecting herself and the need for her guardian figure to protect her. She is worried about taking care of herself, she voices that her major concern is uncommitted lovers, those that *"have the voice of lions and the act of hares"*, these she considers *"monsters"*. Troilus does not understand; he feels that there are no monsters in Cupid's pageant. When Cressida confesses her love and verbally bullies Troilus to talk about his thoughts and feelings *"To angle for your thoughts"*, what Troilus finally confesses is that he is not fearful of any weakness in himself but rather of women's inconstancy (3.2.156)

> *To keep her constancy in plight and youth.*

Troilus confesses to being a simple man. Hector has already pointed out his immature reasoning skills. Troilus, himself, admits to his lack of sophistication (4.4.83-90)

> *In this I do not call your faith in question*
> *So mainly as my merit. I cannot sing,*
> *Nor heel the high lavolt, nor sweeten talk,*
> *Not play at subtle games – fair virtues all,*
> *To which the Grecians are most prompt and*
> *pregnant.*
> *But I can tell that in each grace of these*

> *There lurks a still and dumb – discoursive devil*
> *That tempts most cunningly. But be not tempted.*

Troilus' education is not yet well rounded; he sees temptation in life's joys. Troilus could almost be viewed as a type of religious fundamentalist, perhaps like a Puritan projected onto the Ilium stage. Troilus does as he is told, he respects his elders. He is immature in his reasoning and tends to act according to his feelings. He is not evil nor is he open-minded. He is still young enough to see things in black and white. This is useful in war but less so in love.

So in the end Cressida is afraid of 'uncommitted lovers' and Troilus is afraid of 'inconstant women' [2]. Sadly Troilus' commitment will fail before Cressida's fidelity. The morning brings fresh doubts to Cressida (4.2.17-19)

> *You men will never tarry.*
> *O foolish Cressid, I might have still held off,*
> *And then you would have tarried!*

When news arrives that she has been traded for Antenor and must immediately leave for the Grecian camp one can only imagine the betrayal she feels and the lessons pertaining to trust that have been reinforced. Her immediate departure is likened to death (4.4.49-50)

> *Some say the Genius so*
> *Cries 'Come!' to him that instantly must die.*

This metaphor of physical death has, throughout the play, been likened to falling in love, making love, and love being taken away. It speaks of love's transcendent quality, a quality beyond the normal day to day existence. As Troilus and Cressida part, Troilus either consciously or unconsciously harps on the need for Cressida to be true (4.4.73)

> *O heavens! 'Be true' again?*

This may just speak of Troilus' insecurity or it may reveal the conditional nature of his love. He will only love her if she is true to him – a condition of honour imposed on her by him. Troilus does not say 'be careful' or 'take care of yourself', his concern is not for Cressida but for himself – his honour. The plot reveals this to be the case. When Troilus spies on Cressida's behaviour in the Greek camp (5.2) it is enough to kill any love he has for her. He will not respond to her letter, her mere words. He tears it up. He focuses on Cressida's actions which he considers unfaithful. He never reflects on the fact that all he offered Cressida was words and that his failure to act brought them to this situation (3.2.54)

Words pay no debts; give her deeds.

The Cressida he loved is now dead to him. She only lives on as an ethereal image in his mind; he idealizes the Cressida he loved, the faithful version. He psychologically dissects Cressida into 'two Cressidas' – his is the Madonna, the spiritual Cressida; the other, Diomed's, is the Whore, the earthly Cressida.

The Making of Heroes

The transcendent quality of love relates emotionally to an equivalent experience in war; that of heightened physicality and intensity that occurs in hand to hand combat. This is where the play now shifts its focus, to the storyline of Hector's battle with Ajax.

As Cressida is welcomed into the Greek camp so too is Hector (4.5), his challenge has been accepted by Ajax. Both Cressida and Hector have crossed boundaries, this is what heroes do. Both are received with good manners by the Grecians but good manners are not morality, only the temporary façade of morality. The orderly ceremoniousness of the greetings/combat appear to reconcile the conflicting interests of the different groups but it doesn't take long before the forces of discord show themselves.

Both Hector and Cressida, as it turns out, will face a 'maiden battle' as they attempt to gain the respect of their hosts – Hector in a physical bloodless battle with Ajax – Cressida in a battle of wits with the Grecian generals.

Everyone discusses how honourable Hector is. Ulysses comments that Hector is merciful to the defenseless (a quality not shared by Troilus) (4.5.106-107)

> *For Hector in his blaze of wrath subscribes*
> *To tender objects.*

Ajax recognizes this gentle side in Hector as well (4.5.140-2)

> *Thou art too gentle and too free a man.*
> *I came to kill thee, cousin, and bear hence*
> *A great addition earned in thy death.*

It is a quality that Troilus fears in his brother for he thinks it may be his downfall. Troilus feels pity has no place in war, that mercy is a vice (5.3.37-38)

> *Brother, you have a vice of mercy in you,*
> *Which better fits a lion than a man.*

Both Hector and Cressida go through an examination by the generals; their assessment reveals similar concerns. They are examined like enemies. Hector and Achilles regard each other (4.5.235; 238; 239)

> *Let me look on thee.*
> *As I would by thee, view thee limb by limb.*
> *O, like a book of sport thou'lt read me o'er.*

Cressida is assessed by Ulysses (4.5.58)

> *At every joint and motive of her body*

and she too is examined like a book (4.5.61-62)

> *And wide unclasp the tables of their thoughts*

To every tickling reader!

The experience of Achilles meeting Hector mirrors Ulysses meeting Cressida. Both have met persons that they regard as their enemies and in many ways their equals.

Cressida has adopted a defensive strategy in her new situation. She loves Troilus but he did not protect her and now cannot. He lies in her past. The present situation demands her attention. She must make the best of it. She does not know it but she is Ulysses' worst nightmare; a desirable, independent, uncontrolled female capable of using her wit. Her beauty makes her divisive in this all male camp and her wit borders on disrespect. Ulysses sees her as dangerous as Achilles, an independent male who uses his strength and reputation as a weapon and who doesn't respect or respond to any social constraints. Ulysses sees the pair of them as insurrectionists chipping away at the Greek ordered state.

Worldly Decisions

Cressida appears to be more aware than Hector of the danger of being a stranger in an enemy's camp. The Greeks are being gracious but they are looking for weaknesses and ways to exploit the newcomers. Ajax was hoping to steal honour from Hector, Achilles was hoping to preview Hector's weaknesses. Cressida is remaining aloof, charming but distant, knowing that the market value of an object is always determined by how badly more than one person wants it. The only example she knows of a foreigner in a foreign camp is Helen. Cressida's best survival tactic is to be fought over. She is making worldly decisions and not spiritual ones. Ulysses' reasoned vision of an ordered universe does not mean much to someone who is at the bottom of that status system (female, outsider, daughter of a traitor). Ulysses' ordered structure offers nothing to her, there is no way for her to climb the social ladder. She, like Achilles, operates outside the bounds of social order. Honour plays no role in her situation; she is not seen as possessing any honour (Ulysses, Thersites and probably others regard her as a whore) so she cannot be controlled by it. What Cressida has to fight is being defined by what others think. Her self-knowledge, i.e., her sense of herself, is the only weapon she has against others' expectations.

Hector finds himself in the same situation as Cressida. Achilles is bullying him, trying to project a future onto him (4.5.242-243)

> *Tell me, you heavens, in which part of his body*
> *Shall I destroy him?*

Hector does not care what Achilles thinks (just as Cressida must not care what Ulysses thinks). Hector is wise enough to let the future write itself (4.5.252-253)

> *Wert thou the oracle to tell me so,*
> *I'd not believe thee.*

The two scenes resonate off one another. Cressida and Hector are foreigners in a foreign camp. The Greeks are trying to assign them an identity as victims rather than as heroes. Cressida and Hector both offer resistance to being defined, both are heroic in their own way, but Hector gets to leave while Cressida must come to some permanent solution to her problem.

Cressida solves her problem in much the same way Troilus solved his. She too decides to separate the spiritual Cressida from the earthly Cressida. Her concerns in the Greek camp are for her physical self. Her betrayal by the Trojans has hardened her defensive strategies. She believes that love must be demonstrated through actions, that love is a present tense activity, and that love has both earthly requirements and rewards. Cressida has used her past experience to redefine the 'rules of engagement' when it comes to love. The men must wait their turn. We see this in her interaction with Diomedes (5.2). She has convinced him that he has to compete for her love; that he cannot just take her being with him for granted. Diomedes attempts to prove his love through battle during which he captures Troilus' horse. He uses this as a sign of physical proof of the actions he will perform for Cressida (5.5.4-5)

> *Tell her I have chastised the amorous Trojan*
> *And am her knight by proof.*

By doing this Diomedes shows that he understands the concept of *discordia concors*, a central concept to chivalry, and that he will protect Cressida and serve her. Diomed is capable of crossing over between the Martian and Venerean battlefields. His actions indicate that he is a more dedicated lover than Troilus. Troilus responds to Diomed's actions by challenging him (5.6.7-8)

> *O traitor Diomed! Turn thy false face, thou traitor,*
> *And pay the life thou owest me for my horse!*

Troilus, at this point in the play, appears to be more concerned about his property than anything else, even if one reads 'horse' as a pun on 'whore' meaning Cressida it hardly raises Troilus' estimation in the eyes of the audience. Troilus has moved on. Cressida was only property to him, only a reflection of his honour taken, an excuse for a fight.

If Troy was Cressida's spiritual home then the Grecian camp is her earthly one. She does not resist this idea but accepts the compromises that come with living in the physical realm. Her last lines of the play confirm this, she understands that any decisions she makes that takes into account the real sensual world will always involve some degree of moral compromise (5.2.117-118)

> *O, then conclude:*
> *Minds swayed by eyes are full of turpitude.*

This conclusion mimics Ulysses' understanding of the world as well for we have come to know him as a character who has given up Prudence in favour of Cleverness, he too has chosen earthly goals.

Compromise and Uncertainty

"Events seem to conspire to prevent the achievement of an expressed purpose." A.S. Knowland points this out in his paper, *Troilus and Cressida* (Shakespeare Quarterly, Vol.10, No. 3, 1959). He feels that Time and what it brings with it in the form of chance often interposes itself between the characters' aims and their achievements; what they imagined to be the outcome and the real outcome. A type of corruption inserts itself between their 'best laid' plans and the results of those plans. Cressida has concluded that this uncertainty is the natural consequence of any plan that takes into account worldly concerns. To be compromised is our natural state. G. Wilson Knight (*The Wheel of Fire*) comes to similar conclusions; he feels that every character in the play is compromised, that their human values are compromised by their human failings.

What is common to all these points of view is time or, really, change. Time is a condition of life. It brings with it flux and uncertainty. Its only constant is change. So time is associated with change and change is associated with corruption and corruption is the natural state in the physical realm. Ulysses is fighting change. He wishes to maintain the order and structure he sees reflected in the universe, he wants to keep the order of degree. Achilles and Cressida both threaten his vision of stasis. Both characters are corrupting figures because they question the decisions made by the majority, they are insubordinate characters that don't know their place and they are divisive characters because they infect others with their example. They untune the string. Achilles and Cressida behave as individuals; Achilles is an insubordinate individual who will not do what his society requires of him, Cressida is an individual who has been forced to comply, against her will, to the wishes of her society. Both Achilles and Cressida attempt to maintain their individual rights in a society that would strip those rights from them.

Troilus is the Trojan equivalent of Ulysses; he too argues for and accepts decisions made by the council. Troilus, just like Ulysses, is terrified by inconstancy. Troilus fears inconstancy in women, Ulysses fears change of all kinds; all of it bodes disaster to him. The fact that they buddy up in the Grecian camp merely confirms their like natures. When Troilus spies on an adapting Cressida he makes an intellectual speech not unlike Ulysses' speech on the order of the universe. Troilus divides Cressida into a heavenly Cressida, free from sin, idealized, and an earthly Cressida, corrupt. Ulysses' speech too spoke of the heavens' idealized order and the dangers posed by corruption. The play leaves us with the impression that the ideal has little place on the earth.

Honour and War are community activities; both require the agreement of a large number of people. Honour is earned in the eyes of the community; it is both bestowed and taken away by the community.

Love and revenge are individual activities. Love defines a relationship between individuals and revenge usually defines the type of retribution an individual seeks in return for an isolated wrong.

Troilus and Hector both live up to their ideals of honour but they do so at the expense of love. Hector's unrestrained honour is exercised over his love for his wife, sister, father, and even his own self-preservation. Hector's idealistic belief that honour can bring some order to the horror of war puts him in harm's way; because of it Hector does not take advantage of a disadvantaged Achilles (5.6.15)

> *Pause, if thou wilt.*

Hector's fault lies in possessing excessive honour.

Troilus fails at love because he chooses to obey the will of council, to respect degree, over his own desires. He lets Cressida be taken away from him. He accepts the community's wishes over his own and over

Cressida's, he chooses not to honour their love or the commitments he has made to her. He breaks his oath of love in deference to degree and decree. Troilus fails to break away from the pack and Cressida is betrayed in the process.

Achilles is not controlled by honour and because of it he succeeds in his limited plans. He plans to kill Hector. He sacrifices his honour in order to accomplish this. He strips himself of his ideals to attain his goal, revenge. Achilles also reveals something about war to the audience. That war is just killing, often done to achieve political goals but sometimes it can be used to also achieve personal goals. Achilles was willing to sacrifice his honour to achieve some personal justice.

Cressida too has managed to adapt to reality. She learns to cope with her circumstances. She does what a hero should do; she does what needs to be done. In this aspect she again is like Achilles, he had to lose his honour – she her constancy, but both achieve their limited goals.

Achilles and Cressida are alike in one other surprising aspect: love. Achilles sacrifices his honour not out of hate for Hector but out of love for Patroclus. Achilles goes back to the battlefield only to avenge his friend. Rage born out of love. Earthly love requires earthly actions, on this Achilles and Cressida agree. Troilus did not live up to this requirement for Cressida; he let her go, he did not hold on, he did not act to keep her. Diomedes, on the other hand, appears to be actively engaged in proving his love for Cressida as he performs acts of knightly proof.

Cressida is an abandoned character who is left to her own devices, her survival depends on her ability to do what needs to be done, to adapt to changing circumstances. The 'status quo' is not her friend. She is, in this sense, a modern character for she is forced to live in the constantly changing present. Her past is gone and of no use to her. What Ulysses has said about honour also applies to Cressida's view of lovers (3.3.146-151)

> *Time hath, my lord, a wallet at his back,*
> *Wherein he puts alms for oblivion,*
> *A great-sized monster of ingratitudes.*
> *Those scraps are good deeds past, which are*
> *Devoured as fast as they are made, forgot*
> *As soon as done.*

Cressida is a fresh slate in the Grecian camp. Cressida has learned hard lessons in life and has been abandoned by her society, her uncle, and her lover. If she had abandonment issues before (from her father, Calchas, leaving her) one can only imagine how she feels now. For her, love requires both action and continuous action. Ulysses' words can be used to describe Cressida's feelings about love as much as they do Ulysses' feelings about honour (3.3.151-153)

> *Perseverance, dear my lord,*
> *Keeps honour bright; to have done is to hang*
> *Quite out of fashion.*

Ulysses' words when they are applied to the concept of love instead of honour help explain Cressida's behaviour. Cressida has been forced to live in the constantly changing present and so must fly on the wings of time to get what benefits she can. When Troilus abandoned her she had to greet the next in line (3.3.166-169)

> *For Time is like a fashionable host*
> *That slightly shakes his parting guest by th'hand,*
> *And with his arms outstretched as he would fly,*
> *Grasps in the comer. Welcome ever smiles,*
> *And Farewell goes out sighing.*

She, like Time, must keep moving. To love Cressida is to prove it every day. Cressida is not unfaithful rather those who lose Cressida are unfaithful to her keeping. She is not only honour personified but love personified. To serve her is to protect her, keep her, and love her; it is a present tense activity.

Lust and Rage

Women in *Troilus and Cressida* may be understood as objects of attraction, objects to lust after. Men are drawn to them initially on an instinctual level, at a level that does not engage their reason (3.2.151-152)

> *for to be wise and love*
> *Exceeds man's might.*

Attraction can be seen as a form of animal instinct. It is difficult to know if any of Cressida's suitors feels anything more than this. Love requires much more of someone than does lust. Diomedes is starting to perform the actions that indicate a level of commitment that are indicative of love; Troilus, however, failed to perform any protective behaviour when it came to Cressida, he was talk without action, a hare with a lion's roar.

The primal nature of lust gives us some understanding of why Ulysses is threatened by Cressida's presence in the Grecian camp. Not only does he have to concern himself with Achilles' insubordination but he now has to contend with another divisive presence, as the men secretly start to compete for Cressida's attention. Ulysses understands order, he can work with reason but both lust and love lie outside these parameters. Cressida represents a force Ulysses cannot control, a force he sees as destabilizing to his society [3].

It is important not to blame the messenger; Cressida is the source of lust in others; she is not intentionally harmful. She is divisive not through her own planning but through her very presence. She is not necessarily responsible for the chaos she introduces to the Greek ranks but through self awareness and planning she may be able to capitalize on it. Cressida is not actively subversive like Achilles but Ulysses does not distinguish between the two. Both individuals introduce an element of chaos into his structured military world.

Homer's *Iliad* begins with the word Rage. *"Rage – Goddess, sing the rage of Peleus' son Achilles"*. Rage is also an instinct felt but not controlled by man. It is Achilles' fault, his weakness. It is what makes him insubordinate, uncontrollable, it is what clouds his mind (3.3.309-310)

> *My mind is troubled, like a fountain stirred,*
> *And I myself see not the bottom of it.*

> *Pride is Achilles' sin but rage is the way his pride is manifest* (2.3.169-173)

> *Imagined worth*
> *Holds in his blood such swoll'n and hot discourse*
> *That 'twixt his mental and his active parts*
> *Kingdomed Achilles in commotion rages*
> *And batters down himself.*

Achilles is torn between pride and love and he rages within. His pride and the generals' lack of respect for him cause him to rage at their ignorance. His love for Patroclus and Polyxena leads him to withdraw from the battle that his pride hungers for; again the frustration can only find relief in his rage. Achilles is insubordinate and infects others with this same arrogance but he is oblivious of his effect on others. He is not actively trying to destroy society, he is merely withdrawing from it.

The same could be said of society's effect on Cressida. They did not intend her harm, nor did they care. When Cressida was traded the only thing her society considered was the good they would derive from the trade and not the harm they would inflict on one of their own.

The Challenging Universe

Troilus and Cressida was written slightly earlier than 1603, after the writing of *Hamlet*. It was a time when the structure of the universe was being contested both in public debates and in writings dating from that period. Ptolemy's well ordered, hierarchical view of the cosmos where the earth lied motionless at its center was being displaced by a view of the cosmos first promoted by Copernicus and soon defended by and expanded on by others such as Giordano Bruno and Thomas Digges. The Copernican view demanded a shift in our 'point of view'. We had to see the rest of the cosmos relative to our point of view on earth, an earth that orbited the Sun just like the other planets. This required a shift in our thinking, we had to learn to see what the cosmos would look like from a new perspective, one that was in constant motion. Bruno and Digges expanded on Copernicus' ideas; they understood that his ideas led to an infinite universe where the earth was neither at the center of the solar system nor was that solar system at the center of the universe. Every star could be a sun and each of these suns could have their own solar system. In an infinite universe there was no center. When the structure of the cosmos changed, questions began to be asked about the relationship between the macrocosm and the microcosm. If the macrocosm was not ordered the way we thought then maybe the microcosm was not ordered the way we initially imagined. Since the earth was no longer at the bottom of a hierarchy of planets, and since those planets were no longer made up of an ethereal quintessence but rather the same four elements as our earth, it had consequences to our world view; questions arising from our astronomy rippled through our theology and our psychology. If we are not the center of the universe then maybe we are not the center of God's attention. If matter in heaven is made up of the same matter as our earth then maybe the world is not a corrupt place and maybe flesh does not taint the soul. If there is not a hierarchy to our heavens maybe there should not be a hierarchy on earth. Absolute knowledge of an absolute universe had to give ground to the relative knowledge obtained from a moving perspective. Our point of view affected what we were seeing.

These are the questions that form the backdrop to the 1600s and these ideas are reflected in *Troilus and Cressida*. This play is perhaps the most interlaced play Shakespeare wrote. Each scene, each character is echoed in another. Concepts related to war and love are interlaced. Ideas of individuality are interlaced with concerns of the community and vise versa. Nobody is a villain, nobody is wrong, it all depends on the perspective one takes, on whose point of view is used to examine the scene. Shakespeare often muddies the moral waters, for instance in a play like *Macbeth* his central character is a murderer, but we are always aware of how wrong Macbeth is even as we sympathize with his problems. The moral center is not removed from *Macbeth*. In *Troilus and Cressida* this moral center is missing. This is why it becomes such a difficult play to discuss, from whose point of view do we discuss it?

In *Troilus and Cressida* Ulysses argues that 'the good' proceeds from God downward. As institutions and individuals move further from God they become more corrupt. This is why Kings had command over individuals, they were higher up the chain of being, less corrupt. Erasmus compared 'reason in the mind' to the 'king in the state' and considered the mind's low passions as comparable to 'the common rabble'. This is the form of hierarchy we see questioned in *Troilus and Cressida*. The institutions and generals are revealed to be no less corrupt than the individuals they govern. Thersites offers us some insight into the problem of degree (2.3.50-52; 56-57; 59-62)

> *I'll decline the whole question. Agamemnon*
> *commands Achilles, Achilles is my lord, I am Patroclus'*
> *knower, and Patroclus is a fool.*

> *Agamemnon is a fool, Achilles is a fool,*
>
> *Thersites is a fool, and, as aforesaid, Patroclus is a fool.*
>
> *Agamemnon is a fool to offer to command*
>
> *Achilles, Achilles is a fool to be commanded of*
>
> *Agamemnon, Thersites is a fool to serve such a fool,*
>
> *and Patroclus is a fool positive.*

What Thersites does is that he first shows the order by degree, next he states his conclusion that all are fools, then he tells us why they are fools. What he also shows is the inherent danger in such a system of being under the command of a fool.

If the infinite universe is not ordered in a hierarchy then maybe the rules associated with a hierarchy no longer apply to the microcosm. Maybe the new universe speaks in favour of an emancipation from this hierarchy.

In Troilus and Cressida I would propose that the play's fragmentation offers us a clue to its meaning. Hierarchy by degree is one way to organize a society but whether degree is recognized or not societies can also organize themselves by distinction, by individual areas of specialization, and by competence. This is the point of Agamemnon's and Nestor's speeches early in the play (1.3.17-30). Both speak of how fortune tests our resolve, how life's trials separate the bold from the coward, hard from the soft and wise men from fools. This process can be understood as pragmatic, the best rise to the top through the 'hard-knock' school of real life. Nestor and Agamemnon are triumphing individual merit. Real leaders emerge from within instead of by appointment as occurs in a hierarchical structure. Real life competence as opposed to appointment by heredity or class. Ulysses' speech on order follows these speeches. Ulysses implies that if degree is not respected then all hell will break loose but we know from Agamemnon's and Nestor's speeches that life will itself impose an order, one based on ability, and not necessarily the one based on survival of the fittest that Ulysses fears. Shakespeare is introducing us to the forces that are available and that are capable of organizing a society. He is not making any moral judgments. He has also introduced the idea of testing an individual or society in the play. This concept of challenge is central; he does this with the story of Hector's one-on-one challenge to the Greeks, with Achilles' challenge of the Grecian generals' authority, with the story of Troilus' love and how it will be challenged, and with the debate that takes place in Troy and the challenging of their decision to keep Helen. This idea of challenging individuals, societies, and the decisions they make gives rise to the very concept of the play and its moral ambiguity. It also provides the play with a rebellious undercurrent that is everywhere apparent.

Combinatorics: Creating a Relative Perspective

Societies, just like individuals, can be tested as to whether their goals are aimed at 'the good'. All parts of society from kings to peasants can be examined as to whether they serve 'the good'; everybody's 'merit' can be tested. This is what we see occur in *Troilus and Cressida* – both communities and individuals are divided into their nobler and baser parts. The play does not show us harmony, it shows us dissent. Individuals subverting the decisions of the community and the community ignoring the wishes of individuals. We are witnessing both a power struggle and the abuse of that power between two groups, between the community and the individual. Both sides offer a unique point of view; the communities' interests are championed by Ulysses. His world view is the classical Ptolemaic world view; order and degree leading to harmony. This is the 'top-down' view, considering the interests of the powerful over the weak. The tools it employs to control others are honour and shame. These ideas can be used by the few to control the many.

Cressida affords us a 'bottom-up' point of view. She is an individual that is being coerced by her society. She is forced to take action in her own best interests. She affords us the chance to identify with an individual. She experiences the consequences of her society's decisions. She is an innocent that no one defends. Her rights are not protected and she is abandoned by her society. As a consequence she becomes isolated and the center of her own universe. The tools an individual can employ against their community are those that champion the individual's worth, ideas like these tend to promote insubordination and seed insurrection.

The moral ambiguity of the play comes from these differing perspectives. Do you believe in the rights of society over the individual, always? Or only when the individual is interfering in the rights of others? What about when the individual is right and society is wrong? Then what?

Achilles is the man who untunes the string in the Grecian camp, he abuses his power as an individual and his actions encourage both insubordination and insurrection; he is a force of chaos in the Grecian camp. Achilles is the pinnacle of pride; self-interested and self-involved; he is beyond community control (the twinned powers of honour and shame have no effect on him) and he feels no obligation to his community. Achilles is an easy target, he clearly doesn't care about the interests of his society or the consequences his withdrawal from the battlefield has on his fellow Grecians. It is very easy to identify with Ulysses' speech and to appreciate that Achilles must be disciplined. It is only as the play develops that we begin to see how unscrupulously Ulysses exploits the different individuals. The machinations of society are seen as less than honest and in no way just. Achilles and Ajax are being used as dumb oxen to *"plough up the war"* (2.1.103-104); Ajax is being pitted against Achilles so the *"two curs shall tame each other"* (1.3.391); and Ajax is being set up to battle Hector, a battle he may not be ready for (1.3.382-385). As an audience we begin to see that society's greater good comes at a cost to the unappreciated (*oxen, curs, brainless*) individuals.

As the play proceeds, the State is seen as less benevolent and more tyrannical, it is presented as having the right to oversee everyone's life (3.3.198-199; 207-208)

> *The providence that's in a watchful state*
> *Knows almost every grain of Pluto's gold...*
> *All the commerce that you have had with Troy*
> *As perfectly is ours as yours, my lord.*

In the above quotation, Ulysses has effectively threatened Achilles with the power of the State. He has let Achilles know that the State is well aware of his correspondence with Troy and its effects on his behaviour. He is demonstrating that Achilles has no private life, no secrets, from the State.

Cressida, however, is a better example of an individual who is abused by power. Cressida is not a member of the military, she is a civilian and yet her community trades her for a captured soldier. Her wishes are of no import, she is the proverbial pawn. Her community feels no obligation to her and her interests are not protected. She is sacrificed for the greater good. She, unlike Achilles, has committed no sin. She is not puffed up with pride, she is not divisive in her community nor has she, like Helen, brought a war upon them. The council's decision is like fate; they take control over Cressida's life and override her will. This betrayal by her community comes as a shock to Cressida; she has always believed that her community was there to protect her (1.2.251-255). The hierarchy she describes is similar to

Ulysses: the individual protects themselves, family protects each member and the community protects the families. Cressida is a member of the community that is forced to become an individual. She is literally forced into looking after her own interests. Her community has abandoned her to the Greeks and she is not a part of their community, she literally stands alone, as self-interested now as Achilles, forced to look after herself.

Our Baser and Nobler Halves

Community indifference to its members breeds insurrection and excessive self-interest amongst its members destroys the community. The balance between these forces is the line along which civilizations can grow. In *Troilus and Cressida* it is not only the balancing of these interests that we see depicted but also the challenging of every decision and action into its nobler and baser parts. This creates the dyadic entropy of multiplicity. Everything in the play is divided into these parts. This is the force that creates infinite possibilities. We see it early on in Nestor's speech (1.3.45-47)

> *Even so*
> *Doth valour's show and valour's worth divide*
> *In storms of fortune.*

and we see it near the end of the play as Troilus dissects Cressida into these respective halves (5.2.153;155-156)

> *This is and is not Cressid.*
> *Of this strange nature, that a thing inseparate*
> *Divides more wider than the sky and earth.*

One can go through the play parsing it successively into community interests and individual interests and parsing each of these into their nobler aspects and their baser aspects. This theme carries through right to Pandarus' final soliloquy where he speaks of panderers and turncoats and how both groups carry the stigma of disapproval even though individuals and societies benefit from their services. This attitude seems to stem from a resentment towards the idea that personal profit is made from a service that should be a part of one's duty to a friend or to an ideal. Personal profit has made base their valuable service. This same resentment can also be seen towards the rulers of a society that profits by achieving excessive gains at a cost to the individuals under its care. Society's greater good, if experienced by a diminishing few, can make base even a noble enterprise.

Whether something said or done by someone is proper or not, whether it is noble or base, can only be determined if we can examine the motive of the individuals involved. Is it done to secure some greater good, avert a greater evil, or is it done out of personal interest or for personal benefit?

One can examine all aspects of the play in this manner. The war can be divided into its noble aspects and its base aspects; love too finds representation in both the noble and the base. The list goes on, society's interests can be classified as noble or base; so too an individual's interests. Even a person's Passions can be assessed as noble or base as can their Reason; if it serves 'the good' it is noble if it is self-serving it is base. Nothing is good in and of itself; only in its application can one determine its value, noble or base.

A society that serves a base goal is not noble. Hector tries to point this out to the Trojan council. He argues that Troy is interfering in a man's marriage and should let Helen go because it is morally wrong to keep her (2.2.183-186)

> *If Helen then be wife to Sparta's king,*
> *As it is known she is, these moral laws*
> *Of nature and of nations speak aloud*
> *To have her back returned.*

Hector is pointing out that the aim, the goal, determines if actions are noble or base. Thersites, the cynic, also sees the war as ignoble *"All the argument is a whore and a cuckold"* (2.3.69-70). Again pointing out that it is not wise to fight for a bad cause.

We can see this analysis also applied to Reason, which is not good in and of itself. For example, Ulysses employs reason with base goals in mind. We see him try to convince Achilles to return to the battlefield by attacking his self-worth, we see him connive to let Ajax fight Hector without any respect for Ajax's life. Ulysses shows himself to be clever man who uses reason for base goals.

Even honour has base and noble aspects. Hector is an honourable man but he is 'unrestrained with respect to honour'. He values it over love. From Roman iconography we know that love guides the virtuous man to honour (*The French Academies of the Sixteenth Century*, Yates, Routledge, 1988, p. 144). To place honour above love is a mistake, a form of pride; it makes honour into a dishonourable thing. In the play it leads to Hector's death.

This obsessive examination of every motive and action in the play whether performed by an individual or a society creates a morally ambiguous play. The central question is easy – is an action noble or base; but the consequence of this examination means that societies can be moral sometimes and base at other times, as can be individuals, as can be honour, or reason, or any particular virtue or vice. Everything becomes subject to analysis, everything can be challenged. One cannot say Achilles is evil or dishonourable. True, he kills Hector in a dishonourable way but Achilles has sacrificed his honour for his love of Patroclus. Achilles wishes to avenge the death of a loved one regardless of the personal cost to himself or his honour. Achilles employs his rage in service of his love. If one can have 'noble rage' then Achilles does. This propensity towards mixed messages occurs throughout the play, as when Paris describes the feeling of Aeneas to Diomedes as *"the noblest hateful love"* (4.1.35).

The moral rules of finding an action noble or base are clear but the assessment of these actions requires an appreciation of the motivation or the end goal, something that is not always apparent to everyone looking on. This study of combinations, or combinatorics, is what creates the resulting moral relativism. It also enhances the fragmented nature of the play.

Shakespeare has taken pains to fragment almost everything in the play into parts. This increases the moral confusion exponentially. For instance Ajax is broken into his Greek and Trojan parts (4.5.120-139). This causes confusion for Hector who wishes to cause no harm to that part of Ajax which is related to him (4.5.86)

Half heart, half hand, half Hector.

Moral confusion also results when we break society down into the individuals from which it is made. Some of these individuals command others, for instance Achilles governs the Myrmidons. Moral complexity results when Achilles issues immoral commands. Is it moral or immoral for the Myrmidons to follow their superior? Or we can return our focus to the larger society; what happens if that society makes immoral decisions? Are those that obey that authority then immoral? Is Hector immoral for continuing to fight in a war he knows and has argued to be both morally wrong and one which can be easily stopped?

This fragmentation is intentional, it results from challenging every decision, action, and character in the play, it is not however an extension of the idea of ranking everything by degree akin to Ulysses' speech. Ulysses' system is a hierarchy which carries with it an associated moral hierarchy. The fragmentation we observe functions to subvert the idea of authority, by making every aspect of society subject to the same judgment – is this action noble or base? This simple action takes an ordered system and explodes it into an infinity of possibilities and combinations. The permutations become infinite. Are we moral if we follow the orders of an immoral government? Are we immoral if we oppose this immoral government? Is it moral to do immoral things if we achieve moral ends? The resulting moral confusion is not to frustrate us but to moderate our judgment, our certainty, to make us a little more empathetic. An ordered world of black and white is easy to navigate but ours is a world of ordered chaos rendered in shades of gray. It is difficult to see any clear heroes or villains in *Troilus and Cressida* and this is the point of the play.

The love story within the play is the story that most engages the audience. The question posed – 'Is Cressida false?', Is the one that causes the most debate. The reason being is the moral relativism that Shakespeare has created around this incident. When Troilus honours the wishes of a dishonourable society can we still see him as honourable? When Troilus does not defend the wishes of Cressida is he honourable? Is Cressida false to look after her own well being especially after her own society and those she loved have demonstrated no interest in protecting her? In the end Troilus' and Cressida's actions must speak for themselves. Both are compromised by their own wishes and by the demands of their societies. Both are divided individuals sometimes noble and sometimes base. He is and is not Troilus; she is and is not Cressida. Both carry on with their lives. To live is to be compromised (1.2.94)

> To say the truth, true and not true.

Conclusion

Troilus and Cressida begins as a noble play about war and love but ends in a mire of base compromise. What starts out as a story of heroes and lovers ends as a story of humans trying to get by. The clear morality we would like to believe in proves inadequate to the task put before it. Noble goals and Base goals are easy to identify but it is their repeated application upon every action in the play that creates the infinite permutations on the theme of morality that renders everything and everyone morally grey. Individuals and their actions, when understood in the context of the actions of their societies, can have their most noble actions made base and their base actions made noble.

The play forces us to adopt contrary points of view. First by seeing society's concerns through Ulysses' eyes then seeing the individual's concerns through Cressida's eyes. The play does not provide us with the balance; this we must determine for ourselves. Society's concerns are based on order by degree and are championed by Ulysses. It involves a system of morality that is imposed from the top-down. It involves acceptance to its principles with very little accountability for its actions. The second system is one that projects our own personal prudence onto our culture. This is a morally accountable system in that the culture we produce becomes an extension of our own personal morality. If we all act with wisdom we produce a wise society. Creating the 'just society' in this case is a ground-up exercise based on individual morality that iterates through the community. It is as accountable for its actions as the individuals that create the community. It requires individuals to act for 'the good' and to be judged on their merit, i.e., to do good.

What is subversive about *Troilus and Cressida* is that it forces the Elizabethan audience to analyze everyone and their actions in the play as to whether they are noble or base in their intent. What this inevitably leads to is the questioning of those in authority to account for their actions. It puts in place the psychological tools necessary to replace a hierarchical system with one based on merit. I should point out that both systems regarded 'the good' as their ideal so both systems could be regarded as equally moral but that only one system, a system based on merit, could be held accountable for its actions. This meant that Cressida, Troilus, and the Trojan council could all be held accountable for decisions they had made and whether or not these decisions served 'the good'. By encouraging people to challenge the decisions made by others and to realize the effect that others' decisions could have on their own morality was the first step in challenging the order of the universe and reassessing our place in it.

Troilus and Cressida appears as a fragmented work; from simple beginnings every action and interaction becomes more complex and the possibility of understanding the moral consequences less likely. The simple story slips out of our hands and is replaced by one of infinite complexity. The story we hoped would reflect a simple truth has become a hall of mirrors increasingly difficult to navigate. The story of the war is reflected in the love story; society's concerns are reflected in individual concerns and vice versa. The simple authority of those governing falls into question and the actions of each individual is challenged. *Troilus and Cressida* is a self-referential and integrated play both possessing a poetic unity and moral ambiguity all at the same time.

> *Like or find fault; do as your pleasures are;*
> *Now good or bad, 'tis but the chance of war*
> (Prologue, 30-31).

Footnotes

[1] It was felt that the proper discipline to educate the young be focused on guiding their desires. The passions were not seen as evil but rather as the raw energy that kept us engaged in life. The job of education was to direct this raw energy in the right direction. The passions could all be turned into virtues through correct education and training.

Remember the virtues were seen as the mean between two extremes, for example, fortitude is the mean between fear and recklessness. Cressida and Troilus can be heard debating this particular idea as he attempts to temper her fears of falling in love with his loving recklessness (3.2.66-72).

Achilles' rage or anger offers us another example of energy that needs to be re-directed. Anger's virtuous form is in severity. Severity of the type needed to maintain a just society by both punishing the lawless and preventing crime. This is the virtuous mean between the vicious extremes seen in either the tyranny of rulers or the rebellious violence of subjects. Both extremes are presented in the play; tyranny is displayed over Cressida as she is traded, against her will, for Antenor and rebelliousness is displayed by Achilles as he boycotts the war. It shows the singleness of virtue and the doubleness of vice.

Again it is the goal to which passions are harnessed that makes them into virtues or vices. If the goal is 'the good', the mean, then they are virtues. The young were seen as not yet possessing enough life experience to control their passions.

[2] Constancy in an inconstant world. It is difficult to know if this is a theme or sub-theme or just a line of harmony that runs through the play but it is an idea that keeps recurring.

Agamemnon laments that Jove's trials are to find the "*constancy in men*" (1.3.21).

Troilus' hope is to find a constant woman (3.5.153-158).

Cressida's fear is of men's lack of commitment (4.2.17-19).

Ulysses' speech on the order of degree (1.3.101-110) is all about maintaining stability in the world.

All these characters hope to find something constant in an inconstant changeable world. All will be faced with disappointment.

[3] *"the soul must begin by warring against itself...and the one part of the soul must win victory over the others, which are more in number. It is a feud of one against two, the one part struggling to mount upward, and the two dragging it down."*

(*Hermetica*, Vol 1, p. 393, Walter Scott translation)

This section of the *Hermetica*, as Scott explains, is referring to a battle of the mind against self-assertion (desire for honour) and desires of the flesh. The mind against two forms of passion. What it has to do with *Troilus and Cressida* is that it helps explain why Ulysses (ordered mind) is threatened by Achilles (self-assertion) and Cressida (sexual desire).

This battle, according to Scott's translation (*Hermetica*, Stobaei Hermetica, Excerpt II B. Hermes to Tat, p. 391), all takes place in a world where *"there is nothing real here below"* a world considered to be all an illusion. This world of illusions is the same one that Pandarus and Thesites champion. They too, see love and honour as just an illusion.

I do not wish to leave the impression that Shakespeare has produced *Troilus and Cressida* as an allegory of the battle for the soul for Ulysses is not without fault and Achilles and Cressida are not without virtue, but he may have used this Hermetic understanding of the tripartite soul to set up a dynamic for their relationships.

Bibliography

1) *Troilus and Cressida*, W. Shakespeare, edited by David Bevington, The Arden Shakespeare, Third Series, 1998.

2) *Beyond Fate*, Margaret Visser, House of Anansi Press Inc., 2002.

3) *Troilus and Cressida*, A.S. Knowland, Shakespeare Quarterly, Vol. 10, No. 3 (Summer, 1959), p. 353-365.

4) *The Father and the Bride in Shakespeare*, Lynda E. Boose PMLA, Vol. 97, No. 3 (May, 1982), p. 325-347, published by Modern Language Association.

5) *The Nicomachean Ethics*, Aristotle, transl. H. Rackham, The Loeb Classical Library, 1956.

6) *The Elizabethan World Picture*, E.M.W. Tillyard, Vintage Books, 1958.

7) *The Wheel of Fire; Interpretation of Shakespearian Tragedy*, Chapter 3, 'The Philosophy of Troilus and Cressida', G. W. Knight, Routledge Classics, 2001.

8) *The Iliad*, Homer, translated by Robert Fagles, Penguin Books, 1998.

9) *Hermetica*, Hermes Trismegistus, edited and translated by Walter Scott, Shambhala Publications Inc., 1993.

10) *The French Academies of the Sixteenth Century*, F. Yates, Routledge, 1988.

Abstract for *The Taming of the Shrew*

Kissing the Blarney Stone

Understanding *The Taming of the Shrew*

The Taming of the Shrew is on its surface a sexist play, it has always been so. Its chauvinism is employed to create dramatic tension in order for the comedy to work. The goal of the play is not to put people in their place but rather to emancipate them.

By examining the art of acting Shakespeare demonstrates to us the role it can play in transformation. Through the art of acting Katherine's solid single identity is transformed into many Kates. Katherine's spirit is not broken in the play but her words and wit are finally set free to soar.

Kissing the Blarney Stone

Understanding The Taming of the Shrew

Introduction

The Taming of the Shrew is a sexist play and has always been a sexist play; even in Shakespeare's time it was insulting to women. We know this because in the early 1600s John Fletcher wrote his response or reply to Shakespeare's play by writing his own sequel to it called *The Tamer Tamed* or *The Woman's Prize* (1611). Fletcher's play was written and performed during Shakespeare's lifetime. This tells us that there was a ready-made audience for Fletcher's work. His play shows Petruchio getting his comeuppance and in the work Fletcher argues for an equality in marriage. If these ideas did not carry currency the play would not have been written or performed, nor would it have found an audience. Clearly, Petruchio's actions were not considered appropriate even by Elizabethan standards. The sexism of the work, however, is a surface characteristic; it is perceived by everyone but it does not explain the purpose of the play nor does it dismiss the value of the work. To understand Shakespeare we must always go beneath the surface to find the core and this particular play is all about the deceptive nature of surfaces.

The second idea we must keep in mind to understand Shakespeare's work is that *The Taming of the Shrew* is a play-within-a-play. It is the play performed for Sly in the Induction scene. *The Taming of the Shrew* is a fiction based on a folktale told to a group of men. This is the setting of the work: a dissimilation within the dissimilation of the Induction; a dream within a dream as Sly would see it.

117

The final thought I wish you to continually keep in mind while considering this play is the concept of 'inner essence versus the outward show', i.e., surfaces deceive [1]. This concept is applied like an iterative principle throughout the play. What we see on the outside seldom reflects truthfully what is on the inside.

The deceptions pile up starting from the Induction scene: Sly is a drunkard who is dressed up to appear to be a lord, his wife is not his wife but a Pageboy dressed up to look like a woman, the play they watch performed is not a slice of reality but a fiction put on by actors.

As the audience, we are in on the setup. We are in fact witnessing a de-construction. Shakespeare is telling us very straight forwardly that Katherine is not Katherine but an actor playing Katherine.

These are the ideas we must keep at the front of our minds as we attempt to appreciate this play: the play is sexist, it is a fiction, and the surface of things does not reveal their essence (truth is not linked with appearance).

Looking at Structure

What a play means, what a playwright intends to communicate, can often be conjectured from its structure and central metaphors. These typically repeat to reinforce an idea. When I say they are structural I mean just that, they physically hold up the idea of the play, they repeat just like bearing walls in a building. By noticing these repeated ideas we can begin to appreciate the concepts that the playwright felt were necessary, that could not be ignored, that were central to her/his vision.

Themes and metaphors may be repeated by different characters in different plot lines; this does not matter. It is the repeat, reflection or echo that is of concern. Allusions function in a similar fashion only they link the stories inside the play to stories outside the play, again echoing or reflecting the author's intent.

Let us start examining Shakespeare's play by looking at the Induction scene. It is set in our reality. Sly is a drunkard whose drinking is cut off by the Hostess, a woman, who calls in his tab. She threatens him and exercises control over him. He passes out. Along comes a lord and his hunting party and they decide to relocate him, dress him as a lord, and treat him as such in order to determine whether (IND.1.39)

Would not the beggar then forget himself?

They are conducting a social experiment centered on one's identity to test both its permanence and its flexibility. Does Sly remain Sly the drunken tinker or does he rise to the occasion and transform himself into Sly the lord?

Sly is not the only character in the Induction that is transformed. The lord transforms himself into one of Sly's servants and the lord also transforms his page into a woman (IND.1.103-104)

Sirrah, go you to Barthol'mew my page,
And see him dress'd in all suits like a lady.

The lord not only requests this transformation but he also provides his page with a cultural script (IND.1.108-115)

He bear himself with honourable action,
Such as he hath observ'd in noble ladies
Unto their lords...
With soft low tongue and lowly courtesy,
And say 'What is't your honour will command,
Wherein your lady and your humble wife
May show her duty and make known her love?'

What is interesting about this script is that it is given by a man to another man instructing him on how to play a woman. Gil Harris ("*The*

Taming of the Shrew, An Authoritative Text, Sources and Contexts, Criticism, Rewritings and Appropriations", edited by Dympna Callaghan, Norton Critical Edition, p. 246) has suggested that "*both nobility and femininity are not natural identities, but socially scripted roles*". Both Sly and the page are essentially instructed on how to behave like cultural stereotypes or ideals.

As Sly is introduced to his trappings and the options available to him for his 'Lordly day' he is also told of his paintings. These depict scenes of Adonis, Io, and Daphne, all subjects of Ovid's poetry and personages that were transformed; Adonis into a flower, Io into a cow, and Daphne into a laurel tree (*The Metamorphoses of Ovid,* translated by Allen Mandelbaum; Book X, p. 356; Book I, p. 26-29, 21-24). This central theme of transformation is repeated innumerable times in the Induction and is carried forward into the play with equal frequency as characters adopt disguises.

The Taming of the Shrew play within the Induction can be regarded as a keystone metaphor to the play as a whole. It is a play-within-a-play. It involves actors playing characters. This is hidden from no one, especially not the audience. Karen Newman in her article ("Renaissance Family Politics and Shakespeare's *Taming of the Shrew*", Norton Critical Edition, p. 247-261) points out that Sly is presented with two illusions or dreams; first, he dreams that he is a lord and secondly he dreams that a man can tame a woman (that Petruchio can tame Kate). Both are illusions. Both are examples of theatre, the result of actors role playing.

Illusion and transformation hold this play together. They are concepts easy to forget as we get caught up in the action of the play and the actor's craft. As we examine the play I will be drawing your attention away from the action, destroying the illusion, to reveal possible reasons for it. This is what the Induction was set up to do. This is what Shakespeare intended.

A Play-within-a-Play

Laurie Maguire in her article ("The Naming of the Shrew", Norton Critical Edition, p. 123-137) highlights a production of *The Taming of the Shrew* performed by the Oxford Stage Company in 2006. The production was directed by Chris Pickles. Her description of the production points out two key features that make Pickle's direction important. Firstly, he keeps the Induction scene, the scene where Sly, the comatose drunk, is relocated to a manor house, dressed as a lord and then awakened by his supposed servants. Many versions of the play cut these scenes. This is a mistake. The Induction scene sets up the central metaphors that will play out in the larger work: how our understanding of ourselves is affected by how others treat us, how we see ourselves, and where we fit in society.

Secondly, Pickles has cleverly created a bridge between the Induction scene and the play within this Induction scene. The play performed for Sly is *The Taming of the Shrew* but in Pickle's version the cast is short one member and so they recruit Sly to read the parts this missing cast member would have acted. By so doing Pickles has integrated the two parts of Shakespeare's play – that often exist in isolation from one another – into a coherent whole.

By making Sly an active cast member in the 'Shrew Play' Pickles constantly reminds the audience that *The Taming of the Shrew* is in fact a play within Sly's world, that the roles are performed by actors, some of the roles being played by Sly himself. This deconstructs the play for the audience by constantly reminding them of its construction. In a play so focused on transformation this gives the audience a helping hand.

They can begin to see through the layers of actor, character, and the disguises each character adopts.

A play-within-a-play is a construction created to serve the enclosing structure. In *Hamlet,* the *Murder of Gonzago* serves the story of *Hamlet;* in *A Midsummer Night's Dream* Bottom's play *Pyramus and Thisbe* serves to reinforce ideas about the role of the imagination that were presented in the main play. The play-within-a-play is usually a minor work housed within a major work. With *The Taming of the Shrew* we are looking at a major work housed within a minor work, the Induction Scene. This creates a problem for audiences in that as they get caught up in the action of this play they forget it is a fiction held within and intended to inform the Induction scene or the Sly-Frame. The genius of Chris Pickle's production is that it constantly reminds the audience that they are watching a performance within Sly's world.

The Induction, Sly's world, is not inherently sexist. The Hostess who manages the Inn is a strong woman who exercises control over Sly. She has both a good job and power. Within the Induction the only sexist elements are when the lord describes how he thinks a lady should behave. He does this in order to guide the page's performance, but it must be remembered that he is also creating a fantasy for Sly.

This does mitigate some of the sexism inherent in the work. We are in essence being told a sexist folk tale with fairy tale overtones within the Sly-Frame (E.M.W. Tillyard, "The Fairy-Tale Element in *The Taming of the Shrew*", The Norton Critical Edition, p. 261-266).

Ovid's Seductions and Transformations

Within the fiction of *The Taming of the Shrew* there are two plot lines. The transformation of Kate and the seduction of Bianca. Kate's storyline is described as having evolved from the folktale tradition (Jan

Harold Brunvand, "The Folktale Origin of *The Taming of the Shrew*", Norton Critical Edition, p. 266-273) and Bianca's storyline comes from the Italian tradition (George Gascoigne, *Supposes*, Norton Critical Edition, p. 94-106).

Bianca's tale follows the literary conventions of a fairy tale romance whereas Kate's tale has the more pragmatic realistic feel of a folk tale. Kate's tale more than Bianca's is grounded in the times and place of Elizabethan England.

In the Sly-Frame attention was given to Ovid's *Metamorphoses*, poems about transformations but in *The Taming of the Shrew* attention is also given to Ovid's *Ars Amatoria* (1.1.33) (4.2.8). Ovid's *The Art of Love* was a group of poems themed on the art of seduction or on 'how to woo'. These poems explored the romantic notions associated with the Bianca plotline. Ovid's *Metamorphoses* examined the ideas of transformation more appropriate to the Kate plotline. Both sets of poems provide the background ambiance or the mood to the play, both sets of poems are themed to one or the other plotline but are not exclusive to either. Love finds Kate, and Bianca's story is full of transformations.

Supposes

In Gascoigne's Prologue to *Supposes* he states that *"a suppose"* is *"nothing else but a mystaking or imagining of one thing for another"* (*The Taming of the Shrew*, edited by Brian Morris, The Arden Shakespeare, Introduction, p. 119).

This is the iterative principle for Shakespeare's entire play. It applies to both the Sly-Frame as well as to *The Taming of the Shrew*. This principle will show up over and over creating an uncertain world where expectations and assumptions are almost always misleading.

Lucentio is the first character we meet in 'the play'. He has come to Padua on the expectation of pursuing (1.1.9)

A course of learning and ingenious studies

but promptly finds himself pursing his passions as he falls instantly in love with Bianca (1.1.146-147)

I pray, sir, tell me, is it possible
That love should of a sudden take such a hold?

He changes his plans as quickly as his identity. Lucentio becomes Cambio (Italian meaning "to change or exchange"), a Latin teacher. Lucentio also gives up his identity as master to his servant Tranio, who will now act his part (1.1.236)

Tranio is chang'd into Lucentio.

Lucentio has decided to humble himself, to (1.1.219)

be a slave, t'achieve that maid.

Although this is part of the Bianca plot line it possesses many features in common with Ovid's *Metamorphoses*. In Ovid it is common to find stories of gods who fall in love, often at first sight, with mortals. These gods then go on to transform themselves (humble themselves) by taking on a disguise in order to obtain the lover. This formula is followed by Lucentio. Lucentio's tale also alerts us to the fact that we are operating within a world where 'love at first sight' is possible, a world of romantic possibility.

Outward show is being used to hide the inner essence. This practice of adopting disguises will run rampant through the Bianca plotline. Lucentio disguises himself as Cambio, Tranio becomes 'Lucentio', Hortensio will adopt the persona of Litio, and a pendant will be asked to impersonate Vincentio. All these counterfeits are employed to fool the observer of surfaces. Truth is separated from appearance. By using subterfuge these deceivers accomplish their goal (5.1.107)

While counterfeit supposes blear'd thine eyne.

The action of the play occurs below the visible surface.

While deceit and sexual peak-a-boo play their standard role in the Bianca storyline a heavier more realistic tale unfolds in Katherine's plotline. Shakespeare loves the Katherine character. In many ways she is an embodiment of his Sonnet 130, *"My mistress' eyes are nothing like the sun"*. This sonnet was written in response to all the overblown purple prose typically written by a lover, like the poetry Lucentio recites about his vision of Bianca (1.1.174-176)

> *I saw her coral lips to move,*
> *And with her breath she did perfume the air.*
> *Sacred and sweet was all I saw in her.*

Shakespeare's Sonnet 130 exposes these sentiments for the vapid nonsense they are. His lover is a real woman

> *Coral is far more red than her lips' red...*
> *And in some perfumes is there more delight*
> *Than in the breath that from my mistress reeks...*
> *I grant I never saw a goddess go -*
> *My mistress when she walks treads on the ground.*

As romantic and ethereal as Bianca is Kate is the opposite. She is drawn from the real world not a fairy tale. She possesses real faults. The audience can and does relate to her, that is why her fate is so important, why the sexism in the play carries so much sting.

Petruchio is introduced to us as a mercenary. He appears to be only after one thing: wealth (1.2.64-75). The wooing of Kate takes on the features of a commercial venture. Hortensio and Gremio agree to bear the cost of his courtship of Katherine (1.2.213-214). Petruchio will marry Katherine (for money) so that they are free to pursue Bianca. We fear for Katherine.

At this point we must remind ourselves that Peturchio's character, like Bianca's and Katherine's is only a surface feature. All the characters possess a hidden depth that is yet to be revealed. This is the iterative feature of the play, mathematical in its purity, it cuts through every aspect of the work; inner essence does not match the outward show. Whatever we see is a deception, a false front – counterfeit supposes blear our eyes.

Baptista falls victim to this truth. He is so preoccupied with the commercial aspects of Bianca's marriage agreement and his attention is so consumed by imposters that she is stolen right under his eyes. He is so distracted by 'false players' that he does not see the 'false players' seducing his daughter. Baptista's problem is the audience's problem as well; the surfaces deceive and distract us from looking below the surface to the heart of the play.

Bianca: Below the Surface

Bianca is a more nuanced example of the separation between surface and essence. She conforms to the lord's definition of how a lady should appear and behave as offered in the 'Sly-Frame'. She is modest, quiet-spoken, and elegant but she is not obedient. She is not obedient to her father (she elopes without his consent) and she is not obedient to her instructors.

Patricia Parker in her article ("Construing Gender: Mastering Bianca in *The Taming of the Shrew*", Norton Critical Edition, p. 192-209) sheds much light on the Bianca plotline. I would, however, like to focus on just her discussion of the 'Latin lesson'. Initially Bianca interrupts a discussion Cambio and Litio are having on the proper order of the arts. By interrupting this discussion and telling them of her wishes she is also rejecting the proper order in the master-pupil relationship (3.1.16-20)

> *Why, gentlemen, you do me double wrong*
> *To strive for that which resteth in my choice.*

I am no breeching scholar in the schools,

I'll not be tied to hours nor 'pointed times,

But learn my lessons as I please myself.

The pupil will be master of the Masters [2].

As Parker points out in her analysis of the 'Latin lesson' Cambio uses a text from Ovid's *Heroides* (*Heroides, i.* 33-34). It is from a section concerning Penelope's complaint. In it she grieves of having to hear the story of Troy second hand and having to wait twenty years for her husband's return. These passages evoke images of Penelope being placed under siege by her suitors but it also evokes images of how the Walls of Troy were breached by deception. Both images are directly relevant to what is occurring in Shakespeare's play – Bianca is isolated but for her suitors and these suitors have breached the walls of her father's house by deception.

The next line Cambio draws from this translation of *Heroides* appears to be "*illic Aeacides, illic tendebat Ulixes*" but he translates it wrongly as "*sure Aeacides / was Ajax*" where it should be "*sure Aeacides / was Achilles*" (3.1.50-51). Bianca recognizes this error and it reinforces her suspicions as to his true identity "*I know you not...I trust you not*" (3.1.40-41) but she acquiesces to his mistake in order to take control and end the session (3.1.52-54)

I must believe my master, else, I promise you,

I should be arguing still upon that doubt.

But let it rest. Now, Litio, to you.

Katherine will repeat this process in the 'Sun-Moon' scene with Petruchio. By agreeing to his 'mistakes' she can take control of her journey. The appearance of control, of being master, belongs to the men, the actual control lies below the surface and belongs to the women.

Understanding Petruchio

Petruchio is the villain of the piece or the hero if you see the play as a comedy. I believe there is every reason to see it as a comedy; the love matches made are happily in place at the end of the play, no one is harmed, and the iterative device used consistently throughout the play tells us that we cannot believe the outward show. This means that our first impression of Petruchio as a 'land pirate' willing to marry just for money is undoubtedly a false impression.

Petruchio belongs to the realistic side of the play. We do not expect a romantic device such as 'love at first sight' to occur in his story line but we do expect a more realistic affection to grow and evolve into love. We also expect to discover who Petruchio is over time. In Shakespeare's work, I am not convinced that characters evolve so much as they are revealed. The great tragic characters in Shakespeare do not change, that is the source of their tragedy, but they do reveal themselves throughout the play. This I believe to be true of Petruchio as well.

When he brags about his exploitative goals with regards to marriage he shocks his friend Hortensio but not his servant, Grumio. So the materialistic drive, the drive for commercial success is certainly one of Petruchio's core characteristics. Petruchio has also revealed a recklessness in his character, he is a risk taker, he does not fear consequences perhaps because he has a confidence in his ability to face uncertainty (1.2.197-209).

Petruchio is also disrespectful of others, he demonstrates this several times in the course of the play. Gremio tries to correct his forward nature (2.1.45)

You are too blunt, go to it orderly.

Petruchio does not respect order. He describes himself as *"peremptory"* (2.1.131), he is bold and sees his command as absolute. All these behaviours manifest themselves early in the play before he adopts his scheme to 'outshrew the shrew'. We can regard them as the characteristics he is choosing to present to others, they represent his outer persona.

When Petruchio witnesses Katherine's 'devilish spirit' I believe he recognizes a 'kindred spirit' for he is struck with affection for her (2.1.161)

> *I love her ten times more.*

Katherine's disrespect and recklessness are attractive to him. This is presented honestly to the audience. He is not performing for anyone so we can trust this first blush of affection.

A fable has an internal logic to it. Even before Petruchio has met Katherine we know he harbours a sincere affection for her. We also know Petruchio is driven to 'improve' things. He wishes to improve his lot in life just as he has already improved on his inheritance (2.1.117-118)

> *Left solely heir to all his lands and goods,*
> *Which I have better'd rather than decreas'd.*

Within the 'fable logic' Petruchio's goal is to better Katherine. Harm is never intended. What he loves in himself he has already witnessed in a raw form in her. Before they have met he already loves her spirit.

Petruchio and Kate: Fire and Fire

Petruchio renames Katherine when they first meet, he calls her Kate and then puns her name into "*cates*" (2.1.189) which means a type of household commodity (Natasha Korda, "Domesticating Commodities in *The Taming of the Shrew*", Norton Critical Edition, p. 149-164). Katherine responds in kind referring to Petruchio as "*a movable*" (2.1.197) meaning a piece of furniture. This banter continues; each a verbal match for the other. Their dialogue exploits the physical and sexual tension between them.

Petruchio sees his job as one of domestication to (2.1.270-271)

bring you from a wild Kate to a Kate
Conformable.

This is Petruchio's way of dealing with the world. He takes command of situations. This appears to be Katherine's strategy as well, she likes to have control and in her culture this has resulted in her being labelled 'a shrew'. It is her visible fault. Petruchio does not see it as such (2.1.246-247)

Why does the world report that Kate doth limp?
O slanderous world!

Petruchio recognizes her domineering spirit (2.1.283-285)

Yourself and all the world
That talk'd of her have talk'd amiss of her
If she be curst it is for policy

and understands that her behaviour is intended 'for policy' or to take tactical advantage. This is the same strategy Petruchio has employed so far in the play, bold/agressive. He understands that her behaviour is not getting her the results she wants. She wants control. She wants command. But insulting and abusing others (a hammer is the only tool she has in her toolbox) is not giving her the control she seeks.

The taming Petruchio has in mind may be better understood as educating. Just as a falconer does not wish to destroy a bird's instincts or aggressiveness but merely to redirect these strengths to more appropriate goals so too Petruchio has no intention of destroying Katherine's spirit, he only wishes to focus that energy.

The idea of 'mistaking one thing for another', the theme of *Supposes,* has led to Katherine being mistaken for a shrew and

Petruchio being mistaken as a *"half lunatic"* and *"a madcap ruffian"* (2.1.280-281). Our job is to look for the essence beneath the surface.

We are made aware of Petruchio's hidden depths from an oath made by one of his friends (3.2.22; 24-25)

> *Upon my life, Petruchio means but well,*
>
> *Though he be blunt, I know him passing wise*
>
> *Though he be merry, yet withal he's honest.*

Petruchio's presence in Katherine's life begins to bear fruit very early on. Because of Petruchio's odd behaviour he becomes the focus of gossip instead of her. Katherine begins to be the object of sympathy from others, perhaps for the first time (3.2.27-28)

> *Go, girl, I cannot blame thee now to weep,*
>
> *For such an injury would vex a saint.*

As the community condemns Petruchio they begin to redefine Katherine. Petruchio is described as (3.2.151-153)

> *A grumbling groom...*
>
> *Cruster than she...*
>
> *Why, he's a devil, a devil, a very fiend.*

Gremio who previously called Katherine a *"fiend of hell"* (1.1.89) now sees her as (3.2.155)

> *a lamb, a dove, a fool to him.*

In order to adopt a new persona it often helps if the community accepts that change. If everyone calls you a shrew and treats you like a shrew it is difficult to see yourself as anything but a shrew.

Petruchio has helped to start the reinvention of Katherine by presenting himself at the wedding, publicly, as such an outrageous character that he has managed to shift the focus away from her. She can now be seen as *"a lamb"*. If Katherine is to transform having the community ready to accept this transformation is half the battle.

Petruchio, following the wedding, abducts Katherine from her confused but slightly protective community. He declares her his chattel, his property, his anything. Petruchio presents his actions as 'protective' of her. In the days to come nothing is good enough for her – at least in his eyes. His perfectionism prevents her receiving adequate food, shelter or rest but also leaves him blameless in her eyes (4.3.12)

He does it under name of perfect love.

We know Petruchio's violence is an act; he has revealed this part of his plan in his soliloquy (4.1.184-196). His servants have discerned the change in his behaviour and they remark that *"he is more shrew that she"* (4.1.76). Petruchio has however created an atmosphere of violence even though behind the scenes he attempts to make up for his antic behaviour to those he harms, as when Hortensio is instructed to pay the tailor and apologize for the clothing that Petruchio has both insulted and damaged (4.3.163-164)

Tailor, I'll pay thee for thy gown tomorrow.

Take no unkindness of his hasty words.

So as an audience we know Petruchio is not as controlling or as violent as he appears, but Katherine does not. His particular performance is done just for her (the play-within-a-play has a performance of Petruchio's own private design within it). Petruchio's 'set piece' does yield some results, Katherine has been given a chance to show her better qualities, such as her empathy, when she intercedes between an inappreciative Petruchio and one of his staff (4.1.143)

Patience, I pray you, 'twas a fault unwilling.

Katherine, under his mild deprivation, has also been reminded of how privileged her life has been (4.3.6-7)

But I, who never knew how to entreat,

Nor never needed that I should entreat.

These behaviours reveal who Katherine is to the audience, they are not the consequence of training, they merely come to the surface as a result of the circumstances in which she finds herself. These behaviours reveal her inner self her true self.

How Katherine copes with Petruchio's artificial world and what Petruchio's ultimate goals are determines how offended we will be with Shakespeare's play. This is the turning point, the answer to these questions determines what kind of play we are watching.

Katherine's Response

At this point Katherine has been transformed into Kate, a chattel, an object. Petruchio has ignored her words, pretends he does not hear them or hears just the ones he wishes to.

Katherine's moving speech (4.3.73-80) leaves us with the clear understanding that she must *"be free...in words"* or her spirit will be destroyed, her heart will break. How one reads the next few scenes determines if we see Katherine as redeemed or destroyed. It determines if we see the play as a tragedy or a comedy.

Petruchio has committed himself to a process we may define as positive reinforcement training with regard to his interactions with Kate. He avoids confrontation with her by ignoring her words; he doesn't rise to her insults or engage her in argument. He uses only positive descriptions of her in front of others. This part of his plan was outlined in his soliloquy (2.1.170-180)

> *Say that she rail, why I'll tell her plain*
> *She sings as sweetly as a nightingale*
> *Say that she frown, I'll say she looks as clear*
> *As morning roses newly wash'd with dew*
> *...etc.*

In public he always depicts her as *"the kindest Kate"* (2.1.300). Even at the wedding he draws attention to himself with his bad behaviour but he has nothing but good things to say about her (3.2.191-193)

> *I thank you all*
> *That have beheld me give away myself*
> *To this most patient, sweet, and virtuous wife.*

Petruchio is trying to draw attention to those positive aspects possessed by Kate that she may not have acknowledged or heard acknowledged in years.

Petruchio appears to be a man capable of seeing beyond the surface affectation (3.2.115)

> *To me she is married not unto my clothes*

it is an insight he shares with Katherine (4.3.169)

> *For 'tis the mind that makes the body rich.*

Perhaps Petruchio is trying to free Katherine of her obsession with the surface of things. He wants her to look below the surface (4.3.172-173)

> *What is the jay more precious than the lark*
> *Because his feathers are more beautiful?*

Petruchio also offers himself as Katherine's scapegoat. He is willing to accept the blame for any outward appearance Katherine may feel ashamed of. In this way he frees her from any responsibility for the offence (4.3.178-179)

> *If thou account'st it shame, lay it on me.*
> *And therefore frolic.*

He is encouraging Katherine to *frolic*, a term meaning to be playful and full of pranks. He wishes Katherine to shed some of her seriousness or sense of responsibility.

Petruchio has shown us (the audience) that he is both an actor and an improvisor. We have seen him adopt at least one role that we know to be different from his normal behaviour, that of the 'über-shrew'. We have also seen him adopt strange dress and play the role of 'pirate and protector' when he appears at the wedding and subsequently abducts Katherine from the celebration. Petruchio appears to be full of pranks and living his life by the very adjective '*frolic*'.

If one were to be generous, you could view Petruchio as an actor teaching Katherine his craft – how to use her imagination – how to improvise – her taming lesson may in fact be a lesson on how to free herself of this reality and begin to fashion a new one of her own making.

Up to this point in the drama we have seen several characters choose to play the part of others. Lucentio is acting the role of Cambio (the man of letters), Hortensio has been playing Litio (the musician), and Tranio is acting the role of Lucentio (his master). Most of the characters have adopted roles more suited to achieving their goals. Even Petruchio's antic behaviour has been chosen by him as the role most likely to help him achieve his goal.

Bianca, too, is playing a role albeit one assigned to her by her culture. Her role does not attract any attention because she appears to be what others expect her to be. Katherine, however, has chosen a role for herself that does shock her culture and this has both sidelined her and made it difficult for her to achieve her goals.

The question Petruchio explores with Kate is the same question the lord explores with Sly in the Induction scene – *Does a person have a solid-single-identity or can they change and learn to improvise on a newly adopted role?* This does not require the destruction of Kate's persona so much as it requires her to free herself from her own limitations.

Juliet Dusinberre ("*The Taming of the Shrew*: Women, Acting, and Power", Norton Critical Edition, p. 219-237) explores the idea that *The Taming of the Shrew* is not just a play-within-a-play but that it would have been a play in which the Elizabethan audience would have recognized the actors who played the various parts. This meant that their presence as actors was never completely concealed behind their masks or the roles they played. The audience would have always been aware of their dual identity and sometime triple identity (for example they knew the name of the actor who played Lucentio even as he pretended to be Cambio) within the play.

Dusinberre points out that in the play there is a power of emancipation that comes from this role playing. Tranio must oscillate between the subservience he must show in his social role (servant to Lucentio) and the confidence he must project when he is acting the role of Lucentio. In this role he acts as the master would and becomes friends with his social superiors. This role playing affords him increased status by the end of the play, at the final feast we find he still maintains friendships he forged while pretending to be Lucentio and that he can still share in a jest at the expense of and with his betters (5.2.49-62).

Acting a part makes others see you in that role and treat you as that person. By acting we can change who we are socially. This is the idea explored in the Induction scene. The lord attempts to see if he can improve Sly the drunk by convincing him he's Sly the lord. Social improvement is the theme we see enacted in both parts of this play.

Petruchio puts Katherine's wish 'to be free in words' to the test when he challenges her to see the Sun as the Moon or otherwise (4.5.1-25). He is challenging her skill to improvise, to play and be playful, to free herself from this reality. How an actor plays this scene is important – is it enacted as Petruchio bullying Katherine into compliance or is it presented as a scene of encouragement, encouraging Katherine to 'come play with me' in an absurdist game of make believe?

The context helps us with this question. The play is clearly a comedy with dramatic tension. The Sly-Frame of the Induction is clearly a comedy. The play within this Sly-Frame is a blend between a folk tale and a fairy tale – no ill will is intended – no dark purposes lurk behind any one character. The play contains a double marriage both lending a different flavour to the happy-ever-after-ending: Bianca's tinged with a naïve romanticism and Kate's showing a more realistic partnership. To render this play into a tragedy glosses over too much of the mitigating text, it demands reading Petruchio in a too one dimensional way. The overriding metaphor of 'outward show versus inner essence' so widely applied throughout the text would have to be ignored.

The play is a farce and a comedy with the drama lending the necessary tension for the comedy to work. Knowing this helps us to understand the Sun-Moon scene.

The Penny Drops

Petruchio is offering Katherine control but only on the condition that she pay attention to his lead (4.3.189-190)

> *Look what I speak, or do, or think to do,*
> *You are still crossing it.*

This advice creates the dramatic tension required for the comedy of release to follow. We are still unaware of Petruchio's motives – is he just trying to exert his control or is he planning for Katherine's freedom?

The advice given is the type of advice a good actor would give to an apprentice, i.e. follow my lead, be prepared to react to what I say or do. Good acting is reacting. Good acting depends on action-reaction, you must behave as if you are seeing it for the first time, you must be flexible in your response.

The next scene (4.5) has Petruchio calling the Sun the Moon. Katherine's ire begins to rise and she starts to engage him in an argument then slowly it dawns on her – both the chance for control – and the chance to play. By exercising both her love of words and her wit she can gain control of her situation. Petruchio has listened to her and has given her a wedding gift [3].

By the time Vincentio shows up the game of make-believe is in full bloom. She is going to improvise on Petruchio's lead. When Petruchio call Vincentio a young virgin Katherine hams it up embracing and embellishing the idea as she goes. When Petruchio changes the game saying Vincentio is actually an elderly gentleman she convincingly backtracks in a most playful way. She is *frolicing*.

The gift Petruchio has given Kate is not just freedom to use her words but freedom to act and achieve. He paraphrases this in his comment (4.5.24-25)

> *Thus the bowl should run,*
>
> *And not unluckily against the bias.*

The bias – the oblique line or the prejudiced view. Petruchio is telling both Katherine and the audience that if we avoid our natural tendencies, our single mindedness, our prejudices, we may have more luck achieving our goals.

Harold Bloom (*The Taming of the Shrew* from his work *Shakespeare: The Invention of the Human*, excerpted in the Norton Critical Edition, p. 187-192) has sensed this playfulness in the script. He has sensed but not argued why the vignette on the street in Padua is so moving. It is the scene where Petruchio asks Katherine for a kiss (5.1.130-138). He does not take it, the kiss is hers to give. She responds by playing with him. This time she is changing the Sun into the Moon.   There is real affection here, she understands the gift Petruchio has given.   She can be 'many Kates' now and not just the single-minded shrew.   She is free as never before.   Her words can play and frolic and help her to achieve her goals which, in this instance, is to kiss Petruchio with love and appreciation [4].

The Wedding Feast – The Bridal Roast

The actors' gift – the gift of the mask – has been given to Katherine.   She can hide behind it, she can change it, she can use it to accomplish her goals.

The last scene (5.2) of the play lends itself to the most controversy. Within the structure of Shakespeare's work it can perhaps be better appreciated.   The play has equipped us for this last scene.   Its first lines (5.2.1-2)

At last, though long, our jarring notes agree

And time it is, when raging war is done

refer more to Katherine's and Petruchio's struggle than to anyone else's.   We know Petruchio brought insight and understanding to Kate by 'outshrewing the shrew' (4.1.167)

He kills her in her own humour.

So we may now expect that such a method may be used by his apprentice, Kate, to help her solve her problems.

At Bianca's wedding feast Hortensio's wife, the widow, insults Petruchio (5.2.20)

He that is giddy (dizzy) *thinks the world turns round.*

No one picks up on this insult except Katherine; she asks the widow to repeat it and explain herself (5.2.22)

Mistress, how mean you that?

She explains by both insulting Petruchio, calling him hen-pecked, and Katherine, calling her a shrew (2.2.28-29)

Your husband, being troubled with a shrew,
Measures my husband's sorrow by his woe.

For Katherine to be revenged she is going to 'out-submissive' the 'submissive' wives. This is completely within Katherine's normal behaviour, she intends to win, and so defend both her and her husband's reputations. She will no longer be typecast as a shrew and she will not be insulted. She does, however, now possess the tools necessary for her to accomplish her goal in a civil manner.

Katherine's speech of submission, like all aspects of this play, is not what it appears to be on the surface. Truth is separated from appearance. The 'speech of submission' is a 'speech of revenge', it is a defense of a husband and a vindication of herself. It is delivered in response to an insult with the intent to accomplish a goal.

Katherine manages to shame both Bianca and the widow with their own words or words similar to the ones they would espouse to reflect their views or at least those of the role they are playing. The submissive wife is a total fiction in this play.

Katherine's speech need not be examined in detail. It is a re-hashing of parts from the *Book of Common Prayer* and even older more archaic works (Lynda E. Boose, "Scolding Brides and Bridling Scolds", Norton Critical Edition, p. 174-186, specifically p. 177). The point of the speech is that it is ultra-conservative and serves to redefine Katherine's social role. She has used words to 'duff-in' the widow and Bianca. She has achieved her goal of revenge without raising either her voice or her hand in violence. By choosing to go against her bias she managed to score a goal for herself.

It should be noted that the women take the brunt of Katherine's revenge but that the women were also the source of the insult. The men pay too and are made to suffer financially for their chauvinism (betting on their wives).

The power couple that emerge triumphant from the drama are Katherine and Petruchio, two actors adept at improvising to achieve their goals. The fact that Kate's 'revenge speech' should have such positive consequence for both of them is an ironic high note on which to end the comedy.

Conclusion

"All three strands of the sixteenth-century play (the gullying of Sly, the wooing of Bianca and the taming of Katherina) involve pretence, deception, and the acting out of roles to achieve particular ends". Marea Mitchell ("Performing Sexual Politics in The Taming of the Shrew", Norton Critical Edition, p. 237-247).

The Induction scene focuses our attention on the fact that actors are going to play the roles of Petruchio, Katherine, etc. in the play-within-a-play. We can also note that within this fiction when the Page or Katherine or Lucentio play a role they play a stereotype of it, i.e., the Page plays a stereotype of what a lord's mistress would be; Katherine plays the stereotype of a shrew; Lucentio plays the stereotype of a teacher. This strategy informs us that Katherine will also adopt a stereotype in her performance of the 'submission speech' (I would prefer this speech to be called the 'revenge speech' for reasons of intent afterall the speech is about achieving revenge, it is not about submission).

By alternating 'real' characters with their 'stereotype' creations it is possible to orient oneself in the various aspects of the play. These levels of performance help an actor portray a character who has adopted a different role.

The Induction scene is important to understanding *The Taming of the Shrew* because it focuses our attention on actors and acting. It forewarns us that role-playing is going to be central to any understanding of the play. It warns us that the surface of the thing is not indicative of its true essence. The Induction scene has shown that 'truth can be separated from appearance' as soon a Sly the tinker becomes Sly the lord. It tells us that Sly or anyone else can be separated from their identity. This separation is reinforced and maintained throughout the production of *The Taming of the Shrew*.

The sexist play is not sexist, Petruchio is not a chauvinistic villain, Katherine is not a shrew and Bianca is not spineless. The surface of the play deceives us at every opportunity. Uncertainty and worry for the characters builds the dramatic tension. This tension makes the comic relief work.

Katherine has learned of the subversive nature of language, she has become 'free in her words' – her heart will not break – she has learned how to be subversive, she has learned how to create a character and to use language to achieve her goals. The gift of blarney – the gift actors have – is now hers to use and abuse; she can become anyone, anytime. Her imagination is set free. She is now 'many Kates'.

Footnotes

[1] A Possible Source of the Iterative Principle

In Plato's *Symposium* Socrates was called first a Marsyas and later described as a 'Silenus figure'. A 'Silenus figure' was a deceptive contraption sold in statuary shops. The figure had the outer appearance of an ugly man or a monstrous creature playing a flute but when opened proved to be full of gods. Outwardly poor, inwardly rich.

Both Silenus and Marsyas were followers of Dionysus/Bacchus. Ovid writes about the flaying of Marsyas in his *Metamorphoses* (Book VI, p. 192-193). It is a horrific tale about the Dionysian rite of purification. The outward man was thrown off to reveal the beauty of the inward self. By shedding our mortal flesh, our worldly preoccupations, we could free our souls. The physical body was sacrificed so that the heavenly body could be free.

Marsyas was tortured by Apollo, the god who both inspired him and who freed him of his limitations. In the legend Marsyas, who played the flute (symbol of uncontrollable passions), challenged Apollo, who played the lute (symbol of contemplation), to a contest. Apollo was judged the winner and Marsyas was punished for his presumption. It was a tale dramatizing the imperfections of our outer physical bodies and celebrating our inner essence. Although the outward tale is horrific the Dionysians interpreted it as a hopeful tale of transformation into an enlightened state.

The Taming of the Shrew depends on this same principle. The outward show always hides the inner essence. This is true both of the play and throughout the play. The surface never truly reveals what is beneath the surface. The Marsyas/Apollo story is repeated with Katherine and Petruchio. Katherine is freed of her limitations by Petruchio who appears to torture her.

[2] Power and Control

This discussion of being 'tied' to a 'choice' (3.1.16-20) is a reprise of an earlier scene (2.1) where Katherine physically 'ties' Bianca's hands and asks her which suitor is her 'choice'. The unspoken answer in both cases is the same 'the choice is mine and not thine'. This infuriates Katherine (as it is intended as an insult) but is accepted by Cambio and Litio who both only hope to spend some time with Bianca (whose perfection is an illusion). They are frankly under her spell and would do anything for her.

These two scenes draw our attention to the methods people use in order to gain control. Katherine, at this point, uses <u>force</u> in attempt to control another person's choices. Cambio, Litio and Bianca have chosen to use guile or <u>deception</u> in order to gain control of a situation. Finally, this scene also hints at the power of <u>love</u> by showing that people in love will willingly do anything for their partner.

[3] A Religious Parallel Helps Tell the Story

When Petruchio and Katherine begin their journey back to her father's house we are immediately reminded of the conversion of St. Paul on the road to Damascus. We know the play is about transformation, all the allusions from Ovid have made this point, the Induction scene has also made it abundantly clear we are dealing with a story of transformation of identity so it should come as no surprise that Katherine's epiphany should come on a road trip just like St. Paul's (Acts 9, 1-9). Here both see the light and change their ways:

and suddenly there shined round about him

a light from heaven (Acts 9,3)

which is comparable to (4.5.44-45)

Pardon...my mistaking eyes,

that have been so bedazzled with the sun.

This is a hint Shakespeare has given us to help interpret the text. Katherine is not being forced into compliance by Petruchio rather she has seen the wisdom in what he is doing. He is freeing her from her old self, her old ways of doing things (he does not tell her he shows her). He is not destroying her spirit but rather letting it soar.

[4] Dramatic Tension - Comic Release

Comedy depends on dramatic tension. Petruchio sets a stage for Katherine. The atmosphere he puts Kate into is one of unpredictable violence and abuse. This is to put both Katherine and the audience on edge. Its purpose is to crank up the dramatic tension. If we examine the sequence of events in the play it is apparent what Shakespeare is trying to achieve:

(4.3.189-190) *Look what I speak*...here dramatic tension is being built up. We think Petruchio is bullying Kate.

(4.5.2) *How bright and goodly shines the moon!* Again the scene begins with tension as we think Petruchio is being unreasonable. Katherine thinks so too and begins to argue (4.5.5) *I know it is the sun*...Dramatic tension is racketed up. Violence could be eminent.

Katherine has an epiphany, she begins to recognize she has control; all she must do is be free with her words, (4.5.12) *Forward, I pray, since we have come so far*. She begins to play, reservedly at first, but it brings about the desired goal. They are off to see her family. By the time Vincentio shows up she understands the word game and hams up her response. She is frolicking in word play.

At the end of act 5 we see a new development. Petruchio asks for a kiss but this time Kate decides to play. She is the one who cranks up the dramatic tension by denying it; she then playfully lets the tension fall away as they return to the familiar game they have previously established.

Comic release requires dramatic tension; it requires us to be suspicious of Petruchio's motives. Petruchio's character can only be slowly revealed to us or the play loses its ability to keep our attention, if it loses its tension it loses its comic potential. If there is no believable threat then there can be no comedy. This is also the reason the play must appear sexist. If it is revealed too early that the sexism is only a surface characteristic, if the insult to Katherine is not perceived as real then you remove the tension which allows the audience to relax. This is counterproductive to the comedy and to the conclusion of the play.

Bibliography

1) *The Taming of the Shrew*, W. Shakespeare, edited by Brian Morris, The Arden Shakespeare (3rd Series), Thomson Learning, 2006.

2) *The Taming of the Shrew; An Authoritative Text, Sources and Contexts, Criticism, Rewritings and Appropriations*, edited by Dympna Callaghan, Norton Critical Edition, W. W. Norton & Co. Inc., 2009.

3) *The Metamorphoses of Ovid*, translated by Allen Mandelbaum, A Harvest Book, Harcourt Inc., 1993.

4) *The Art of Shakespeare's Sonnets*, Helen Vendler, First Harvard University Press, 1999.

5) *Pagan Mysteries in the Renaissance*, Edgar Wind, Chapter XI, *The Flaying of Marsyas*, The Norton Library, W. W. Norton & Co. Inc., 1968.

6) *Giordano Bruno and the Philosophy of the Ass*, Nuccio Ordine, translated by Henryk Baranski and Arielle Saiber, Chapter 11, *The Ass in the Guise of the Sileni: Appearances are Deceptive*, Yale University Press, 1996.

7) *Ovid, The Art of Love and Other Poems*, translated by J.H. Mozley, revised by G.P. Goold, Loeb Classical Library, Harvard University Press, 2004.

Abstract for *Antony and Cleopatra*

Immortal Longings

Antony and Cleopatra is the very human tale of aging and making an accounting of your life. Using Plutarch as his guide Shakespeare has employed not just his historical accounts but also his metaphysics in the play. Shakespeare's characters Octavius, Antony and Cleopatra derive their motivation from concepts such as The One and The Indefinite Dyad while they move the story to its ultimate conclusion in the reconciliation of contradictories.

Immortal Longings

Understanding *Antony and Cleopatra*

Introduction

Antony and Cleopatra tells the story of Antony, a man slightly past his prime, who is forced through circumstance to discover what he truly values in life. The play is both a tragedy – in that our hero dies, and a comedy – in that our hero obtains his desire.

Antony's journey takes him from the Roman world of small minded limitation, towards the Egyptian world of infinite possibility.

The Roman world, Octavius' world, is limited by the whims of Fortune but Antony finds he can move even beyond the reach of Fate with Cleopatra's help. *Antony and Cleopatra* is a love story with Cleopatra the star of her own drama and Antony her chosen leading man, and lead him she does into a world beyond his imaginings.

How Antony moves from the limited physical world of discrete forms into the syncretistic world of the imagination is the topic of this essay.

Our Chaotic World and the Creation of Multiplicity

In *Antony and Cleopatra* Shakespeare engages in a process that is very dear to his poetic heart; he actively creates variations on a theme. He does this not only at the level of individual words but also with actions and with his allegorical allusions. In each case he takes one aspect of the word or action and applies it to a specific situation. Later he will use the same word or action or allegory and apply it to a new situation. This way he carefully expands the meaning of the word/action/allegory. As the play progresses these individual meanings begin to build up and inform or broaden our appreciation of the repeated element. The repeats create both a familiarity and a foreignness as the concepts are broadened to include an ever widening number of possibilities.

As the number of possible meanings increases a type of syncretism occurs – the various meanings find a harmony together – they achieve a type of simultaneity where they can take on all possible meanings at once creating a poetic unity as it were.

The story of *Antony and Cleopatra* provided an appropriate subject for these variations because Shakespeare's audience was well acquainted with the story. It was a very popular subject explored in many different works: Robert Garnier's *Marc Antoine* (1578), the Countess of Pembroke's *Antonius* (1592), and Samuel Daniels' *Cleopatra* (1594). Shakespeare's main source for the work was Sir Thomas North's translation of Plutarch's *Parallel Lives of the Greeks and Romans* (1559) which was itself a very popular book.

This familiarity is important for variation. A musician can do variations on a well known theme and the variations are amusing because the structure beneath it can be recognized and the musician's playfulness acknowledged. Variations on an unknown work are less successful because the joy of recognition is removed. Shakespeare's subject, Antony and Cleopatra, was so well known that when he played with the contents the audience could enjoy and recognize these changes without losing touch with the familiar storyline. His changes would stand out against a very familiar and perhaps now bland backdrop.

Variation on the Meaning of a Word

In *Antony and Cleopatra* a simple example of Shakespeare's use of a single word to mean different things can be seen in his use of the word 'square' (2.3.6-7).

I have not kept my square, but that to come

Shall all be done by th'rule.

Here 'square' means the square of prudence or the rule of reason as a guiding principle, i.e., using practical wisdom.

'Twere pregnant they should square between themselves. (2.1.46-47)

In this context 'square' means square-off or fight.

In the brave squares of war. (3.11.40)

This relates to the above meaning but expands on it by describing the way troops were drawn up in a quadrilateral formation before war.

Mine honesty and I begin to square. (3.13.42)

The word here means that his honest views and his actions are going to come into alignment with each other as in 'the theory squares with the facts'.

She's a most triumphant lady, if report be square to her. (2.2.194-195)

'Square' meaning an honest assessment or measuring true.

Beyond these definitions the word 'square' also carries with it visual baggage. Square implies rigidness and a mechanical nature, it implies rigor. The square is not an organic form; it is seldom seen in nature. It is a man-made product, the product of precision and measurement, the product of reason.

When a poet introduces a single word that means different things they often want the reader to hold all the definitions and images in their imaginations at once. This way each time the word is encountered the possible interpretations expand giving rise to the poetic experience.

Shakespeare does not repeat many words and when he does it is usually for some thematic effect; it is a practice he has carried over from his sonnet writing.

Many critics, including Northrop Fry (*On Shakespeare*, in his essay *Antony and Cleopatra*, p. 137) feel that the metaphors associated with Rome are of a geometrical nature. They see the use of the word 'square' as a Roman characteristic since Rome is associated with rule, measure, solidity, and reason. Egypt is seen as liquid, languid and spiritual.

These repeated words draw our attention to where Shakespeare wants it to go. By paying attention to these we can sometimes intuit the nature of the work, the purpose of the play.

Caroline Spurgeon (*Shakespeare's Imagery and What it Tells* Us, p. 352) mentions the word 'world' is used 42 times in *Antony and Cleopatra* more than twice as often as in his other plays. She believes this is to give us the sense of grandeur, power and space taken up in the play. I feel that Shakespeare is also alluding to what's at stake in the play – the world – not just in the military struggle but also on an individual level; Antony is both forced by circumstances and by volition to give up both 'the' world and 'his' world. In this way it is similar to the play *Hamlet* in that we are witnessing in Antony a type of letting go.

Variations on an Action

In *Antony and Cleopatra* there are many actions that can be considered thematic – that are repeated by different characters in different ways at different times. Janet Adelman points out that *Antony and Cleopatra* is one of the few plays Shakespeare wrote where we are not afforded a dominant point of view. We are instead exposed to multiple and competing points of view throughout the play. This multiplicity lends itself to variation (*The Common Liar*, p. 45-47).

Desertion is a type of action that presents itself in many and escalating ways through the course of the play. As the play begins we are aware that Antony has in effect deserted his wife Flavia and is currently living with Cleopatra. Antony has also turned his back on Rome and entertains very little business with it. On news of Flavia's death Antony decides he must *"break off"* (1.2.135) from Cleopatra least his idleness cause even more harm.

These 'leave-takings' or desertions are sometimes voluntary, as Antony leaving Cleopatra, and sometimes through death but each time a character is left increasingly isolated. We, the audience, are repeatedly exposed to this action seeing slight variations each time.

We witness peasants desert Octavius in favour of Pompey (1.4.37-38) and later see Pompey's servant desert him. Menas leaves Pompey because he perceives in him a lack of determination (2.7.82-84). Following this we see Lepidus desert Octavius in favour of Pompey only to meet with defeat (3.5.6-12). Antony deserts Octavia (3.6.65-69) and then his own men at Actium (3.10) for Cleopatra. This has the consequent effect of Antony's land forces surrendering to Octavius and it leads to a cascading series of desertions by various kings against Antony (3.10.33-35).

The number of desertions increases in rapidity after this point in the play. Antony finds his personal servants and forces are deserting him. Enobarbus plans his desertion from Antony (3.13.67-69) and *"the god Hercules, whom Antony lov'd / Now leaves him"* (4.3.21-22). Finally, it even appears that Cleopatra has deserted Antony (4.12.9-15).

This process of desertion, 'leave-taking', is repeated over and over. The motives differ, each time is slightly different but the variations continue throughout the play. They isolate Antony and they also create a sense of instability. Partnerships are not certain, friendships can be set aside. The world is temporary and in a constant state of flux.

This is the consequence of variation. As we saw earlier with words, as a single word is repeated but each time with a new definition we saw how variation led to expansion – the word's meaning expanded.

So too with a repetitive action like leave-taking. We see it applied to various situations in an increasing number of different ways. The action is no longer a simple act; variation allows for expansion – expansion of interpretation – expansion of meaning. It is Shakespeare's way of achieving MORE.

Variations on Allegory

Antony and Cleopatra can be viewed as a play about Antony. He is the character that changes and grows. He represents the variable that is manipulated between the two fixed points of Rome (Octavius) and Egypt (Cleopatra). Antony's journey is the journey of everyman – his triumphs are in his past (3.13.147-148), he sees himself as old compared to Octavius (3.13. 16-19), and he knows he is heading towards his own death (4.14.63-69). Antony must decide, as we all must, what things in life he values. He must set his priorities in order. He's reached that point in life when he must make an accounting.

Adelman points out that *Julius Caesar,* a play which deals with similar historical matter, has almost no mythological allusions in it whereas *Antony and Cleopatra* has at least 39 classical allusions (*The Common Liar*, p. 79). This clearly means that the classical gods play an important role in understanding these characters – that these allusions provide a shorthand to understanding them.

The general type of allusion that Shakespeare does variations on is of 'a man that is seduced by a beguiling and enslaving lover'. Just like all variations on a theme we will see both a familiar story and one that is slightly different each time. The stories mainly reveal something about Antony but they also contain content pertaining to Cleopatra.

a) Circe and Odysseus

The first of these allusions comes from Homer and *The Odyssey*. It is the story of Odysseus' captivity by Circe on the Isle of Aeaea, the

154

death-island. Circe was a goddess of love – of degrading love – and was known for her evil spells. She cast spells on anyone who landed on her island and turned them into animals. She turned Odysseus' men into swine. Odysseus escaped this fate but spent years with Circe forgetting both his wife and country (*The Odyssey*, Book X, lines 146-552).

This story summarizes the Roman view of Antony, a man seduced by a witch, forced to live like an animal and forgetful of his obligations to wife and country.

The Romans promote this view of Antony in the play: that he is trapped by his animal passions and is a slave to his fundamental instincts – nutrition, self-protection, and procreation. Octavius views Antony as less than Roman, a sorry combination of human vice (1.4.9)

> *A man who is the abstract of all faults*
> *That all men follow.*

b) Dido and Aeneas

The story of Dido and Aeneas is told by Virgil in *The Aeneid*. Virgil wrote during the reign of Augustus (a.k.a. Octavius) so his story can be seen as reflecting the Roman point of view.

Aeneas left Troy, after the fall, with the remaining Trojans in search of a new fatherland. When Aeneas and his crew were shipwrecked in Carthage, he fell in love with Queen Dido. If Aeneas had remained with Dido he would not have gone on to found Rome so the gods, in a vision, instructed Aeneas to continue his journey to Italy.

Aeneas, obedient to the gods, decided that founding an Empire was more important than his love of Dido and so abandoned her. Aeneas triumphed over his passions, his human frailty, in order to accomplish something great for his community. The establishment of Rome symbolized the rule of law and reason triumphing over an individual's passion.

When Antony recalls this story (4.14.51) he thinks only of their love and not of Aeneas' betrayal of Dido nor of how Dido turned her back on Aeneas when she encountered him in the underworld (*Aeneid*, Book VI, lines 450-474). Antony remembers the story only as a romance.

The threat Dido's passions posed to the founding of Rome were of the same type as Antony's passion for Cleopatra. His passions were threatening Rome's world of law and reason; his happy life was a mockery of their world view.

Rome saw Antony's dalliance with Egypt as an act of rebellion similar to Pompey's. In (1.4) not only is Pompey's rebellion brought up as a topic but so is Antony's wantonness; both are seen as threats to Octavius' Rome. Pompey thrives because Antony is idle. To attack Roman culture is to attack Rome.

Rome was founded because it and the idea of it could overcome an individual's passions. In the tale of *Antony and Cleopatra* passion threatens to undo what discipline has created. The Roman way of life was being drawn into question because Antony was living his life in mockery of its principles. He was neglecting public affairs, the values of civilization, in favour of his individual freedom.

The type of gossip we see spread about Antony at the beginning of the play is identical to the gossip Rumour spreads about Aeneas and Dido (*Aeneid*, Book IV, lines 193-195).

> *The couple are spending the winter in debauchery,*
> *the whole long winter,*
> *forgetting their kingdoms, rapt in a trance of lust.*
> *Such gossip did vile Rumour pepper on every mouth.*

Cleopatra, a foreign queen, was seen as the new Dido and Antony's passion for her as a threat to Roman values. The threat was real; Antony had turned his back on Rome *"Let Rome in Tiber melt"*

(1.1.34) and he had embraced Egypt *"Here is my space"* (1.1.35). Antony had made the choice Aeneas did not - Antony had chosen love over country.

c) Hercules and Omphale

Ovid tells a story of how Hercules was subjugated by Omphale, the Amazon Queen of Lydia (*The Greek Myths,* 135d, 136). In the tale, Hercules is made a slave to Omphale where he is dressed in women's clothes and made to perform domestic chores.

Antony is an analogue of this Hercules and in the play is subjected to a similar description by Cleopatra (2.5.21-23)

> *Ere the ninth hour, I drunk him to his bed;*
> *Then put my tires and mantles on him, whilst*
> *I wore his sword Philippan.*

Octavius reaffirms this understanding (1.4.5-7)

> (Antony)...*is not more manlike*
> *Than Cleopatra; nor the queen of Ptolemy*
> *More womanly than he.*

The Egyptian Antony is seen as effeminate by the Romans and under Cleopatra's control (1.1.12-13)

> *The triple pillar of the world transformed*
> *Into a strumpet's fool.*

The allegory implies that love has enslaved Antony to Cleopatra and robbed him of his reason and judgment.

d) Hercules at the Crossroads

Cleopatra regards Antony as a descendent of Hercules (1.3.84-86; note 85). Xenophon tells us the tale of *Hercules in Bivio* or *Hercules at the Crossroads* (*Memorabilia*, 2.1.21-34, Arden p. 65). In the story, Hercules is said to have sat at a crossroad wondering which road to take when two women approached him. One was modest, serious, and dressed in white while the other was voluptuous and provocatively dressed. Vice offered Hercules a life free from hardship and devoted to the pleasures of food, drink and love while Virtue offered him only hardship and toil which would lead him eventually to glory.

This, of course, mimics Antony's choice in the play. The play's turning point is where Antony must choose between a life with Octavia, the definition of virtue, (2.2.251-253)

If beauty, wisdom, modesty can settle

The heart of Antony, Octavia is

A blessed lottery to him

or Cleopatra. Antony chooses Cleopatra (2.3.37-39)

I will to Egypt;

And though I make this marriage for my peace,

I'th'East my pleasure lies.

Clearly from the Roman point of view Antony has chosen a life of debauchery but Shakespeare is not a Roman and an allusion does not tell the whole story.

e) Venus and Mars

In the opening lines of the play Antony is seen as a retiring Mars (1.1.2-10) but there are no lack of allusions pointing out this connection. Antony is (2.5.116-117)

painted one way like a Gorgon

The other way's a Mars.

In the play Mars becomes a captive of Love. This is an old theme for Shakespeare. He used it previously in his poem *Venus and Adonis* (103-110)

Over my altars hath he hung his lance,

His batter'd shield his uncontrolled crest;

And for my sake hath learn'd to sport and dance,

To toy, to wanton, dally, smile and jest,

Scorning his churlish drum and ensign red,

158

Making my arms his field, his tent my bed.

Thus he that overul'd I oversway'd,

Leading him prisoner in a red rose chain.

Venus makes Mars lay aside his weapons, sword or lance, and armor. Botticelli's painting *Mars and Venus* visually depicts this scene showing Mars' tools of warfare become toys in the hands of Venus' infant satyrs.

Cleopatra, the goddess Isis, easily fits into the role of Venus. Apuleius (*Metamorphosis* XI, 5) points out that Venus, Minerva, Diana, Proserpina, Ceres, Juno, and Hecate are all names for the divinity whose real name is Isis. Shakespeare had used Apuleius as a source in the past for his play *A Midsummer Night's Dream* so this information would not have been new to him.

Antony's emasculation by Cleopatra was understood as an insult to Antony by the Romans, as a jest by Cleopatra, but it was seen as a weakness by Antony himself after his loss at Actium (3.11.65-68)

You did know

How much you were my conqueror, and that

My sword, made weak by my affection, would

Obey it on all cause.

Antony's loss at Actium revealed to Antony his absolute devotion to Cleopatra, something he may not have been aware of before. She has become his purpose for living (3.11.69-71)

Fall not a tear, I say; one of them rates

All that is won and lost. Give me a kiss. [They kiss.]

Even this repays me.

This is one of the great epiphanies in the play. Antony recognizes a personal truth – his utter devotion to Cleopatra – that she has become his world. He has discovered he loves her to the betrayal of even himself.

Edgar Wind has examined the various meanings associated with Venus' and Mars' relationship (*Pagan Mysteries in the Renaissance*, p. 85-96). It was said that the union of Venus with Mars led to the birth of Harmony – the doctrine of contraries uniting in concord.

This idea was the fundamental principle behind all creation. Pico della Mirandolla (*Pagan Mysteries in the Renaissance*, p. 89) stated:

"...Empedocles spoke more perfectly when he introduced discord not by itself but together with concord as the origin of all things, understanding by discord the variety of elements of which they are composed, and by concord their union...since in the constitution of created things it is necessary that the union overcomes the strife (otherwise the thing would perish because its elements would fall apart) – for this reason is it said by the poets that Venus loves Mars".

That the world can maintain form and order, that the world can regenerate itself, is only because of the tension between opposed principles – discord and concord – Mars and Venus.

The balance of discord and concord is not static but rather dynamic. At times Mars must subordinate the effects of Venus or nothing would die and return to the elements. Venus and Mars are the forces of Life and Death.

The story of Venus and Mars reveals that Love is a fundamental constituent of the universe, in fact, responsible for its existence. This raises the allegorical status of Antony and Cleopatra easily to the status of cosmic forces if not gods. However not all interpretations of this myth are so clear cut. Natale Conti (*The Common Liar*, p. 86) saw the conjunction of Mars with Venus as morally evil, as it represented adultery, but also as a cosmic good, as it represented the forces of generation and creation.

Shakespeare's play follows the broad strokes of this allegory. Harmony does result from the union of Antony and Cleopatra although as an ironic side effect. Cleopatra's influence on Antony has resulted in Antony's defeat and subsequently led to Octavius' victory making him sole ruler of the world and the bringer of world peace.

f) Isis and Osiris

Plutarch was Shakespeare's major source for *Antony and Cleopatra* but he was not just his source for the historical narrative (*Parallel Lives of the Greeks and Romans*) he was also his source for its more abstract philosophical structure (*Concerning the Mysteries of Isis and Osiris*).

The central myth of Isis and Osiris concerns Isis' devotion to her husband Osiris. Osiris was killed by Typhon (his brother and rival) and cut up into 14 pieces which were scattered over the land. Isis searched for these pieces and reconstructed Osiris such that he might gain immortality. This is, in part, a lunar myth whereby the 14 pieces represent the 14 days it takes for the full moon to wane into a new moon. The reconstruction of Osiris by Isis is represented by the following 14 days where the new moon waxes back into a full moon.

In *Antony and Cleopatra,* Cleopatra mimics this process. After Antony has been discredited and cut down in stature by the Roman Octavius she re-imagines or reconstructs his greatness and turns the dead Antony into an immortal myth.

These variations on the theme of 'enslaved lover' give us varying perspectives. Every interpretation brings out a different level of meaning. The allegories are not as simple as a witch controlling a hero to act against his better judgment. Elements of each tale are present in Shakespeare's play. No single myth fits all the details of the play. This is the strength of employing multiple points of view. The tale becomes richer and more nuanced. Cleopatra is both Circe (the witch) and Isis (the devoted lover). Antony is both the immoral adulterer and the faithful hero to Cleopatra.

Achieving Ambiguity

Antony and Cleopatra is a problematic play because of this technique of variation – where something is many things simultaneously. Adelman's book *The Common Liar* goes a long way in uncovering other techniques Shakespeare has employed to create this ambiguity. I will briefly outline some of these techniques of obfuscation as I believe that Shakespeare was interested in embodying the concept of 'multiplicity' in his play for reasons I will discuss later.

Creating 'variations on a theme' is one way to achieve multiplicity. You witness how a word, action or allegory can be viewed in different and sometimes opposing ways. The variations broaden possible interpretations.

A second technique Adelman sees Shakespeare using is that of uncertainty. The play fails to give us concrete information. What it offers most often is gossip or someone's opinion of the events or characters we encounter. These opinions change as the source of the opinion changes.

Lack of certainty permeates the play. Just as characters in the play must make guesses as to what is happening so must we as an audience. We must guess at a character's motives from their actions. There are very few soliloquies in *Antony and Cleopatra* so as an audience we are left in the dark as to a character's motivation, inward struggle or beliefs.

Adelman points out (*The Common Liar*, p. 24-30) that the play begins with an argument "*Nay, but...*" (1.1.1). The very first words in the play are contesting someone else's opinion. This pattern continues with both major and minor characters arguing about what is happening. Antony argues with Enobarbus about Cleopatra (1.2.135-162), we see Octavius and Lepidus argue about Antony (1.4.1-33), and during the course of the play we even witness two watchmen argue as to whether or not Enobarbus is dead (4.9.27-40). The play is full of this kind of uncertainty. It, in fact, makes mockery of even the most certain judgments, as when Pompey predicts Antony's behaviour – behaviour that has already been confirmed as typical of Antony by both Octavius and Antony himself and yet even as Pompey is describing what Antony is likely to do a messenger arrives to tell him he is wrong. Antony is no longer behaving like the person Pompey knew (2.1.11-35).

Even intimate characters are uncertain about each other; Antony even after spending years with Cleopatra has his doubts about her love for him (4.14.15-16)

> *I made these wars for Egypt, and the queen,*
> *Whose heart I thought I had, for she had mine.*

Truth appears momentary – the characters believe what they say when they say it – but it is not necessarily any indication of future beliefs. People and situations are dynamic. The information we are presented with may not be accurate or timely. There is a degree of uncertainty to every decision made in the play.

Adelman points out that *Antony and Cleopatra* has a repetitive structure within it that is similar to a play-within-a-play (*The Common Liar*, p. 31). Often a group of minor characters discusses the actions of the major characters. It is as if these minor characters are an audience to the actions in the play and are free to discuss it. It insures that we get as much information from minor characters as we do from the principals. Adelman points out that this pattern occurs in at least 12 scenes. A few examples of this type of commentary are:

(1.1) Demetrius and Philo comment on the scene Antony and Cleopatra play out before them. They are like a prologue and epilogue to the scene itself.

(2.2) Enobarbus and Lepidus discuss Antony and Octavius' coming meeting and project their own feelings onto it.

(2.6) Pompey, Antony, Octavius and Lepidus meet while Enobarbus and Menas discuss related events.

(2.7) Servants discuss their drunken leaders.

(3.13) Enobarbus provides commentary on four separate actions within this one scene.

These are just a few examples of scenes utilizing this type of framing structure. This play-within-a-play format necessarily creates multiple points of view and by doing so increases the uncertainty as to whose point of view is most accurate or the least tainted.

In addition to variations on a theme, uncertainty of information, and multiple points of view, Adelman also points out that obfuscation can occur through poor lines of communication.

Messengers abound in the play – 8 characters are designated as just 'messenger' and 7 more are identified: Alexas, Menas, Varrius, Thidias, Mardian, Proculeius, and Dolabella. Their role is as often as not to carry false information. Cleopatra's messengers carry false information of her death (4.14.27-34) or they carry messages that are altered according to the mood of the receiver of these messages (1.3.1-6) or they deliver messages that are massaged to match her expectations (3.3.1-36).

Often messages arrive too late to be useful. The news that Cleopatra is not dead arrives too late to prevent Antony's suicide (4.4.120-130). Sometimes messengers take their own initiative as when Dolabella, Octavius' messenger, betrays his master and delivers truth instead of the reassuring lies he is expected to confirm (5.2.108-109). Agrippa refers to this 'fog of war' that exists in the play when he talks of rumours being regarded as truths (2.2.141-142)

> *Truths would be tales,*
> *Where now half-tales be truths.*

Isolation

At the same time that Shakespeare has introduced variation he has also been careful to include some directionality into all this change. We witness each character in the play become increasingly isolated. Desertions do not just leave Antony alone but they also isolate Cleopatra. Octavius, even though he is the victor, is also now the lone leader of the world. We can sense his isolation when he eulogizes Antony; he has lost an opponent but also an equal (5.1.39-48).

a) Isolation due to Plot Momentum

The play begins with three Triumvirs controlling the world, a world that contains a degree of diversity, with Pompey and Antony representing a type of opposition to the status quo. Pompey rebels against the concentration of power and Antony rebels against Roman culture and tradition.

The Triumvirs first make peace with Pompey (2.6) (2.7) only to isolate and destroy him later in the play (3.5). These subsequent wars against Pompey are used to both exploit and then to betray Lepidus. By (3.5) the world is in the control of two leaders (3.5.13)

Then, world, thou hast a pair of chaps, no more.

Octavius isolates and then destroys his enemies. We see him weave his strategies well in advance of acting on them. Following the removal of Lepidus, Octavius begins in earnest his propaganda campaign against Antony maligning him first before the Roman people (3.6.1-22) and then before his sister, Antony's wife (3.6.65-77).

Following Antony's defeat at Actium and the several desertions that follow (3.10), Antony is forced into a smaller and smaller corner of the world. His options become increasingly reduced until finally his defeat is certain.

Octavius becomes the sole ruler of the world. During the course of the play the number of Triumvirs is reduced from 3 to 2 to 1, a movement from multiplicity to unity. It also marks a transition from the chaos of war to a world experiencing universal peace.

b) Isolation due to Instability

There is a dynamism in the plot right from the start. Multiplicity and uncertainty add to this feeling of instability but so does the number of stable relationships that are overturned. Shakespeare has taken care to create a number of triads, relationships of three characters, with two extremes and an intermediary. Octavius - Antony - Cleopatra can be seen as one of these triads where Antony is the intermediary between the extremes of Octavius (Roman Ideals) and Cleopatra (Egyptian Ideals). The Triumvirate itself of Octavius - Lepidus - Antony is another example. Here Lepidus is the intermediary between the extremes of Octavius and Antony. A similar triad exists in Octavius - Octavia - Antony where Octavia plays the moderating role between Octavius and Antony.

Normally a triad is a very stable structure, the extremes being moderated by the mean. In Shakespeare's play all these triads are overturned, balance cannot be reached. When we examine this last triad Octavia's role is not much different than Lepidus'. She is the glue to cement relations between Antony and Octavius, her marriage to Antony is designed to make them brothers (2.2.133-135)

> *To hold you in perpetual amity,*
> *To make you brothers, and to knit your hearts*
> *With an unslipping knot, take Antony*
> *Octavia to his wife.*

Octavius (Caesar) describes Octavia as the mean between them (3.2.27-33)

> *Most noble Antony,*
> *Let not the piece of virtue which is set*
> *Betwixt us, as the cement of our love*

> *To keep it builded, be the ram to batter*
> *The fortress of it. For better might we*
> *Have loved without this mean, if on both parts*
> *This be not cherished.*

As an audience we are never sure if the marriage was a sincere offer on Caesar's behalf or whether it was always intended to be a trap, so that any betrayal by Antony could be seen as an insult to Caesar and be used to justify his use of force against Antony. What we do know is that rather than establishing harmony this triad leads to instability; Octavia views her position as untenable (3.4.18-20)

> *Husband win, win brother,*
> *Prays and destroys the prayer; no midway*
> *'Twixt these extremes at all.*

The play will not allow for balance to be struck between the extremes. There is to be no compromise. This is true of all the triads. Lepidus is expelled from the Triumvirate and Antony is never to resolve the cultural differences between Egypt and Rome. The play is not about balance or compromise; it is more focused on extreme goals.

The play sets out physical goals and spiritual goals. Octavius cannot see past the physical. He is fixed on his goal of obtaining sole custody of the world. Antony and Cleopatra, by the end of the play, have both given up their claims to the physical realm and are focused on obtaining a spiritual unity.

These goals allow no balance to be struck *"for where your treasure is, there will your heart be also"* (Matt 6:21). Antony can no more care about the pragmatic, day to day, running of government than can Octavius care about the imaginatively fanciful. Rome and Egypt can only exist in isolation there is; *"no midway 'Twixt these extremes at all"*.

Unity

Octavius is what Antony was. Antony has become a changed man in Egypt. It is only upon the news of Flavias' death that Antony entertains '*Roman thoughts*' again. These thoughts are about control and limit. He feels he should have controlled Flavia and his brother (1.2.93-99) (2.2.47-49) and not allowed Pompey to grow powerful (2.2.174; note 174). He also fears more harm will come to others if he remains in Egypt (1.2.136-137). The Roman that has been reawakened in Antony is no longer the Antony that is. He discovers this when he gives up everything to be with Cleopatra. It is his religious epiphany. When he realizes the extent of his love for Cleopatra his infinite longings finally take charge of him. His goals change; he only wants to be with Cleopatra and he begins to imagine how to make this possible. Late in life Antony wants to grow from a Roman into a true Egyptian.

a) Beyond Self

Adelman argues (*The Common Liar*, p. 121-144) that Rome represents a culture of measured behaviour with measured responses based on planning while Egyptian culture is one of excess representing the hyperbolic and magnanimous. Because of this she feels that Egypt is more at home with the Spiritual and the excesses that come with it like an all encompassing Love or an overflowing Grace.

Antony is at war with his Roman nature. At the beginning of the play we find he is afraid of his obsession with Cleopatra (1.2.123)

> *These strong Egyptian fetters I must break,*
>
> *Or lose myself in dotage.*

He is possessed with an obsession that "*O'er flows the measure*" (1.1.2).

Antony's reasonable self – his prudent self – his measured self – his Roman self – is not his true self. Over and over again the play shows us that Antony is a man of excess.

To set a limit on how much he loves Cleopatra there would have to be new worlds discovered (1.1.16-17). He sees himself and Cleopatra as *"peerless"* (1.1.41). Octavius sees Antony not just as a flawed man but an excessively flawed man (1.4.8-9)

> *A man who is the abstract of all faults*
> *That all men follow.*

That Cleopatra sees him in excessive terms *"The demi-Atlas of this earth"* (1.5.24), a veritable Jove (5.2.78-91), is no surprise since she too is a creature of excess but the fact that others see Antony in heroic or despotic terms is revealing. Pompey sees Antony as twice the soldier as Octavius and Lepidus combined (2.1.35-36)

> *His soldiership*
> *Is twice the other twain.*

But he also sees Antony as the definition of decadence (2.1.38)

> *The ne'er-lust-wearied Antony.*

Antony recognizes this tendency, in his past, towards excess but promises Octavia that in the future he will hold himself in check (2.3.6-7)

> *I have not kept my square, but that to come*
> *Shall all be done by th'rule.*

This is a promise Antony is incapable of keeping. No sooner has it left his lips than he realizes what he desires (2.3.39)

> *I'th'East my pleasure lies.*

Antony's excesses appear to be instinctual, part of who he is, and something he cannot control even when it betrays his own sense of self (3.4.22-23)

> *If I lose mine honour,*
> *I lose myself.*

His excessive obsession with Cleopatra causes him to flee from battle at Actium. This leaves his men dumbfounded (3.10.22-24) and the action is a disgrace to himself (3.11.7-8)

> *I have fled myself and have instructed cowards*
> *To run and show their shoulders.*

Antony had not, until that moment in the play, recognized or acknowledged to himself how deep his love for Cleopatra was. It surpassed his love for kingdoms, it was more than his love of honour. His love reached beyond worldly excess and personal esteem (3.11.69-71).

> *Fall not a tear, I say; one of them rates*
> *All that is won and lost. Give me a kiss* [They kiss.]
> *Even this repays me.*

This loss of self has led Antony to something even greater than himself. Only when one is selfless can one truly find love. Love is a transcendent experience which forces the lover to go outside of the self, to transcend the ego. Antony has shed his and this epiphany has simplified his life. He now 'knows himself' something he did not know at the beginning of the play. Antony is no longer torn between Rome and Egypt.

b) Beyond Boundaries

Breaking through boundaries has been foreshadowed since the start of the play when Antony instructed Cleopatra to find new heavens (1.1.17). Breaking boundaries is a different concept from hyperbolic living, immoderate excess or magnanimous giving. It is about breaking through the boundaries that define or restrict us. It is spiritual in its nature.

An example of this occurs when Octavius blurs the line between Antony and Cleopatra. It is meant as an insult (mythically speaking it alludes to fulfillment, Wind p. 92-94). Octavius claims that Antony (1.4.5-7)

> *is not more manlike*
> *Than Cleopatra, nor the Queen of Ptolemy*
> *More womanly than he.*

Antony, because of his search for an identity, is aware of these boundaries and the limitations they place on him. He discovers through the play what his true self is. Following his epiphany he begins to imagine the form of this new true self. At one point he imagines himself like a cloud capable of taking on different shapes – of merging with other clouds (4.14.12-14)

> *now thy captain is*
> *Even such a body. Here I am Antony,*
> *Yet cannot hold this visible shape.*

He sees himself becoming indistinct and lost in the larger cosmos "*As water is in water*" (4.14.11).

By recognizing this dissolution he can imagine a life beyond the physical, a life intermingled with Cleopatra, a life of spiritual unity. Mardian offers Antony some reassurance of this hope (4.14.24)

> *No, Antony,*
> *My mistress loved thee and her fortunes mingled*
> *With thine entirely.*

Antony, knowing he was not betrayed, happily accepts his death as a chance to be reunited with her (4.14.100-103)

> *But I will be*
> *A bridegroom in my death and run into't*
> *As a lover's bed.*

Antony has admitted to a belief in an afterlife earlier in the play when he described a crocodile (2.7.40-46)

> *It is shaped, sir, like itself, and it is as broad*

as it hath breadth. It is just so high as it is, and
moves with it own organs, It lives by that which
nourisheth it, and the elements once out of it, it
transmigrates.

The description contains no information – it is completely ambiguous except for one clear fact – when the crocodile dies it transmigrates.

The play provides us with another hope that resurrection is possible. When Antony dies, Cleopatra faints. Because we have previously witnessed Enobarbus die of a broken heart (4.9.26) we, as an audience, are not assured that she will recover. When she does it provides us with an image of, and a hope for, an afterlife.

The water imagery that Antony employs when discussing the dissolution of personal boundaries *"As water is in water"* stresses the unity that is to be experienced in the afterlife.

Water carries much symbolic baggage (Cirlot, p. 345). Water has always been associated with creation; it was considered the generative source of all life. Clouds were symbolic of the Upper Waters; they represented potential, that which was possible, while the Lower Waters represented that which was actual, what was already created. Antony, when he sees himself like a cloud (4.14.12-14), is reflecting on a future potential and not just his present state.

Water was seen as the transitional element (liquid) between the solid element (earth) and the ethereal elements (fire and air). Water connected life with death, the earthly to the spiritual. It was said that Death was the first mariner because he carried souls across the river Styx. Because of water's role in transition, immersion in water often represented a type of rebirth into a new spiritual life.

As the boundaries break, a spiritual unity forms. Male and female become one sex. Death becomes dissolution and a type of intermingling. The cacophony of differing opinions and the clashing of personalities falls away as Antony and Cleopatra are united in one person and in one death.

c) Melting

The play offers us examples of the dissolution of personal boundaries but it also provides several examples of the physical world melting away

> *Let Rome in Tiber melt (1.1.34)*
>
> *Melt Egypt into Nile (2.5.78)*

and at Antony's death Cleopatra announces (4.15.65)

> *The crown o'th'earth doth melt.*

The melting represents a turning back to a primal state, a liquid state from which new worlds can emerge. It represents the value Antony and Cleopatra have placed on Rome, Egypt, and power. These are all things that will pass away, that hold little value to them (1.1.36)

> *Kingdoms are clay!*

Cleopatra knows where her heart lies but it takes Antony the course of the play to discover just how much he loves her (3.13.163)

> *Not know me yet?*

Cleopatra has treasured Antony and when he is gone she is alone (4.15.69)

> *there is nothing left remarkable*
>
> *Beneath the visiting moon.*

Cleopatra views death as the final dissolution, a return to the primal sea (3.13.167)

> *Dissolve my life!*

Cleopatra understands the Egyptian/Hermetic view of death as does Shakespeare (*Corpus Hermeticum*, Libellus, XII,ii,16).

> *"The living creatures do not die, my son; but they are composite bodies, and as such, they undergo dissolution. Dissolution is*

not death; it is only the separation of things which were combined; and they undergo dissolution, not to perish, but to be made new".

Dissolution is a return to unity where all the contradictions of life are resolved.

d) Men, Heroes and Gods

The distinction between men and gods is deliberately blurred in the play. There are many allusions to the gods and sometimes Cleopatra and Antony are described as Venus and Mars or as Isis and Hercules. On Cleopatra's part there is no deceit, she regarded herself as Isis; Egyptian royalty always thought of themselves as gods so there is no reason to think Cleopatra would not. Antony has longings to be more than he is. Pompey accuses him of this (2.6.14-19). Pompey felt that Antony supported Julius Caesar's attempt to make himself more powerful than the Senate and in effect a supreme power and dictator for life. Pompey felt that Cassius, Brutus and the Senators had murdered Julius Caesar in order

> *that they would*
> *Have one man but a man*

and not allow an individual to claim such inordinate powers for themselves. Pompey sees such longings still in Antony.

Antony is a creature of excess and Pompey's suspicion is certainly correct.   Antony is from the previous generation.   He was a contemporary of Julius Caesar and Pompey the Great (Pompey's father) both men who had also been amorously involved with his Cleopatra. They are all bigger than life characters and none had trouble accepting Egypt's hyperbolic excess.

Heroes are characters of excess, excess valour, but as Adelman points out (*The Common Liar*, p. 132) characters such as these no longer fit within the Roman ideal of measure and moderation.

Ventidius (3.1) demonstrates this new Roman ideal of moderation. He is careful not to rise above his station (3.1.13-15)

> *For learn this, Silius:*
> *Better to leave undone than, by our deed,*
> *Acquire too high a fame when him we serve's away.*

Personal greatness is no longer a safe goal. This type of moderation is also seen in young Pompey; his honourable act of not killing his guests is reduced only to a wish that he had not been consulted beforehand (2.7.62-81).

Enobarbus is also of this younger generation. He is a figure of moderation in the Egyptian world of excess. Enobarbus understands the danger of remaining with Antony as Antony's situation deteriorates. But when he finally acts on his reason and deserts Antony, Antony's response of generosity and respect reveals to Enobarbus the pettiness of his own decision.

In *Antony and Cleopatra* the great actions, the heroic actions, are reserved for Antony (1.4.57-72). Octavius is the "*boy Caesar*" who will not meet Antony in heroic hand-to-hand combat (4.1.1-6). He is of the new generation of measure and moderation.

Antony embodies a type of striving for more. He is greedy for life and for experience (1.1.47-48)

> *There's not a minute of our lives should stretch*
> *Without some pleasure now.*

Cleopatra, when she eulogizes Antony, speaks of him moving dolphin-like through life, rising from this world into the next, striving to be more than he was (5.2.87-89)

> *His delights*
> *Were dolphin-like: they showed his back above*
> *The element they lived in.*

Antony is a figure of transcendence – he wishes to go above and beyond limits. Like the Nile overflowing its banks, Antony too is a figure difficult to contain.

This movement of Antony from a man to more than a man to hero is what Plutarch might describe as the ascent of man (*The Middle Platonists*, Chpt. 4, Plutarch of Chaeroneaia and the Origins of Second-Century Platonism, p. 219). Plutarch believed in a scale of promotion. He did not believe in a static universe but rather one in which there was a continual promotion and demotion:

"so the better souls obtain their transmutation from men into heroes and from heroes into daemons. And from the daemons...to share completely in divinity".

This is the path that Cleopatra sees for herself and Antony. It is an escape from the world of Fate and into a world of divinity and Unity.

Cleopatra views Octavius as a petty bureaucrat and a puppet to Fate (5.2.2-4)

> *'Tis paltry to be Caesar.*
> *Not being Fortune, he's but Fortune's knave*
> *A minister of her will.*

She sees herself and Antony as rising above this, as taking control over their destinies. By so doing they raise themselves above Fate and need no longer answer to her (5.2.4-7)

> *And it is great*
> *To do that thing that ends all other deeds,*
> *Which shackles accidents and bolts up change,*
> *Which sleeps and never palates more the dung.*

Antony is dead and she plans to join him momentarily. From a world of accident, change and uncertainty she plans her escape to the certain and constant world of death.

Death is not an end in Cleopatra's mind but a promotion. Isis was the goddess of the moon – every month the moon died and every month it was resurrected. She was the goddess of generation – after the flood the crops were renewed. Resurrection appears to be her right. It is as Enobarbus says of Cleopatra (1.2.148-151)

> *I have seen her die*
>
> *twenty times upon far poorer moment. I do think*
>
> *there is mettle in death which commits some loving*
>
> *act upon her.*

Cleopatra saw herself as leaving the world of change and entering the unity of the spiritual world to become an immortal being beyond change and beyond Fate (5.2.238-239)

> *Now from head to foot*
>
> *I am marble-constant. Now the fleeting moon*
>
> *No planet is of mine.*

Multiplicity and Unity

In *Antony and Cleopatra* Shakespeare has created a play where two strong forces are at work. Multiple points of view, variation, and uncertainty create a multiplicity, a type of chaos, that permeates the play. It creates a fog that works to prevent understanding. On top of this, the forces of instability act in such a way as to isolate each character and prevent any chance of communication.

In opposition to these physical forces of discord there are spiritual forces at work that imaginatively melt, dissolve or break down the physical boundaries that separate characters. These spiritual forces are romantic in nature in that their goal is unification – concord.

In order to understand these forces of multiplicity (discord) and unity (concord) we need to examine these philosophies in more detail and in ways appropriate to each culture.

a) Plato's Philosophy and the Roman Condition

Plato's views on certain basic questions are generally agreed upon. Some of the main features of his ideas on multiplicity and unity can be seen reflected in his mature dialogues such as the *Republic*, *Philebus*, *Timaeus*, and *Laws*. Essentially the idea is as follows (*The Middle Platonists*, p. 3-4): The Unity is everything, all that was, all that can be. Nothing exists outside the Unity. Everything is enfolded into the Unity. It is neither good nor evil since it is superior to these concepts and the cause of them. They are enfolded within it.

From this everything, this Unity, arises a pair of opposed first principles – The One and The Indefinite Dyad.

The One is an active principle imposing limit on the formlessness of the opposite principle, the Indefinite Dyad. The Indefinite Dyad can be simultaneously infinitely large and infinitely small. It is the principle of infinite divisibility. It is reflected in Nature as continuous magnitudes, excess and defect (deficiency), which has to be continually checked by the imposition of correct measure or limit since infinitely small and infinitely large things do not exist in Nature. Nature always exists in a limited form.

This carries with it an implied morality as Virtues are seen as the correct measures since they represent the mean (average) between the extremes of excess and defect.

The Indefinite Dyad is primarily the basic unlimitedness on which The One acts. It forms the substrate (pre-physical matter/energy) on which The One will impose limits (ideas) in order to give rise to the physical world (the cosmos).

Plato's philosophy can now be used to understand the characters of Antony and Octavius and how they relate to each other and the play.

These principles of The One and The Indefinite Dyad come to life in the Roman portion of the play – that part of the play involving Antony and Octavius. If one were to assign them Platonic roles then Octavius is clearly The One, the man who imposes limits, the man who takes the moral high ground. Antony is The Indefinite Dyad, the excessive character upon whom limits must be placed.

The plot bears this out. Octavius places limits on Antony. At first these are moral limits, as he marries Antony to his sister Octavia in an attempt to cut off his relations with Egypt. When this doesn't work he then engages in a propaganda campaign against Antony in order to disgrace his behaviour in front of the Roman people. Octavius tries to bring Antony into line with the norms of Roman behaviour. Finally when moral limits and public shame do not work Octavius feels forced to use military power to physically limit Antony's size.

Octavius embodies the concept of measure and limit, essentially the properties of The One. The Roman people as a whole represent this ideal. Their respect for the virtue of prudence (practical wisdom) places them in this camp. The One has an air of goodness about it and I dare say smugness, as it looks down its nose disapprovingly at both Antony and Egypt.

When we examine Antony we discover in the first sentence of the play that his dotage "*O'erflows the measure*" (1.1.2). Already Antony is associated with excess. But not only does his love overflow the measure so does his courage and generosity. Antony's bounty overflows even to those disloyal to him. Antony rewards Enobarbus for his years of good service even after he deserts (4.6.20-23)

> *Enobarbus, Antony*
> *Hath after thee sent all thy treasure, with*
> *His bounty overplus.*

Adelman (*The Common Liar*, p. 135) points out that Hercules is an analogue for Antony and that Hercules was known not only for his excesses – excess rage – excess strength – but also for making good on his claims – achieving excess.

Antony, by the end of the play, achieves the excess he has the hereditary right to claim. He chooses death and escapes the world of limit and by so doing achieves the infinite possibility he was seeking throughout the play.

Antony represents The Indefinite Dyad – the limitless – just as Octavius represents The One and the idea of limit.

b) Plutarch Interprets Plato for the Egyptians

Plutarch's metaphysics (found in his *Concerning the Mysteries of Isis and Osiris*) deviated from what would be regarded now as standard Platonic beliefs. They gave rise to a unique understanding of Isis by introducing a dualistic complication (*The Middle Platonists*, p. 203-208).

Plutarch's metaphysics created five entities by taking normal Platonic philosophy and subdividing its parts.

The One was subdivided into:

1) The Soul of Osiris: the Divine Mind/The Good.

2) The Body of Osiris: the Platonic Ideas/Ideal Forms.

The Indefinite Dyad was subdivided into:

3) Seth/Typhon: the source of Evil.

4) Isis: pre-physical matter or The World Soul.

Finally when the Body of Osiris (the Ideal Forms) coupled with Isis (pre-physical Matter) it gave birth to their son Horus.

5) Horus: the physical universe/the cosmos.

What made Plutarch's metaphysics unique is that he allowed for the creation of evil by creating Seth or Typhon as a source of this evil.

Plutarch had mixed Zoroastrian theology from the Persian religion with Platonism (Plutarch's ideas were rejected by all subsequent Platonists). Because Plutarch created Seth/Typhon this meant that if Seth coupled with Isis he could bring physical evil into the world. This meant that Isis was morally neutral but could be used to create both good and evil. Plutarch felt (*The Middle Platonists*, p. 203).

"Nature must contain in itself the creation and origin of evil as well as good".

Plutarch continues by describing Isis as not *"evil itself"* but as the *"cause of evil"* even though he points out that she desires *"The Good"* (*Concerning the Mysteries of Isis and Osiris*, LIII.1-2 or *The Middle Platonists*, p. 205)

"Thus Isis is the female principle in nature and that which receives all procreation, and so she is called by Plato (i.e. Tim. 49A, 51A) the Nurse and All-receiving...Imbued in her she has a love of the first and most sovereign principle of all, which is the same as the Good, and this she longs for and pursues. The lot which lies with evil she shuns and rejects; she is, indeed, a sphere of activity and subject-matter for both of them, but she inclines always of herself to what is better, offering herself to it for reproduction, and for the sowing in herself of effluxes and likenesses."

Plutarch places Isis – pre-physical matter, the World Soul, the generative mud – at the disposal of both good and bad forces but tells us she is inclined towards the good. This view of Isis/Cleopatra is seen throughout *Antony and Cleopatra*.

Octavius describes Cleopatra as Isis (3.6.16-18)

She
In th'habiliments of the goddess Isis
That day appeared.

Octavius also demonstrates to us how Isis/Cleopatra can be used by both good and bad forces for if she (3.12.22-24)

> *From Egypt drive her all-disgraced friend*
> *Or take his life there. This if she perform,*
> *She shall not sue unheard.*

Octavius is attempting to bribe Cleopatra so that she will betray Antony. Antony realizes this may be Cleopatra's only chance for survival so he makes sure she hears the ambassador's message (3.13.16-19)

> *Let her know't.*
> *To the boy Caesar send this grizzled head,*
> *And he will fill thy wishes to the brim*
> *With principalities.*

We also know, from foreshadowing in the play, that Cleopatra is not above this type of behaviour and knowing this adds dramatic tension to the scene (2.5.11-14)

> *I will betray*
> *Tawny-finned fishes. My bended hook shall pierce*
> *Their slimy jaws, and, as I draw them up,*
> *I'll think them every one an Antony,*
> *And say 'Ah, ha! You're caught!'*

The action in the play proves that Cleopatra, like Plutarch suggests, is inclined towards the Good (the heroic) and so in the end she does not betray Antony. Cleopatra cannot bear to live a life of limitation under Octavius. For her "*freedom from death is Time – not Life*" (*Concerning the Mysteries of Isis and Osiris*, I.4). To continue to live in a world without Antony would be merely to exist.

Cleopatra can be seen generally as a force of positive creation (2.2.238).

> *He ploughed her, and she cropped.*

Cleopatra was called "*Tethys*" by Antony (3.7.60; note 60). Tethys was the wife of Oceanus, mother of the Nile, and was also another name for Isis. The Nile's swelling and cropping mimicked Cleopatra's own (2.7.20-23)

> *The higher Nilus swells,*
> *The more it promises. As it ebbs, the seedsman*
> *Upon the slime and ooze scatters his grain,*
> *And shortly comes to harvest.*

Cleopatra can be viewed as immortal and the source of the universe (2.2.245-250)

> *Age cannot wither her, nor custom stale*
> *Her infinite variety. Other women cloy (satisfy)*
> *The appetites they feed, but she makes hungry*
> *Where she most satisfies; for vilest things*
> *Become themselves in her, that the holy priests*
> *Bless her when she is riggish. (wanton)*

Shakespeare's Cleopatra, like Plutarch's Isis, can accommodate even the "*vilest things*". It is because Plutarch's metaphysics can accommodate evil that I think Shakespeare used Plutarch's work not only for its historical content but also for it unique philosophical content. The metaphysics found in Plutarch's "*Concerning the Mysteries of Isis and Osiris*" appear to have played a role in the structural features found in the 'Egyptian' portions of the play, just as standard Platonism played a structural role in the 'Roman' portion of the play. The subtle differences between the 'Roman' and 'Egyptian' points of view alert us to the fact that Shakespeare was fully aware of the metaphysics he was dealing with. He used it to enrich his poetry and character studies.

Cleopatra's love of Antony cannot be denied but at times she is also furious with him (love and war – Venus and Mars do not always get along). There are gaps of information in the play where Cleopatra's navy consistently betrays Antony's worldly interests. Twice Antony is betrayed and twice Cleopatra convinces him it was not by her. As an audience we are never sure if she has not been complicit in some way in generating this harm.

Cleopatra, as Isis, as a god, may be spiritually motivated. By denying Antony worldly victory she may be directing him toward spiritual maturity. In the play it is clear that Antony does not know himself, he is torn between Roman and Egyptian values. It is only when he loses all his kingdoms that he realizes that he loves Cleopatra more than all this world (3.11.69-70)

Fall not a tear, I say; one of them rates
All that is won and lost.

Antony's prayers for military success may not have been granted because they may not have been in his best interests (2.1.5-8)

We, ignorant of ourselves,
Beg often our own harms, which the wise powers
Deny us for our good; so find we profit
By losing of our prayers.

That Cleopatra could have her own agenda is generally not acknowledged by critics (she is often seen as merely a corrupting force or a distraction to Antony). By discovering her metaphorical role in the play it may be possible to discern what agenda was assigned to her.

Understanding Cleopatra

In Plutarch's metaphysics Horus (the Cosmos) arose from the coupling of Isis (the generative mud of the Nile) with the Body of Osiris (the Ideals). In our play the Body of Osiris, the ideal, can be seen, at least in Cleopatra's eyes, as Antony. Cleopatra in her eulogy describes Antony as an ideal beyond imagining (5.2.96-99)

> *Nature wants stuff*
> *To vie strange forms with fancy; yet t'imagine*
> *An Antony were nature's piece 'gainst fancy,*
> *Condemning shadows quite.*

She believes that nature normally lacks real objects that can compete with imagined ones but that Antony puts even these imagined objects to shame.

Both Plutarch and Shakespeare have connected Antony and Cleopatra with Osiris and Isis. In the legend when Osiris is killed and torn into pieces by Typhon it is Isis that reassembles him and makes him immortal. So too in Shakespeare's play it is Cleopatra that reassembles the memory of Antony into a legend (5.2.81-91).

The love story is so effectively told that very few audience members would deny that Antony and Cleopatra are made for each other. All take solace in the hope that they may be together for eternity. The premise voiced at the beginning of the play that a great soldier has been made into a strumpet's fool does not ring true by the end of the play. Antony has grown, he has broken boundaries, his excesses nicely fit in with the god he has become.

In both Platonic Philosophy and Plutarch's variation of this philosophy Cleopatra/Isis is seen as either the Indefinite Dyad or an aspect of the Indefinite Dyad; the Indefinite Dyad being characterized by excess. In Plato the Indefinite Dyad is the infinite substrate (the pre-physical matter) on which The One must impose limits. The One imprints ideas onto this substrate in order to create physical reality. The Indefinite Dyad could be said to represent the 'infinite potential' of the universe. The Indefinite Dyad, being infinite, is always greater than the finite created world. In this sense the Indefinite Dyad is comparable to the unlimited imagination.

In *Antony and Cleopatra* the lovers are associated with the imagination. Their's is the hyperbolic world of exaggeration, where everything is possible for it is a world without limit. Paradox is accepted because anything Cleopatra says or does is allowed in this world of infinite possibility (2.2.245-246)

> *Age cannot wither her, nor custom stale*
> *Her infinite variety.*

Cleopatra can make *"defect perfection"* (2.2.241) for she inhabits infinite possibility.

From a Platonic point of view both Cleopatra and Antony are examples of this excess and are therefore destined for the infinite. To be part of the physical world is to be subjected to Limit, something which does not suit either of their expansive characters.

Cleopatra is not Antony's soul; they are in fact both parts of the World's Soul (another name for the Indefinite Dyad). In the Roman world each is a reflection of this Indefinite Dyad; embodying the idea of excess. The Romans see them as flawed since excess cannot possess the virtue of the mean. They are, in fact, characters that do not fit within the limited nature of the physical world.

In the Egyptian world Plutarch's unique brand of Platonism applies. In this philosophy Cleopatra is still part of the Indefinite Dyad where she takes on the aspect of generation while Antony takes on the aspect of the ideal; together they generate the ideal of excess, the heroic.

An Egyptian Understanding of Octavius

Using Platonic philosophy it is easy to ascribe the role of The One to Octavius. He is 'the one' Triumvir to succeed at the end of the play and he brings about a *"time of universal peace"* (4.6.5). Octavius is all about defining limit and imposing limits on others. Octavius demonstrates measured behaviour. He does not drink to excess (2.7.103)

> *But I had rather fast from all, four days,*
> *Than drink so much in one.*

His military actions are measured and planned. Octavius does not know the abandonment of love; his is an arranged marriage devoid of passion in the Roman tradition. Even when Octavius celebrates it is measured and planned, although still seen as a waste in his eyes (4.1.16-17)

> *...feast the army. We have store to do't*
> *And they have earned the waste.*

Platonic philosophy would assign virtue to the idea of limit for it is the mean between extremes. From a Roman point of view Octavius is a virtuous character.

Plutarch's unique interpretation of Platonic philosophy as employed by the Egyptians puts a taint on Octavius' character. In Plato's philosophy The One sliced off pieces of the infinitely large Indefinite Dyad to give rise to the created world. In Plutarch the role of cutting up the Body of Osiris is given to Seth/Typhon (the Evil One). Plutarch believed that both The Good and Evil must have the ability to create since the Good could not create evil (*Concerning the Mysteries of Isis and Osiris*, XLV.8).

> *"For if nothing has been naturally brought into existence without a cause, and Good cannot furnish cause of Bad, the nature of Bad as well as Good must have a genesis and principle peculiar to itself".*

Since Seth/Typhon is a force of evil his actions puts a taint on creation. It also puts a taint on the action of 'cutting up' or limiting. Metaphorically it puts a taint on Octavius for from an Egyptian point of view Octavius can be seen as Seth.

Shakespeare appears to be aware of this possibility for he makes Octavius more evil than the Octavius Plutarch describes in his *Parallel Lives of the Greeks and Romans*. Shakespeare exaggerates Octavius' evil perhaps to make this point. Octavius commits several acts of evil in the play:

(3.5.6-12) Octavius uses Lepidus to fight Pompey and then betrays Lepidus and has him banished.

(4.6.8-16) Octavius is not gracious in his use of Antony's deserters. He places them in the vanguard of his attack against Antony. Octavius also executes Alexas (one of Antony's deserters) even after he proved himself useful.

(5.2.130-131) Octavius threatens to execute Cleopatra's children if she does not comply with his wishes.

(5.2.335-336) Octavius plans to parade Cleopatra in his triumph even though he promised her he would not (5.1.61-65).

So from an Egyptian point of view Octavius is seen as a source of evil that limits the potential of the creation. Cleopatra is seen as the infinite potential of creation and Antony as the ideal form of that creation.

c) Conclusion to Multiplicity and Unity

The forces of multiplicity and unity are concepts that have been regarded as the creative forces of the universe. We encountered these ideas earlier when discussing the allegory of 'Venus and Mars' and the associated ideas of *concord* and *discord* or *unity* and *multiplicity*. Empedocles believed that the forces that unite the elements into compounds (a form of love) must be greater than the forces of strife or multiplicity that would break these composites back into their elements otherwise the physical world would not exist.

In *Antony and Cleopatra* we are presented with both a war story and a love story. I do not think it coincidental that both the romance and the war story end in triumphs for their respective parties. Metaphorically concord (love) and discord (war) have to be balanced for the world to exist. Shakespeare has taken great effort to make it so. He has manipulated the play so that the poetic vision – the lovers being united after death – becomes as plausible to the audience as Octavius' military victory. This emotional reaction is made possible by Shakespeare's deft hand (*The Common Liar*, p. 103-107, 158-161). As the play proceeds the pace slows down. The short, rapid scenes in different locations characteristic of the chaos of war are replaced by longer, slower scenes that take place in a single location. He slows down time. The play moves from the frantic pace associated with living towards the slower reflections associated with eternity.

At the beginning of the play we are prevented from identifying with the protagonists, there are too many contrary points of view presented. At the end of the play we are allowed to see the world through just the lovers' eyes. We can feel what they feel, empathize with their hopes. Shakespeare has saved the poetic language, the richest language, for the lovers while Octavius is left to speak in blank verse.

Shakespeare did not intend for Octavius or the Roman philosophy to come out as morally superior to that of the Egyptian world. To guarantee this he strategically used two philosophies: Plato when dealing with the Roman world and Plutarch's modification of Plato when dealing with the Egyptian world. Because of this juxtaposition of philosophies the idea of limit embodied in Octavius cannot be seen as morally superior to the ideals of infinite possibility embodied by Antony and Cleopatra.

Shakespeare has written a poetic work, a work of imagination. In spite of the fact that Octavius wins the war we sense Antony and

Cleopatra have won something far greater. Shakespeare has shown us emotionally that heroic excess matters more than the limited vision of petty bureaucrats *"Mechanic slaves with greasy aprons, rules and hammers"* (5.2.208-209) unable to see beyond the limits of the physical world.

In the real world discord must periodically triumph over concord or nothing would die. The forces are balanced but in a dynamic equilibrium. Shakespeare has given us a taste of the heroic but at the same time he's written a requiem for such heroic excess. Shakespeare viewed Antony and Cleopatra as the last of the Great Ones. He views their leaving as creating a void (4.15.67-69)

> *young boys and girls*
> *Are level now with men; the odds is gone*
> *And there is nothing left remarkable*
> *Beneath the visiting moon.*

Shakespeare has written a play where both sides obtain their desired goals. Antony and Cleopatra find an infinite home that can house their excessive longings and Octavius wins the physical realm that can house his limited vision. Neither vision can be said to dominate for they are exclusive of each other. There will always be both Life and Death and nothing *"no midway 'Twixt these extremes"*.

Conclusion

The One and The Indefinite Dyad – Concord and Discord – Life and Death can never find a mean. There is no in between. This is true of the play as well. The world of Rome and Egypt are not meant to compromise. Antony is not meant to find a balance between these worlds; he is meant to travel from one to the other. This is the point.

The play follows Antony's life from the confusion of living to the isolation of dying. The question of meaning is found for Antony in Cleopatra, in the infinite possibility of more. This is enough for Antony, the world doesn't matter; love matters. When the play ends we believe the lovers are together in Elysium but we see Octavius alone, isolated by his limited vision of what was possible and what he would allow in his physical world.

The inclusiveness of Egypt, its embracing of overflow, excess, possibility and paradox makes it a poet's dream. Nicholas of Cusa said that in –

"God is the enfolding of all things even of contradictories"

(*On Learned Ignorance*, Book I, Chapter 22, (67:3-4)).

This belief that God could contain all things even contradictions mimics the poetic conceit mentioned earlier when talking about variation on a theme. By embracing all the ideas or definitions of a word at once we can see the poetic possibilities in the everyday.

Syncretism, the reconciliation of opposing ideas, lies in the infinitely possible, in the world represented by Antony and Cleopatra. All the techniques Shakespeare employs like variation, multiple points of view, and uncertainty are designed to create multiple meanings. He goes on to show how in Egypt these meanings can overflow their boundaries, melt and dissolve into each other. Shakespeare's direction was from life to death, from limit to limitless possibility.

The play is designed like life – we move from many locations at a fast pace to a single location and a slower pace. The scenes get longer and more reflective as we move towards death and eternity. Egypt is Shakespeare's idea of a heaven, a place of infinite possibility.

Octavius, the boy Caesar, is still young when the play ends but he too will be faced with the same choices Antony had to make, about what it is he truly values. It is a choice that we all eventually have to make.

Bibliography

1) *Antony and Cleopatra*, W. Shakespeare, edited by John Wilders, The Arden Shakespeare, 3rd series, 2006.

2) *The Common Liar: An Essay on 'Antony and Cleopatra'*, Janet Adelman, Yale University Press, 1973.

3) *The Middle Platonists*, John Dillon, Cornell University Press, 1996.

4) *Concerning the Mysteries of Isis and Osiris*, Plutarch, translated by G.R.S. Mead, Kessinger Publishing.

5) *Narrative and Dramatic Sources of Shakespeare*, edited by Geoffrey Bullough, vol. 5, Plutarch 'The Life of Marcus Antonius' and 'The Life of Julius Caesar' translated by Sir Thomas North, 1964.

6) *Pagan Mysteries in the Renaissance*, Edgar Wind, The Norton Library, W.W. Norton and Co. Inc., 1968.

7) *Antony and Cleopatra: 'What Venus did with Mars'*, Raymond B. Waddington, Shakespeare Studies 2, p. 210-227, 1966.

8) *On Shakespeare*, Northrop Frye, Fitzhenry & Whiteside Ltd., 1986.

9) *Shakespeare Imagery and What it Tells Us*, Caroline Spurgeon, Cambridge University Press, 19th printing, 2005.

10) *In The East My Pleasure Lies and other esoteric interpretations of plays by William Shakespeare*, Beryl Pogson, Quacks Books, 1994.

11) *Nicholas of Cusa on Learned Ignorance, A Translation and an Appraisal of De Docta Ignorantia*, Jasper Hopkins, The Arthur J. Banning Press, 3rd printing, 1996.

12) *The Eclogues, Georgics and Aeneid of Virgil*, translated by C. Day Lewis, Oxford University Press, 1974.

13) *The Odyssey*, Homer, translated by Robert Fagles, Viking, published by Penguin Books, 1996.

14) *Metamorphoses*, Apuleius, edited and translated by J. Arthur Hanson, Loeb Classical Library, Harvard University Press, 2001.

15*) Hermetica; The Ancient Greek and Latin Writings which contain Religious or Philosophic Teachings Ascribed to Hermes Trismegistus*, edited and translated by Walter Scott, Shambhala Publications Inc., 1993.

16) *A Dictionary of Symbols*, J.E. Cirlot, English translation, Routledge and Kegan Paul Ltd., Published by Philosophical Library Inc., 1962.

17) *The Greek Myths*, Complete Edition, Robert Graves, Penguin Books, 1992.

Abstract for *Measure for Measure*

Bodies Unseen in *Measure for Measure*

This essay, *Bodies Unseen,* takes its title from Shakespeare's main character Vicentio, the Duke of Vienna, whose presence goes unseen through most of the play. The Duke's absence, like a light extinguished, allows the play to slip into a state of near tragedy.

By examining ideas on virtue and by appreciating the unseen influences on Shakespeare's poetry by such philosophers as Lucretius, Aristotle, Nicholas of Cusa, and Giordano Bruno we can begin to understand how a human tragedy can turn around and become a story of human triumph.

Bodies Unseen in *Measure for Measure*

Introduction

"nature works by means of bodies unseen"

(*On the Nature of Things*, Lucretius, Book I, line 328)

This quotation from Lucretius summarizes, in my view, much of what occurs in *Measure for Measure*. The play was seen as one of Shakespeare's 'problem plays', i.e., a play manifesting both cynical and morally ambiguous positions around ethical issues. This interpretation arises from the role that nature, or more specifically human nature, plays in the work.

Nature, manifest through birth and death, universally unites humanity. These are qualities all living things share; we come from the dust and we return to the dust. Women, through the act of giving birth, are strongly associated with the created world; they share in the act of physical creation. Men, through their sensual appetites, are tied to this same material world, the world of nature. Both men and women manifest their worldliness through sex. Sex is part of our earthly natures. Death, too, exposes us as material creatures revealing us to be both mortal and finite.

Measure for Measure is a play set against a backdrop of sex and death. This is code for our natural human existence. In the play an old law is enforced making death the penalty for having sex outside of marriage. J. Adelman in *Suffocating Mothers* (Chapter 4, Marriage and the Maternal Body: On Marriage as the End of Comedy in *All's Well That Ends Well* and *Measure for Measure*, p. 76-102), feels that sex in the play is treated like original sin. Knowledge, sexual knowing, is depicted as the sin that drove us out of paradise and introduced death into our world. In the play sex for Claudio has led to a death sentence imposed by law and sex for those who visit the brothels carries with it

197

the implication of death through disease. Within the confines of the play all humans are seen as bawds because all humans have 'earned' their 'living' through sex. This is the taint, the stain, that sex has left on all human creation, this is the mark of original sin. Whether we can bear this mark with pride or shame is a sub-theme of this work. How ashamed should we be of our humanity, of our naturalness?

The play is also concerned with justice and whether that justice should be aimed at divine or human goals. The allegorical nature of the play makes it an easy fit as a parable. The characters tend to embody concepts and the action in the play is deeply integrated with the character-types involved. G. Wilson Knight (*The Wheel of Fire*; '*Measure for Measure* and the Gospels', p. 79-108) tied many of the pivotal ideas in the play to passages from the Gospels. He sees *Measure for Measure* as a uniquely human reinterpretation of Biblical material. These associations tended to give the play the surface features of a morality play. There is little doubt that Shakespeare was drawing inspiration from this tradition but he updated it considerably. He used the judgments Jesus made on earth to inform the character of the Duke and to create a new story about the balance between our human and divine natures. Shakespeare's play thus creates a commentary on human and divine justice.

Aristotle's Balance: The Golden Mean

J.W. Lever, in his introduction to the Arden Edition of *Measure for Measure*, points out that the play is divided into balanced halves: the first part showing a progressive mounting of tensions characteristic of tragedies and the second half reversing the course of events and transforming the play back into a comedy. There is a balance in the conflicting plot elements and there is a balance in the contrary characters that embody the story. The play seems to embrace the

Aristotelean idea of the golden mean; that happiness lies in the balance between extreme positions. This has suggested to some that Shakespeare was incorporating an Aristotelean design into his tragicomedy.

The title *Measure for Measure* does suggest that such a balance was Shakespeare's intention. As one reads through the play this idea of balance is always there; characters are foils of each other; situations often duplicate themselves; and, like a yo-yo, as the plot unwinds it is forced to rewind upon itself. The end of the play brings us essentially back to the beginning only with everybody a little wiser about themselves. The idea of a pair of scales balancing one another is always present. Opposing concepts are often presented together. We, as an audience, are always weighing pros and cons as the action proceeds.

Aristotle's idea of the golden mean, i.e., the balance between extremes was not, however, the only idea around relating to the concept of opposites. Giordano Bruno was also pitching a more dynamic version of a related idea; that of the coincidence of opposites. Where Aristotle's idea reaches a conservative resting point between the extremes Bruno's idea was one of dynamism where both extremes were present in one property and that a dynamic equilibrium existed between these extremes. This meant that change, rather than rest, was the on-going state of things. This idea, I believe, more closely fits the reality depicted in the play.

Bruno's Balance: The Coincidence of Opposites

Giordano Bruno was in England staying with the French Ambassador, Michel de Castelnau, from 1583 to 1585. During this time Bruno wrote six major works. Nicholas of Cusa (1401-1464) had a major influence on Bruno's ideas and Bruno's work brought knowledge of Nicholas of Cusa to England. Central in Bruno's thinking was Casanus' notion of the coincidence of opposites.

Briefly, Bruno believed that contraries convert into one another. Unlike Aristotle, Bruno believed that contraries did not lie at opposite ends of a line but rather that they were at opposite poles of a circle. Bruno saw contraries as conditions of one principle and not two. For instance, cold is the polar opposite of hot; night is the polar opposite of day; hate is the opposite of love. As you move around the circle one contrary becomes the other. The opposites stand in a dynamic relationship with one another – change from one contrary to the other is both fundamental and fluid. There is no resting place. Both extremes are always theoretically present and together hence the coincidence of opposites.

This circular conceit fits nicely with Shakespeare's design for the play. *Measure for Measure* begins essentially as a comedy where an intelligent Duke with competent lords reigns over a kingdom. When the Duke leaves, the play takes on progressively tragic overtones but once the Duke reasserts his control over events in the play it moves back to its comic origins. It forms a complete circle with tragedy and comedy as polar opposites. The play mimics one turning of the wheel of Fortune.

As the wheel turns we realize that the only stability is constant change. Everything moves because nothing is ever truly at rest. Only by realizing that the world is one of constant change is it possible to seize opportunity otherwise the right moment passes by and the chance to grab Fortune is lost. The Duke, in *Measure for Measure,* knows this to be the case. His timing is impeccable. Only by acting at the right time with the right people is it possible for him to reverse the consequence of potentially tragic events.

The dynamism of Bruno's philosophy, of the coincidence of opposites, fits in with the cycle of Nature which moves from generation to corruption, life to death. Shakespeare uses Nature's cycle to structure much of his play. The crime Claudio is convicted of is fornication (sex) outside of marriage. He has made Julietta pregnant and created a new life with her but he is to be executed for this crime. Shakespeare has linked life and death in his play. He has made both concomitant upon a single action. This theme, this cycle, this coincidence of opposites, will be found to reoccur throughout the play. It is one of its fundamental conceits.

Bruno considered unity and multiplicity to be opposites that were coincident (*Giordano Bruno and the Logic of Coincidence*, Chapter 2, 'The Coincidence of Unity and Multiplicity'; p. 109-124). He believed a type of equilibrium existed between the two such that both could exist as opposite entities and yet still exist together. For example a sphere has height, width, and depth; height, width, and depth are three different geometrical concepts but within this context they are all the same. They are distinct and yet the same.

If one thinks of the universe there is a plurality of things in this universe. These things, at any given time, are the universe. The universe is multiple and one. Yet the universe is also eternal while some of the things that make it up are finite – so the one exists eternally while the multiple parts exist finitely. This means that at any given time the one and the many are coexistent and yet still conceptually different. The two ideas exist separately but together; aspects of the same thing. The one is eternal (all that has been and will be) so it is always greater than the many (the multiple parts existing at any finite moment). The many do not define the one nor does the one define the many; the universe and what's in it are distinct but coincident.

This coincidence of opposites is conceptually different from Aristotle's mean between opposites. It is a more dynamic situation; movement is continuous and circular between the extremes. In *Measure for Measure* Shakespeare's poetry matches Bruno's philosophy much closer than it does Aristotles'. Consider what the Duke says about Life and Death (3.1.11-13)

> *thou art Death's fool;*
> *For him thou labour'st by thy flight to shun,*
> *And yet run'st toward him still.*

By running from Death we run towards him; this is a circular conceit typical of Bruno's philosophy.

Shakespeare similarly links the noble to the base (3.1.13-15)

> *Thou art not noble;*
> *For all th'accommodations that thou bear'st*
> *Are nurs'd by baseness.*

In this coincidence of opposites Shakespeare argues that all noble things in life (our clothing, our housing, ourselves) come from the base elements of the earth. Civilizations rise then fall and all their accomplishments are reduced to rubble and from this rubble they rise again. There is a cyclical nature to this inevitability but there is also a coincidence where every noble thing simultaneously carries with it its base origin, i.e., its history.

The Duke continues his argument with Claudio about Life and Death (3.1) but all his allusions link these opposites together. The Duke speaks of death as something that we need not fear (3.1.17-19)

> *The best of rest is sleep;*
> *And that thou oft provok'st, yet grossly fear'st*
> *Thy death, which is no more.*

The Duke is attempting to calm Claudio. To convince him that death is an absence like sleep is in life. Nicholas of Cusa *(On Learned Ignorance*, Book II.172) describes death in a similar fashion.

"Thus, death does not occupy any space, as Virgil says. For death seems to be nothing except a composite thing's being resolved into its components."

This equilibrium, generation and dissolution, the Duke elaborates even more on. He sees in life a constant death. He presents Claudio with the idea that life is lived in the present moment and once that moment passes it can no longer be changed and is therefore dead and a part of the past. Using this idea the Duke argues that life is made up of a series of ongoing deaths (3.1.39-40)

> *Yet in this life*
> *Lie hid moe thousand deaths.*

Claudio accepts this coincidence of opposites (3.1.42-44)

> *I humbly thank you.*
> *To sue to live, I find I seek to die,*
> *And seeking death, find life.*

He takes comfort from the continuous, linked and circular nature of life and death.

The key to understanding *Measure for Measure* is to understand the 'coincidence of opposites' in each of us. Virtues and the opposite Vices are in each of us. The opposites are linked. Angelo, regardless of his wishes, cannot just possess Virtue for in fact Virtue is coincident with Vice. Angelo cannot just pretend that Vice does not exist for to overshoot Virtue means you are coming up on the backside of Vice.

To understand that Virtue and Vice are one thing and not two creates a vigilance and awareness that can be applied to one's life. This is what the Duke is trying to show both Angelo and Isabella. That all the aspects of humanity are within each of us; no matter how we strive Virtue and Vice are common to us all.

In Aristotle's system Virtue lies at the balance point between two Vices. It is the pure point of moderation. For instance, in this play, the Virtue of discipline would lie between the extreme Vices of tyranny and freedom. This system implies Virtues are separate from Vices, that one can remove themselves from Vice. In Bruno's system of 'coincident opposites' Virtues/Vices are one thing, aspects of one property; to have one is to have them both. Bruno's system humbles us – the potential for both good and evil is wholly in all of us continuously.

Angelo and Isabella are on a fool's mission if they think they can avoid the Vice inherent in Virtue. This is what the Duke knows. This is why the Duke planned to be watchful of Angelo.

Measure for Measure can be seen as a metaphor for two weights on opposite sides of a scale or the concept can be understood differently as two ingredients measured out and added to one pot; the sweet and sour being essential to the one dish. Both measures balance out the one flavour. Marianna seems to have this understanding and it is reflected in her plea to the Duke (5.1.437-439)

> *They say best men are moulded out of faults,*
> *And, for the most, become much more the better*
> *For being a little bad.*

The best men are a little bad - opposites are coincident in the play.

Double Time

The idea of the coincidence of opposites, as seen earlier in the discussion of the one and the many, carries with it an assumption about time. Bruno considered time to exist in two ways. For God (the One) time was eternal but for the rest of creation (the many) time was linear and finite. Because of this the One transcended the creation for the creation was only the unfolding of the One at a single moment whereas the One contained all past and future moments - eternity. So at any given time the One and the many exist as distinct elements. When you look at the One you cannot see the many (because there are infinite variations of the many) and when you look at the many you cannot see the One (since it is a snapshot of only one moment and cannot reflect the eternal). The One and the many are coexistent and opposites; the eternal and the finite both exist together.

In *Measure for Measure* we have a play that has two time scales. Critics have called this 'double time' (*Measure for Measure*, Arden Edition, p. xiv-xv) in that the events that occur around Claudio's execution take place over three days and yet the Duke's absence appears to be much longer.

The Duke's time line appears different from the rest of the play. Enough time appears to have passed for Angelo to feel comfortable in resurrecting old laws, for the public to be concerned about the Duke's absence (3.2.85-86), and for various letters sent by the Duke to reach Angelo providing him with mixed messages as to the Duke's whereabouts (4.2.198-202).

The Duke is clearly depicted in the play as a human divinity (5.1.367) possessing a type of secular providence. The Duke goes about fixing the lives of the various characters so it is possible that a more eternal time line was required for him to accomplish his workings. He does in fact operate like a god working around the periphery, in the shadows, and watching what is going on. Northrop Fry argues that the second half of the play can be viewed as a play-within-a-play for during this half the Duke directs and plans the actions of the various characters guiding them to a resolution of his own design. The Duke becomes the Deus of the 'Deus ex machina'.

The presence of two time lines in the play is, in fact, consistent with the other ideas operating in the play. They all fit under the unifying principle of the coincidence of opposites.

The Pious and the Wicked

In *Measure for Measure* the Duke has created a liberal society. He sees himself as Vienna's fond father but now he is having doubts about his permissiveness. He is hoping that by leaving his more conservative staff members in charge that they might correct problems caused by his laxity (1.3.19-21;23-29)

> *We have strict statutes and most biting laws,*
> *The needful bits and curbs to headstrong jades,*
> *Which for this fourteen years we have let slip*
> *...Now, as fond fathers*
> *Having bound up the threatening twigs of birch,*
> *Only to stick it in their children's sight*
> *For terror, not to use, in time the rod*
> *Becomes more mock'd than fear'd: so our decrees,*
> *Dead to infliction, to themselves are dead,*
> *And Liberty plucks Justice by the nose.*

The Duke feels that Escalus (an older Lord) is as well schooled in the theory of government as he is and that it is time to put this Lord's knowledge into practice (1.1.7-13)

> *Then no more remains*
> *But that, to your sufficiency, as your worth is able,*
> *And let them work. The nature of our people,*
> *Our city's institutions, and the terms*
> *For common justice, y'are as pregnant in*
> *As art and practice hath enriched any*
> *That we remember.*

The Duke sees Escalus' potential; he is pregnant in theory and now must give birth to practice. Thought must be turned into action. The Duke also sets Angelo (a young Lord) to stand in his stead during his absence. Angelo is described as precise and emotionally cool. The Duke hopes the two, advisor and Chief Officer, age and youth, will provide for a balanced justice (1.1.43-46; 58-59)

> *In our remove, be thou full ourself.*
> *Mortality and mercy in Vienna*
> *Live in thy tongue, and heart. Old Escalus,*
> *Though first in question, is thy secondary...*
> *To th'hopeful execution do I leave you*
> *Of your commissions.*

This first scene in the first act has given us two key words we will see over and over in the play - pregnant and execution. These words or variations on them pertaining to life and death will make up most of the key imagery employed throughout the play.

Angelo pleads that he be tested before he is left in charge of the Duke's kingdom (1.1.48)

> *Let there be some more test made of my metal.*

Unbeknownst to him this is exactly what is to transpire. This essentially provides the premise of the play. The Duke is to secretly watch over Angelo to see how he manages the kingdom in his absence. Angelo's book-learning days are over and the Duke intends to find out how competent Angelo is in the real world. The Duke wants to see if Angelo's piousness can be applied to benefit the kingdom. He wishes to see if Angelo's sincere righteousness can transform Vienna into a more disciplined kingdom or whether the power of government will transform Angelo (1.3.53-54)

> *Hence shall we see*
> *If power change purpose, what our seemers be.*

Angelo's Justice

Aristotle wrote about the related qualities of Justice and Virtue in his *Nicomachean Ethics* (Book V.i.15,16)

"Justice then in this sense is perfect Virtue, though with a qualification, namely that it is displayed towards others. This is why Justice is often thought to be the chief of the Virtues...because its possessor can practise his virtue towards others and not merely by himself; for there are many who can practise virtue in their own private affairs but cannot do so in their relations with another.

This is why we approve the saying of Bias, 'Office will show a man'; for in office one is brought into relation with others and becomes a member of a community."

The Duke believes that the office will reveal Angelo's character or more precisely that by interacting with others in the community he will reveal himself. The Duke does not wish to judge Angelo on his potential to be a judge but rather on his actions as a judge. Throughout the play the Duke avoids judging the unseen.

Virtues can be selfish and self-aggrandizing but Justice cannot for (*Nicomachean Ethics*, Book V.i.17;19)

"Justice alone of the virtues is 'the good of others', because it does what is for the advantage of another."

"Justice in this sense then is not a part of Virtue, but the whole of Virtue."

Angelo and Isabella are the male and female equivalents of 'vain piousness' at least with regards to their estimation of their own personal virtue. Both wish to use their piety to restrict the freedoms of others. The Duke is actually counting on this from Angelo because he feels he has given Vienna too much freedom (1.3.35). Isabella, however, tries to impose her piousness on an already pious order of Nuns by requesting that even more restrictions be placed on their privileges (1.4.3-5)

> *I speak not as desiring more,*
> *But rather wishing a more strict restraint*
> *Upon the sisters stood.*

Both Angelo and Isabella are young and idealistic so both are attracted to the romanticism of deprivation. This places both of them outside their community and makes neither one a good candidate for the administration of justice. Both are too sanctimonious for anybody else's good.

Justice requires community input and must meet community standards otherwise it becomes a type of imposed tyranny.

Escalus, in his role of secondary, offers Angelo advice in the fornication case against Claudio (2.1.5-16). Aristotle in his *Nicomachean Ethics* (Book VI.xi.6) placed much value on the opinions of the elderly.

> *"Consequently the unproved assertions and opinions of experienced and elderly people, or of prudent men, are as much deserving of attention as those which they support by proof; for experience has given them an eye for things, and so they see correctly."*

Angleo dismisses Escalus' argument that many could succumb to Claudio's sin under the right circumstances by asserting that (2.1.17-18)

> *'Tis one thing to be tempted, Escalus,*
> *Another thing to fall.*

When Angelo says this he is making a reasonable statement – that we should be judged by our actions and not our intents. This is in-keeping with Aristotle's attitude (*Nicomachean Ethics*, Book III.i.1)

> *"Virtue however is concerned with emotion and actions, and it is voluntary action for which praise and blame are given."*

Angelo has used the law and Claudio's actions to condemn him. He has ignored Escalus' pleas to temper his Justice with Mercy. Mercy means empathy for Escalus; it is a projection of ourselves into the circumstances of the accused, it adds the human element to the equation. It asks if the accused acted as we might under similar circumstances.

Angelo makes a poor judge because he cannot empathize. He sees himself as above sin and he projects his piousness onto everyone around him. Angleo is so confident in his ability to resist a sin like that committed by Claudio that he issues a promise (2.1.29-30)

> *When I that censure him do so offend,*
>
> *Let mine own judgment pattern out my death.*

Angelo's poor judgment is a symptom of his lack of experience (*Nicomachean Ethics*, Book I.iii.5).

> *"Again, each man judges correctly those matters with which he is acquainted, it is of these that he is a competent critic."*

It is only when Angelo meets Isabella that he is struck by desire. He realizes for the first time what might have motivated Claudio (2.2.174-175; 185-187)

> *Dost thou desire her foully for those things*
>
> *That make her good?*
>
> *...but this virtuous maid*
>
> *Subdues me quite. Ever till now*
>
> *When men were fond, I smil'd, and wonder'd how.*

Angelo's awakened desire combined with his new powers allows him to plan evil acts (2.4.2-3;6-7)

> *Whilst my invention, hearing not my tongue,*
>
> *Anchors on Isabel...*
>
> *And in my heart the strong and swelling evil*
>
> *Of my conception.*

210

Angelo's evil is conceived just like the baby Julietta carries for Claudio. Throughout the play gestation and growth imagery is employed and balanced against the death imagery.

Angelo makes it clear to Isabella that if she would have sex with him he would release her brother Claudio (2.4.88;96)

> *...to save his life –*
>
> *You must lay down the treasure of your body.*

Isabella, pious as ever, cannot entertain such a violation of her honour, nor does she believe her brother would permit it (2.4.106-108)

> *Better it were a brother died at once,*
>
> *Than that a sister, by redeeming him,*
>
> *Should die forever.*

Rape in an Honour/Shame Culture

Isabella's fear of spiritual pollution was widely held in the Renaissance. It was a society still bound by ideals of chivalry and often motivated by honour and shame.

Surprisingly it is in the stories of the Saints that this fear of spiritual pollution can be seen (*Geometry of Love*, M. Visser, Chapter 10, 'Virgin Martyr: Tomb', p. 235-257). One saint whose plight resembles Isabella's was that of St. Agatha who was murdered during the 3rd century for her religious convictions.

Agatha had decided to remain a virgin in order to dedicate her life to Christ. Quintinian, the Roman administrator of Catania, tried to seduce her in order to deter her from her purpose. She refused his advances so he had her sent to a brothel. There she was miraculously preserved from being raped. After this Quintinian set about torturing her to death.

It was said that Agatha's glory was twofold – she wore the 'double crown' of virginity and martyrdom. This tradition that had to 'miraculously' preserve Agatha from rape did much to undermine the teachings found in the gospels. It was a tradition passed down from the Greeks and the Romans and had little to do with Christian values.

In the ancient Roman and Greek worlds, virginity for a female was the state of being intact, unviolated (symbolic of a fortified city). To lose virginity outside of wedlock could label a woman as spoiled goods and destroy any chance at a future marriage. Loss of virginity outside of marriage was considered a matter of shame. Shame was assigned by others to an individual or to their family. Shame was a form of 'social pollution'; it was a state of being. It was not regarded as something that could be removed except by revenge, i.e., you had to steal honour from those responsible for stealing your honour (a primitive form of justice).

The Greco-Roman tradition required a female hero to keep both her moral and physical integrity intact. The story of St. Agatha is more a Greco-Roman myth than a Christian myth. When examining the list of virgin martyrs one cannot help but notice how many were sent to brothels but were left miraculously inviolate. Their deaths are described in horrible detail but the women were never raped. The Church had a hard time accepting the idea of a 'shamed' Saint.

We know that 'thinking Christians' believed that a raped woman was in no way polluted or reduced by what had been done to her. St. Augustine (354-430 C.E.) spoke of the *"chastity preserved in the spirit"* which could not be destroyed by the physical act of rape. Claudio, in *Measure for Measure,* reasons along this line when arguing that the intended good absolves any sin Isabella would commit (3.1.133-134)

> *What sin you do to save a brother's life,*
> *Nature dispenses with the deed so far*
> *That it becomes a virtue.*

Claudio's quote also contains aspects of Bruno's circular idea of the coincidence of opposites with the deed moving from the pole of vice to the opposite pole of virtue.

These stories of Sainted Virgins in many ways stood as a mockery to Christian revelation. The Christian moral system based on Guilt/Forgiveness was intended to supersede the Honour/Shame culture. The point of Christian forgiveness was that no longer could someone assign shame to an individual. No longer did society have the power to diminish an individual before the eyes of God. Each individual was responsible for their own sins. You could feel guilty for what you had done but these sins could be forgiven if you were truly penitent. Sin and forgiveness was a matter dealt with between God and the individual. Isabella's belief in shame is not unusual but the secretly watching Duke sees this belief as a mistake in her judgment.

Angelo also believes that honour/shame is the operating paradigm for his culture. He fears Claudio will revenge his sister's honour. This is why he proceeds with Claudio's execution (4.4.26-30)

> *He should have liv'd;*
> *Save that his riotous youth, with dangerous sense,*
> *Might in the times to come have ta'en revenge*
> *By so receiving a dishonour'd life*
> *With ransom of such shame.*

Although these ideas of shame and revenge play a central part in the motivation of Isabella and Angelo (the two sanctimonious characters in the play) they do not motivate the Duke's behaviour. He, in fact, quickly removes the thought of honour from Claudio's mind by leading him to believe that Angelo was merely testing Isabella and that he had no intention of ever releasing Claudio. Claudio merely has to come to terms with his own death (3.1.160-162; 165-167)

> *Angelo had never the purpose*

213

to corrupt her; only he hath made an assay of her
virtue...
I am confessor to Angelo,
and I know this to be true; therefore prepare your-
self to death.

Understanding the Duke

The Duke in *Measure for Measure* yearns for a better system of justice; it is part of the reason he decided to test Angelo. He wondered if a more pious, righteous individual would set a better example, both personally and through the laws he would choose to enforce (1.2.64-66)

Your scope is as mine own,
So to enforce or qualify the laws
As to your soul seems good.

By Act 3 the Duke realizes the experiment is over, Angelo is in trouble, and there is much he must now do to set things right.

While in the guise of a Friar he comes upon Escalus who asks him *"What news abroad i'th'world?"* To which the Duke answers (3.2.216-217)

None, but that there is so great a fever on goodness
that the dissolution of it must cure it.

Angelo's excessive piousness has made goodness appear sick. The only way to save both Vienna and Angelo is to kill Angelo's sense of his own goodness. The Duke plans to expose the abuses of the powerful.

What the Duke proposes is what Giordano Bruno proposed in his work *The Expulsion of the Triumphant Beast (Lo spaccio della bestia trionfante*, published in England (1584), sometimes referred to as just *Lo Spaccio).* In this work Bruno calls for a renewal of certain virtues which he feels have been abused; virtues like truth, knowledge, and wisdom. He wishes to see the vices thrown down from the heavens and the virtues put in their stead (*The Expulsion of the Triumphant Beast,* translated and edited by Arthur D. Imerti, University of Nebraska Press, 2004, p. 110).

"The goddess Justice, the goddess Temperance, the goddess Constance, the goddess Liberality, the goddess Patience, the goddess Truth, the goddess Mnemosyne, the goddess Sophia, and many other goddesses and gods, are being banned not only from heaven but also from earth; and in their stead in the lofty places constructed for them as their residences, by exalted Providence, are seen dolphins, goats, ravens, serpents, and other filth, levities, caprices, and frivolities."

Bruno felt the frivolous constellations based on the antics of the gods should be replaced with the virtues so that when humans looked up to the heavens they could find guidance for their actions. Bruno wished to see Ursa, the Bear (representing Callisto, Jove's mistress), replaced by Truth (ibid., p.120-121).

"It is a great ignominy, oh Jove, and a greater one than you yourself are aware of, that you have placed that Ursa in the most celebrated position of heaven...

You have placed that ugly, huge animal in the very part of the sky which sailors consult during the course of their devious and uncertain sea voyages...

I, because it is the most eminent seat, want Truth to make her residence...There she [Truth] will dwell stable and firm; there she will not be shaken violently by waves and storms; there she will be the safe guide of those who go wandering through this tempestuous Sea of Errors..."

Bruno begins his revolution of the heavens by making Truth uppermost and then linking her to the other forms of Wisdom (ibid., p.139, p. 141).

"Above all things...is situated Truth; because she is the unity that presides over all..."

"That goddess who is joined to and close to Truth has two names: Providence and Prudence. She is called Providence inasmuch as she influences and is found in superior principles, and she is called Prudence inasmuch as she is effectuated in us...

Providence, then,...is the companion of Truth..."

Bruno believed that any ethical system had to hold Truth as paramount since all other principles are drawn from it. Providence and Prudence are two forms of wisdom; Providence is Divine wisdom and Prudence is worldly or practical wisdom.

Providence is the venue of the Divine, it is the universal principle of reasoning or forethought, it is part of the infinite knowledge of God. Prudence is the finite aspect of this Divine principle as manifest in humans. Human wisdom participates in Divine wisdom but the finite can only ever reflect an aspect of the infinite.

In *Measure for Measure* the Duke manifests a worldly Prudence as he watches over the actions of Angelo, Isabella, Marianna, and Claudio. He uses his foresight to anticipate the harm awaiting them and applies his practical wisdom to make sure they are kept safe.

The Duke has adversaries in the play just as Prudence does in heaven (ibid., p. 141).

"[Prudence] She has two insidious enemies who are vicious: To her right are found Cunning, Craftiness, and Malice; to her left, Stupidity, Inertia, and Imprudence."

Angelo manifests the cunning, craftiness, and even malice in his relations with Isabella and the stupidity and inertia we find alive and well in the two gentlemen that prefer a world with war to a better one without it, if it requires them to change (1.2.1-40). Aspects of these flaws we also find in Mistress Overdone and Pompey who are slow to adapt to the enforcement of the old law, having been warned two or three times for the same offence (3.2.187-188). Imprudence or being rash and indiscrete is a flaw we can easily assign to Lucio whose slanderous tongue truly galls the Duke (3.2.181-182).

That these general qualities match characters in the play is not such a surprise as the play borrows from the 'morality' tradition where characters often embody certain virtues or vices. What is more interesting is that Shakespeare's play matches a similar intent with that seen in Bruno's work – both seek a new ethic to replace an old one.

In both works Prudence plays a primary role. In *Measure for Measure* it defines the Duke's character (ibid., p. 142).

"[the Prudent] *they doubt nothing, but expect all; they suspect nothing, but guard themselves against everything by remembering their past, planning their present, and foreseeing their future.*"

The Duke trusts Angelo and Escalus; he plans to watch over them but he does not suspect them of evil intentions. Even when Angelo's actions are plain to the Duke he does not intervene. The Duke cares for Angelo; it is not Angelo's punishment he is seeking but his education. The Duke wants Angelo to come out of the experience a better man, a man aware of his weaknesses (Justice is the good of others).

In both Shakespeare and Bruno's works Law plays an important role. For Bruno Law was the daughter of Wisdom (Sophia) and was a servant to the weak (ibid., p. 144-145).

"*Sophia is followed by her daughter, Law: and through Law, Sophia wishes to operate, wishes to be employed; through Law princes reign, and kingdoms and republics are maintained. Law, adapting herself to the complexion and customs of peoples and nations, suppresses audacity through fear, and sees to it that goodness is secure among the wicked...*

Jove has placed her in heaven and exalted her with this condition: that she allow that the powerful be not secure because of their pre-eminence and power; but that by referring all to greater providence and superior law (through which civil law is regulated, as is the divine and natural), she make it understood that for those who come out of spiders' webs there are ordained nets, cords, chains, and fetters since by decree of Eternal Law it is sanctioned that the most powerful be most powerfully compressed and bound...

...she has been ordained...in order that the potent be sustained by the impotent, the weak be not oppressed by the stronger; that tyrants be deposed, just rulers and realms be constituted and strengthened. "

Bruno's vision of the Law and Shakespeare's vision reflected in the drama are similar. The Duke wishes the law to protect the good people (people like Isabella) from the wicked. He also wishes the law to capture the rich as easily as the poor; he wants equality in the law. The Duke refers to this in his soliloquy (3.2.268-270).

> *To draw with idle spiders' strings*
> *Most ponderous and substantial things!*
> *Craft against vice I must apply.*

The Duke's intent is the same as Bruno's, he wants to capture the powerful, the substantial, in the web of the law. Both use spider imagery with respect to discussions on the law.

Bruno also expresses that the Law must adapt herself to *"the complexion and customs of peoples"*. This idea too is reflected by the Duke when first talking to Escalus. The Duke was reassured by the fact that Escalus understood *"the nature of our people"* (1.1.9). Laws are not to be imposed against custom or nature.

The Duke also expresses the thought that one must understand themselves; for it is only by understanding one's own weaknesses that we can be merciful towards others (3.2.258-261)

(Neither) *More nor less to others paying*

Than by self-offences weighing.

Shame to him whose cruel striking

Kills for faults of his own liking!

There is no room for hypocrisy within the Duke's law. Bruno felt similarly *"... no law that is not adjusted to the experience of human society must be accepted"* (ibid., p. 145). He felt laws should work for the betterment of society (ibid., p. 146).

"[Jove] has charged Judgment with the defense of and concern with true law, and the destruction of wicked and fraudulent law."

In *Measure for Measure*, the law Angelo has chosen to enforce is one against human nature and ultimately unenforceable; Lucio points this out to the Duke (3.2.98-99)

but it is impossible to extirp it quite,

friar, till eating and drinking be put down.

Such laws only make a mockery of justice for they are not in anyone's interests. Bruno felt that the Romans understood the purpose of the law (ibid., p. 149).

"For this reason they [the gods] *exalted the Roman people above others; because with their magnificent deeds they, more than other nations, knew how to conform with and resemble them, by pardoning the subdued, overthrowing the proud, righting wrongs, not forgetting kindness, helping the needy, defending the afflicted, relieving the oppressed, restraining the violent, promoting the meritorious..."*

This statement summarizing the 'spirit of the law' is not in any way controversial. One point Bruno does bring up, that might have been surprising to an Elizabethan audience is a call for freedom of speech (ibid., p. 146).

"[Judgment] *should not be concerned with what each one imagines or thinks, providing that words and deeds do not corrupt the tranquil state of affairs.*"

In Bruno's version of the law people's thoughts (and therefore religious beliefs) are beyond the State's judgment. It is only the subversive actions that should be punished. The Duke, in *Measure for Measure,* when he deals with Lucio seems to be thinking along a similar line. Lucio's slanders infuriate the Duke but he is willing to let them pass, or at least acknowledge his inability to legislate against them (3.2.180-182)

> Back-wounding calumny
> The whitest virtue strikes. What king so strong
> Can tie the gall up in the slanderous tongue?

Isabella also argues on Angelo's behalf by using the concept of 'actions taken' as the basis for her plea. She argues Angelo intended evil but accomplished none and so should be set free (5.1.448-452)

> For Angelo,
> His act did not o'ertake his bad intent,
> And must be buried but as an intent
> That perish'd by the way. Thoughts are no subjects;
> Intents, but merely thoughts.

When the Duke finally judges Lucio it is not for his stories and lies but for his actions, those of abandoning a woman he wronged (Mistress Kate Keep-down) and his child by her (5.1.516-518)

> Upon mine honour, thou shalt marry her.
> Thy slanders I forgive, and therewithal
> Remit thy other forfeits.

Bruno's work, like in many of his works, comes down hard on pedants and the intransigent. He wanted an open debate, a free society where ideas could be explored and new truths discovered. Bruno saw all Church authorities as undermining this search for truth by erecting barriers against thought. Bruno was an advocate for change.

The Duke expresses similar views to Escalus, remarking that change is only requested but never put into practice and pointing out that it is dangerous to keep a worn out system. The Duke comments that there is not enough truth in the world to make it safe but more than enough oppression to make societies themselves dangerous (3.2.217-223)

> *Novelty is*
>
> *only in request, and it is dangerous to be aged in*
>
> *any kind of course as it is virtuous to be constant in*
>
> *any undertaking. There is scarce truth enough alive*
>
> *to make societies secure; but security enough to*
>
> *make fellowship accurst. Much upon this riddle*
>
> *runs the wisdom of the world.*

Capricorn Rules

Bruno's *The Expulsion to the Triumphant Beast* not only discusses the purification of Ethics by placing Truth foremost but goes on to discuss at great length the constellation Capricorn and its importance to both humans and gods (ibid., p. 247; note 48 p. 307).

Capricorn was believed to depict Pan, part god/ part animal, and because of this duality it was also seen as a symbol of man. The importance of Capricorn/Pan was that he possessed both a divine intellect and animal passions. Bruno felt that the lesson to be taken from Pan is that sometimes humans rely too heavily on their intellect and neglect their instinctive natures. When this happens they become corrupt. Bruno felt that only by integrating our rational and instinctive natures (coincidence of opposites) could we arrive at our highest understanding of ourselves.

This theme, of the balancing act between the divine and the animal, is found throughout the play *Measure for Measure*. What Angelo lacks is knowledge of his animal-self. His denial of his instinctual nature is what motivates him to resurrect an old law against fornication – the most basic animal instinct. Angelo wishes to direct the citizens of Vienna towards the divine and away from the beast. Lucio feels Angelo must have sprung from a non-human mother and he fears that this sterile man *"will unpeople the province with continency"* (3.2.168). Despite all Lucio's gossip he respects the Duke for having some empathy and knowledge of sex for he felt it moderated his administration of justice (3.2.115-117)

> *He had some feeling of the*
> *sport; he knew the service; and that instructed him*
> *to mercy.*

The Duke is described by Escalus as a man *"contended especially to know himself"* (3.2.226) and *"A gentleman of all temperance"* (3.2.231). These qualities are interesting because the three Delphic precepts were: to know yourself, to be moderate in everything, and to acknowledge God. The Duke can be seen partly as the product of Delphic wisdom. In Bruno's work Apollo is also seen as a wise judge (ibid., p. 126).

"All those who have natural judgment" said Apollo *"judge laws to be good, because they have experience as their end"*.

Earlier in the play the Duke felt his natural judgment, his leniency, was not serving his kingdom's needs. He feared he was giving the citizens of Vienna too much freedom. He believed that Angelo might correct this permissiveness. Now seeing the consequences of Angelo's idealism the Duke realizes that a return to an experienced-based form of judgment is in order.

Although Shakespeare does not mention the concept of Capricorn or Pan in his text of *Measure for Measure,* it is implicitly there for Capricorn/Pan was the sign of Rulers.

"Commonly it personifies Kings, Princes, Dukes, Earls, Judges ..." (*Christian Astrology,* (1647), Chpt. 7, tenth house).

Capricorn (Dec. 21 - Jan. 20), the sign of Patriarchs, was also the sign Jesus was born under. Capricorn/Pan was always chosen to represent the link between the Divine and the human and Shakespeare was clearly aware of these allusions. The Duke in *Measure for Measure* is not just a ruler but Wilson Knight regards him in his essay '*Measure for Measure* and the Gospels' as a stand-in for Jesus himself, often embodying the words Jesus spoke in the Gospels.

This Divine side does not overrule the more physical aspects of Pan, for in Greece he was regarded as a phallic diety with a promiscuous nature. Perhaps this is the gossip that Lucio refers to when he talked of the Duke's past (3.2.113-117)

> *Ere he would have hanged a man for the*
> *getting a hundred bastards, he would have paid for the*
> *nursing a thousand. He had some feeling of the*
> *sport; he knew the service; and that instructed him*
> *to mercy.*

Shakespeare's Duke possesses aspects of the divine but he is also clearly human. The key to the story is the need for both, the human in the divine and the divine in the human – measure for measure – coincident opposites of one quality.

The Profane in the Sacred

Angelo is not evil, he is pious, he is sanctimonious but he is not evil. As the play proceeds Angelo discovers his animal passions; his desires are awakened by the only thing that could arouse a pious man – goodness. Isabella's purity, sanctity and idealism tempt him into sin. Angelo's sin is the excessive love of virtue – by running towards virtue he runs towards vice. These are joined concepts in the circle of the coincidence of opposites (2.2.180-181)

> *O cunning enemy, that, to catch a saint,*
>
> *With saints dost bait thy hook!*

Angelo has not been so overcome by evil as he is ensnared by good, the cause of his fall is his own nature, his lust for virtue.

Angelo lives in his intellect, he believes himself to be a saint, he believes he has divorced his divine nature from his animal nature His desire for Isabella proves to him otherwise. His inability to admit or acknowledge his animal nature drives him to commit further acts of evil to cover up his 'crime' of being human. He is willing to slander Isabella and execute Claudio in order to protect his 'good name', his image of himself. This 'projected image' is more important to Angelo than the welfare of others.

This is a trait that he shares with Isabella who is also willing to let her brother be executed rather than compromise her principles (2.4.183-184)

> *Then, Isabel live chaste, and brother, die:*
>
> *More than our brother is our chastity.*

Both choose ideology over compassion. This is a perverse manifestation of religion where love for an ideal is valued over love of another human being (3.1.145-146)

> *I'll pray a thousand prayers for thy death;*
>
> *No word to save thee.*

Angelo and Isabella both are in need of new wisdom. Fortunately the Duke's concerns lay with the living, he is not an ideologue, he seeks their education, their improvement.

Isabella is a good person placed, through no fault of her own, in a situation she is not prepared for. The Duke knows she has placed 'all of virtue' into the symbol of chastity and that she has failed to act mercifully towards her brother. Later in the play the Duke provides her with a second opportunity. This time she decides to plead for Angelo's life, a man who she thinks has executed her brother and who intended to both violate and betray her. In her pleading Isabella is acting justly, she is doing something for the good of another. This time it is for Marianna who has requested her help (5.1.428-430). Isabel by setting aside her own agenda and doing what she can for another proves she has changed and understands mercy.

Angelo realizes the extent of his crimes and prefers *"death more willingly than mercy"* (5.1.474) so deep is his shame. Angelo realizes he is not worthy of life and certainly not worthy of Marianna (a woman who, in his arrogance, he previously felt unworthy of him (3.1.225-227)). Angelo has acknowledged that he too possesses 'feet of clay'. This self knowledge allows the Duke to pardon him and allow their marriage (5.1.495)

her worth, worth yours.

The two pious characters, Angelo and Isabella, find they are joined in marriage to the two characters that possess earthly wisdom, Marianna and the Duke. The sanctimonious fat has been trimmed from their natures so never again should sanctity interfere with their humanity. The balance between the Divine and the human has been struck.

Claudio and Barnardine

In *Measure for Measure* Claudio and Barnardine personify the same vice in Angelo's mind (2.4.42-46)

> *Ha? Fie, these filthy vices! It were as good*
>
> *To pardon him that hath from nature stolen*
>
> *A man already made as to remit*
>
> *Their saucy sweetness that do coin heaven's image*
>
> *In stamps that are forbid.*

Barnardine, a murderer, has taken away a life already made and Claudio, a fornicator, has created a life that the Church has not permitted. For Angelo both crimes are equal because both involve a life and in Angelo's reasoning both should be punished by death.

The Duke views the two crimes differently. He feels one must take responsibility for one's actions – if a life is created that life must be looked after and the mother taken care of. In this way Claudio is treated the same as Lucio but differently than Barnardine.

In Barnardine's case, he has taken responsibility for his crime, he has agreed to his punishment and he has made no attempt at escape. If any character in the play is an exemplar of a base human it is Barnardine (4.2.140-143)

> *A man that apprehends death no more dreadfully*
>
> *but as a drunken sleep; careless, reckless, and fearless*
>
> *of what's past, present, or to come: insensible of*
>
> *mortality, and desperately mortal.*

The Duke does not believe Barnardine to have been unjustly sentenced to death but he does believe he has been remiss in his treatment of him. To leave a prisoner languishing for nine years does not seem just and he wonders why he *"had not either delivered him to his liberty, or executed him?"* (4.2.130-131). The Duke regrets that Barnardine has been treated like a barnyard animal and that he has now come to act like one. The Duke acquits Barnardine of his "*earthly faults*" (5.1.481) but also provides Barnardine with the assistance of a Friar to help guide him to a better life; responsibility is taken.

Heaven and Hell

The Duke in *Measure for Measure* never speaks of an afterlife even when in the guise of a Friar. The Duke's primary concern is with temporal justice. He is not focused on the life beyond death and never uses religious ideology to justify or pardon his actions. In this sense the Duke is a grounded individual, pragmatic and practical. The Duke judges actions and not intents and his judgments focus on individuals taking responsibility for the consequences of their actions.

Throughout the play we witness the inhumanity of the pious and the kindness of sinners. Wilson Knight points out the gentleness of the gaoler, the honesty in Pompey, and the generosity in Mistress Overdone (3.2.193-196). Human virtue cannot be seen in the outward trappings, only through their actions can they be judged (1.1.32-35)

> *Heaven doth with us as we with torches do,*
> *Not light them for ourselves; for if our virtues*
> *Did not go forth of us, 'twere all alike*
> *As if we had them not.*

Virtues are not to be stored within oneself, they must be acted upon otherwise virtues become the intent to do good rather than the action of doing good. Virtues are divine intellectual concepts that must be applied in the physical world; their nature is twofold. They possess an unseen aspect, the divine intent, and a physical aspect, the thought put into practice. They mimic the creative act where divine thought becomes manifest in the physical world.

Bodies Unseen

I have indicated in this essay several sources that I believe influenced Shakespeare's poetics. His imagery of balance has more to do with Nicholas of Cusa's coincidence of opposites than with Aristotle's golden mean and Shakespeare's understanding of the divine and human links him philosophically with Bruno's writings. Bruno and Nicholas can be viewed as unseen contributors to Shakespeare's philosophy but several other writers can be seen as direct contributors to his plot structure.

The primary story of *Measure for Measure* comes from Giraldi Cinthio's *Hecatommithi* (1565), Part II, Década 8, Novella 5 and George Whetstone's two-part play *The Right Excellent and Famous Historye of Promos and Cassandra* (1578) excerpts of which can be found in the Appendix to the Arden Edition of *Measure for Measure*. Shakespeare has modified these stories by retaining their threat of violence but in removing the actual violence. This made their structure more amenable to his modification of them into a comedy. In Shakespeare's story the Isabella character is not violated and her brother is not executed, as well, the sadism of the Angelo character is removed. Shakespeare also introduces the Duke as a major character that is involved with the action in the play right from its beginning. I would also propose that Shakespeare's play has more to do with mercy than the other plays which seem to stress the virtues of duty and honour. The plot can certainly be traced to these sources but the details, the characterizations, the mood, and the motivations are distinctly different. The purpose, as it were, of Shakespeare's story is not the same as Cinthio's or Whetstone's.

G. Wilson Knight was probably quite accurate in linking *Measure for Measure* with the Gospels but I believe his conception of it as a Christian parable is wrong. Many of the ideas Shakespeare expresses in his poetry come from ideas contributed by Giordano Bruno to the Elizabethan philosophical dialogue. These ideas often reinforce the underlying Christian-humanist ethic but they are not Christian. The shared ethic we are looking at is the 'forgive our debts as we forgive others' type of justice and not the 'eye for an eye' kind of vengeance.

The justice Shakespeare promotes in the play is a measured response to a particular crime with the punishment designed to both educate and rehabilitate the perpetrator using *"correction and instruction"* (3.2.31).

Shakespeare adheres to Aristotle's belief that justice is about the good of others. He is concerned about making a better society. In *Measure for Measure* it is the designated Christians who abuse justice. Angelo abuses justice by exploiting it to serve his own interests. Isabella also fails to treat her brother with justice. She too feels that justice must serve her interests (maintaining her chastity) over her brother's. Both Angelo and Isabella are self-indulgent and fail in their responsibility towards others.

Angelo's and Isabella's self-indulgence stems from a common source, both are pious, both more concerned with the Divine than the human. This dissociates them from the concerns of the world and the concerns of others in their community. From Bruno's writings we can appreciate that it is through prudence (worldly wisdom) that humans participate in Divine Providence. Prudence is an example of our very finite understanding of the infinite mind. If we fail in acting prudently we fail in reflecting what little of the Divinity we can comprehend. Failure in acting prudently is a failure in virtue. Virtue must be understood as a verb and not a noun. Angelo's and Isabella's obsession with piety prevents them from acting prudently and endangers those around them.

The Duke is presented as a prudent man, a man who has no trouble adopting the identity of a humble friar and fitting in with the 'human stew' of his kingdom. The Duke is proud of his humanity just as God was proud to claim humanity in Christ. This dual citizenship in both heaven and earth is what Bruno claimed for Capricorn. Bruno argued that the creation was to be embraced and understood. He felt that our job was to find the divinity that was within the creation (*The Expulsion of the Triumphant Beast*, p. 237-238).

"They did not adore Jove as if he were Divinity, but adored Divinity as it was in Jove, because seeing in him a man in whom majesty, justice, and magnanimity were outstanding, they understood that in him there was a magnanimous, just, and benign god."

This is the Duke's lesson to Isabella and Angelo. You become better people by being better to others. By performing an external act you reform the internal self.

If there is a purpose for writing *Measure for Measure* that purpose must be seen in the Duke's plan. Initially he feels he has made a mistake, become lax in his enforcement of the law. He feels he has failed his kingdom. He is looking to correct this by installing a younger pious Angelo to act as judge. He is hoping the goodness in the man will create an expanding sense of responsibility in the kingdom. Sadly the Duke discovers that the Divinity in Angelo has dissociated him from his humanity. The Duke realizes that the only cure of this problem is in the 'death of good' (3.2.215-225). It is at this point that the Duke understands he must reveal to Angelo Angelo's nature. Only when Angelo realizes that he is not good can he start to become good.

The Duke also realizes that his initial understanding of himself was wrong – his humanity did not thwart his justice. This is where Shakespeare's *Measure for Measure* veers from a Christian parable like that seen by Wilson Knight and begins more to resemble Bruno's poem

The Expulsion of the Triumphant Beast. Christ was human but without sin; the Duke realizes he is better because of his flaws. Vice is a problem in the play as it is in Bruno's poem. Vice is to be thrown from Bruno's heaven just as vice is to be curbed in the Duke's kingdom. Bruno's poem, however, goes on to show that humanity is an important part of divinity (it was Capricorn's animal nature that saved the gods). Bruno's poem also highlights two points; first that nature reveals the divine to humans and second that through prudence (worldly wisdom) humans can participate in the divine mind. Bruno, in all his writings, never saw nature as sinful and this understanding is intrinsic in *Measure for Measure*. Lucio reveals to the Duke the mercy that lies in his humanity (3.2.115-117) and Marianna understands that we are the best for being a little bad (5.1.437-439). Bruno's poem provided an example to Shakespeare of how you could condemn vice while still embracing our humanity. The Divine and nature can be seen as polar opposites of one quality (coincidence of opposites). Bruno described Nature as *"this Nature (as you must know) is none other than God in things"* or *"natura est deus in rebus"* (*The Expulsion of the Triumphant Beast*, p. 235). Bruno describes the cyclical nature that related the two (ibid., p. 236) *"just as Divinity descends in a certain manner...so one ascends to Divinity through Nature"*. To be human was not a sin but only the first step in becoming Divine.

This is why *Measure for Measure* cannot quite be seen as a Christian parable. It draws from the humanity found in the Gospels (forgiveness, empathy, and humbleness) but it does not acknowledge its conceit of a Heaven or Hell.

Unseen Heaven

Heaven and Hell go unseen in the play. Claudio is confused on these issues and the Duke, as friar, makes no attempt to clear things up for him. The Duke, instead, merely gets Claudio to accept death without offering him any comfort of a Heaven (3.1.1-43).

Because of this *Measure for Measure* has been, not unwisely, associated with Epicurean philosophy (*On the Nature of Things*, Book I, line 249; 264).

"Therefore no single thing returns to nothing, but all by disruption return to the elements of matter".

"Therefore no visible object utterly passes away, since nature makes up again one thing from another".

Shakespeare versifies these two ideas neatly as (3.1.19-21)

> *Thou art not thyself;*
> *For thou exists on many a thousand grains*
> *That issue out of dust.*

Epicurus felt that scientific study was useful to free oneself from unnecessary fears and suspicions which disturb the mind, especially the fear of death. For Epicurus death was merely a compound being resolved back into its component atoms – it was nothing to fear (*On the Nature of Things*, Book III, line 830-843).

"Therefore death is nothing to us, it matters not one jot, since the nature of the mind is understood to be mortal; and as in time past we felt no distress (i.e., we felt nothing before our birth)...

so, when we shall no longer be, when the parting shall have come about between body and spirit from which we are compacted into one whole, then sure enough nothing at all will be able to happen to us, who will then no longer be".

L. Martin in his essay *Shakespeare, Lucretius, and the Commonplaces* points out that Lucretius' poem, *On the Nature of Things* (a poem summarizing Epicurean philosophy) was known in Elizabethan times. Spenser and Florio had both translated parts of it, and both Bacon and Burton quoted Lucretius freely in their works.

Giordano Bruno had also incorporated many of Lucretius' ideas into his works (*De l' infinito, universo et mondi* (1584), *De minio* (1591), and *De immenso* (1591)). Bruno as both an atomist and a promoter of the concept of infinite spaces was strongly influenced by Lucretius.

Shakespeare alludes to Epicurean ideas but he does not elaborate on them. The absence of any mention of Heaven or Hell in a scene so clearly concerned with the idea of coming to terms with one's death is perhaps the more revealing; Shakespeare went out of his way not to mention the afterlife.

By avoiding Heaven and Hell Shakespeare was directing his concerns, the Duke's concerns, strictly to the temporal plane. He was concerned with justice on Earth, the good of others in the here and now.

The Duke, even as friar, is not a religious character; he is a pragmatist looking for a measured response, a reasoned response, a prudent response to an act of lawlessness. The Duke is not above deceit if that deceit achieves 'the good of others'. The Duke is not self-serving in his use of deceit. His punishments are also directed towards the good of others.

Measure for Measure is not a Christian parable because it makes too much of an effort to avoid the easy Christian answers. It respects the 'spirit' of the Gospels but it places its hope in humanity and not in Divinity. The play was written with a humanist slant, it acts as an advocate for a human justice, an earthly measured compassionate justice that can be practiced in the here and now. If *Measure for Measure* can be summarized it is that 'Justice can make us divine but a sense of Divinity cannot make us just'.

Seeing Justice

What is revealing in the play is what is unseen in the play. It is the Duke's absence that initially brings about the crisis in Vienna. His void is filled by a character with divine aspirations. The divine in this case only causes repression and fear. It is the unseen Duke's presence in the play that guarantees that justice will prevail. He keeps a careful eye on the situation to makes sure events do not spin out of control.

It is not just the Duke that goes unseen, several physical bodies go unseen. Marianna's participation as an unseen presence is planned out by the Duke. She acts as Isabella's stand-in, freeing Isabella of a moral dilemma while at the same time assuring herself of a just conclusion to her own problem. Barnardine, a man whose presence has gone unseen by the Duke for over nine years, finally sees a just end to his purgatory. Finally, Lucio, an unseen father, is made to take responsibility for his child.

Angelo, a man who publicly projects piousness, hopes his actions go unseen. He takes steps to guarantee this. He plans to execute Claudio in order to keep his actions hidden as well as to prevent any possible vengeance on Claudio's part. He then shames Isabella into silence by using his good reputation and office to bully her.

The return of the unseen Duke is marked by a very public procession accompanied by the blasting of trumpets. His return mimics the Last Judgment *"for there is nothing covered, that shall not be revealed; and hid, that shall not be known"* (Matt. 10:26). The Duke publicly reveals Angelo's crimes, Angelo publicly acknowledges his wrongs – publicly marries Marianna, a woman he publicly shamed. Angelo publicly accepts his punishment and is publicly shown forgiveness. There is nothing hidden in the Duke's justice. Justice is shown to be done.

Religion although not denigrated is not celebrated in Shakespeare's play. The divine in *Measure for Measure* goes unseen except for its actions. The divine is presented as a source of fear and punishment. Angelo's sense of divinity is his source for both his extreme piousness and his repression. He wishes to make Vienna a heaven on earth by casting out all sin. Claudio is the first victim of his pious reform.

In turn, Claudio's fears of death are a result of tales he has heard regarding an afterlife and the possibility of eternal punishment (3.1.117-131). The divine is not presented as acting humanely but rather as acting against human nature.

Conclusion

Wilson Knight is his essay '*Measure for Measure* and the Gospels' points out several of the judgments made by Christ while on earth. I will quickly list a few:

"He that is without sin among you, let him first cast a stone at her".
(John 8:7)

"Neither do I condemn thee: go, and sin no more."
(John 8:11)

"then came Peter to him, and said, Lord how oft shall my brother sin against me, and I forgive him? till seven times? Jesus saith unto him. I say not unto thee, Until seven times: but, until seventy times seven".
(Matt. 18: 21-22)

These are judgments made by Jesus as a man. They are not divine judgments but human judgments based on prudence. The Duke also exercises human judgments, his too are based in prudence. The physical takes priority over the divine while on earth; this is seen in Christ's judgments. They are not eternal judgments he is making but temporal judgments. The Duke concludes that a humanely flawed justice is preferable over divine ideals mercilessly enforced. Angelo's behaviours are pointed out to be god-like and not Christ-like. The play is a triumph of the human and an admonition for the creation of laws that lie within the bounds of commonly held human experience.

Bibliography

1) *Measure for Measure,* W. Shakespeare, Edited by J.W. Lever, The Arden Shakespeare, 3rd Series, Thomson Learning, 2005.

2) *Suffocating Mothers*, Fantasies of Maternal Origin in Shakespeare's Plays, *Hamlet* to *The Tempest*, Janet Adelman, 'Marriage and the Maternal Body: On Marriage as The End of Comedy in *All's Well That Ends Well* and *Measure for Measure*', p. 76-102, Routledge, 2008.

3) *The Wheel of Fire*, G. Wilson Knight, '*Measure for Measure* and the Gospels', p. 79-108, Routledge Classics, 2001.

4) *On Shakespeare*, Northrop Frye, *Measure for Measure*, p. 140-153, Fitzhenry and Whiteside Ltd., 1986.

5) *The Nicomachean Ethics*, Aristotle, translated by H. Rackham, The Loeb Classical Library, Harvard University Press, 1956.

6) *Nicholas of Cusa on Learned Ignorance, A Translation and an Appraisal of De Docta Ignorantia,* Jasper Hopkins, The Arthur J. Banning Press, 1996.

7) *Giordano Bruno and the Logic of Coincidence, Unity and Multiplicity in the Philosophical Thought of Giordano Bruno*, Antonio Calcagno, Peter Lang Publishing Inc., 1998.

8) *The Expulsion of the Triumphant Beast*, translated and edited by Arthur D. Imerti, University of Nebraska Press, Bison Books, 2004.

9) *The Geometry of Love,* Space, Time, Mystery and Meaning in an Ordinary Church, M. Visser, Harper Collins Publishers Ltd., 2000.

10) *On the Nature of Things, De Rerum Natura*, Lucretius, translated by W.H.D. Rouse, revised by Martin F. Smith, Loeb Classical Library, Harvard University Press, 1992.

11) *Shakespeare, Lucretius, and the Commonplaces*, L.C. Martin, Review of English Studies, Vol. 21, 1945, (No. 83, July), p. 174-182.

12) *Christian Astrology* (1647), William Lilly, Astrology Classics, 2004.

13) *The Holy Bible*, King James Version, Zondervan Publishing House, 1962.

Abstract for *All's Well That Ends Well*

Unsatisfied Longings in *All's Well That Ends Well*

The plot source for Shakespeare's *All's Well That Ends Well* is Boccaccio's *Decameron* (Day 3, Story 9) but I will argue that the philosophical source is Ficino's *Commentary on Plato's Symposium on Love* (also known as *De amore*).

By understanding that *All's Well That Ends Well* incorporates an allegory of Pausanias' speech from Ficino's *De amore* it is possible to offer a better explanation of several problematic aspects in Shakespeare's play. For instance, Parolles' discussion with Helena on the topic of virginity takes on much greater relevance; Shakespeare's addition of a murder complication to Boccaccio's plot structure is explicable and it also helps to justify the unsatisfactory nature of the ending.

Unsatisfied Longings in *All's Well That Ends Well*

"Love is, at once, in some degree a thing of Matter and at the same time a Celestial sprung of the Soul's unsatisfied longing for the Good". Plotinus (*Enneads* III.5.9)

Introduction

Marsilio Ficino (1433-1499) wrote a commentary on parts of Plato's *Symposium* entitled *Commentary on Plato's Symposium on Love* which Ficino himself simply referred to as *De amore*. This Latin version was published in 1484. In England Ficino's *De amore* was known as early as 1500 when a copy made its way to Cambridge. In 1578 Guy Le Fevre de la Boderies published a French translation of *De amore* which became widely known in England.

Ficino's work was influential to the writings of several authors notably Giordano Bruno, Philip Sidney, Chapman and Spenser. This essay will argue that Ficino's commentary was also influential to Shakespeare as demonstrated in the contents of *All's Well That Ends Well*. This 'problem play' ceases to be a problem once it is understood as an allegory of Pausanias' speech concerning the roles played by the Heavenly and Vulgar Venuses. Pausanias' speech is contained within Plato's *Symposium* (*Commentary on Plato's Symposium on Love*, Speech II, Chapters 7,8,9).

All's Well That Ends Well in many ways is a feminist play. The main heroine is Helena; she is educated, she takes charge of her life and she makes every effort to achieve her desires. Through her courage and knowledge she creates the conditions that allow her to choose the husband she wishes to wed. She is a woman in control – she controls those events she can control and makes every effort to control events outside her control. Helena's actions create the structure that makes up the plot of the play.

The source of Shakespeare's plot is the ninth novel of the third day in Boccaccio's *Decameron*. Boccaccio's Decameron is a book of 100 stories told by 7 young women and 3 young men who fled from plague-ridden Florence. To pass the time they each tell 1 story a day for 10 days. Shakespeare was probably acquainted with the story through William Painter's translation of *Decameron* (Day 3, story 9) which was presented as his thirty-eighth novel in his *Palace of Pleasure* (1575). This novel is presented in the Appendix to the Arden version of *All's Well That Ends Well*.

The plot structure is part of the intent of the play as are the characters and metaphors Shakespeare employs. *All's Well That Ends Well* is seldom performed or studied and many believe this is because it is so unsatisfying to audiences. For Shakespeare to choose to keep such an unsatisfactory ending reveals that this ending was consistent with his intent for the play. What we as readers or as an audience must try to understand is what purpose this ending might serve.

About the Play

The play was considered one of Shakespeare's problem plays, a play that had an ambiguous morality associated with it. W.W. Lawrence saw the play as a combination of a folktale and a fairytale involving the healing of a king and the fulfillment of a series of impossible tasks. In Shakespeare's *All's Well That Ends Well* the story is realistically told but at times this chafes with its origin in the folk/fairy tale tradition; the realism makes you question its credulity. Because of this credibility gap I believe Shakespeare was more interested in incorporating a particular allegory than he was in keeping the tale believable.

Perhaps the best way to demonstrate this is to discuss the play in the context of Ficino's Commentary and to see how the characters and plot fit within the confines of its parameters.

Shakespeare deviates from Boccaccio/Painter in that he creates two characters: the Countess of Rossillion and Parolles. These characters appear to function as assistants (Cupids) to both the Heavenly and Vulgar Venuses respectively as discussed in Ficino's *Commentary on Plato's Symposium on Love* (Speech II, Chapter 7).

"'On the two origins of love and the double Venus'

According to Plato, Pausanias says that Cupid is the companion of Venus. And he thinks that there must necessarily be as many Cupids as there are Venuses. He mentions two Venuses, whom twin Cupids likewise accompany. One Venus he certainly calls Heavenly Venus born of Uranus, without any mother. The Vulgar Venus was born of Jupiter and Dione."

From this passage dealing with two types of love we can see how an allegory could begin to take shape. Helena, who has no apparent mother in the play, could be seen as an aspect of the Heavenly Venus. Certainly Helena is virtuous and clever. Caroline Spurgeon points out that many of the images and sayings that are applied to or spoken by Helena have to do with stars and heavenly bodies (*Shakespeare's Imagery and What it Tells Us*, p. 273-274). Helena, early in the play, could easily represent an aspect of the Heavenly Venus "*Whom heaven delights to hear*" and whose prayers it "*loves to grant*" (3.4.27-28).

The first Venus (the Heavenly Venus) is the Mind, part of the infinite knowledge of God but which is incapable of procreation, for the Mind is without Matter (Ficino, Speech II, Chapter 7)

"The first Venus, which is in the Mind, is said to have been born of Uranus without a mother, because mother, to the physicists, is matter. But that Mind is a stranger to any association with corporeal matter."

The first act of the play is very much consumed with the ideas of both death and procreation. The play is set up along generational lines. The older generation is dying off. The Countess's husband, Bertram's father, has passed away; Helena's father, the physician, has died and the King is sick unto death. The only cure for death lies not in the mind but in matter; life being a physical affair. Helena clearly states this when discussing her father (1.1.28-29)

He was skilful enough to have liv'd still, if knowledge

Could be set up against mortality.

But, of course, knowledge can only prolong life it cannot cure mortality; only marriage and children can since life is the gift passed on from one generation to the next. This generational theme is hinted at in the play's first line

In delivering my son from me, I bury a second

husband (1.1.1-2).

It is a play on words where delivering alludes to both 'childbirth' and 'giving leave to' and where burying a second husband alludes to the sorrow of a comparable loss. Bertram is leaving home and is beginning to assert his independence. He leaves behind a doting mother and an infatuated lover, Helena.

Helena wishes her thoughts and intents could become a real physical substance. She states (1.1.177-178)

Hel. *That I wish well. 'Tis pity –*

Par. *What's pity?*

Hel . *That wishing well had not a body in't*

Which might be felt.

She wants thoughts (Mind/Heavenly Venus) in essence to become physical. She wants the Heavenly Venus to take on physical form, i.e., to become the Vulgar Venus. This is why Helena's discussion with Parolles about virginity is not out of place. The Heavenly Venus wants to learn physical love; more specifically Helena wants physical love with Bertram (1.1.147).

> *How might one do, sir, to lose it to her own liking?*

Helena's discussion with Parolles deals with procreation – the generation of physical life. Parolles points out that virgins only exist because virginity can be lost (1.1.125-127)

> *Loss of virginity is rational increase,*
>
> *and there was never virgin got till virginity was first*
>
> *lost.*

Parolles in a very crude way is pointing out the connection between heavenly love and physical love. For Ficino this was the connection between the Divine Mind and the Physical creation (Ficino, Speech II, Chapter 7).

> *"The second Venus, which is located in the World Soul, was born of Jupiter and Dione. "Born of Jupiter" – that is, of that faculty of the soul itself which moves the heavenly things, since that faculty created the power which generates these lower things. They also attribute a mother to that second Venus, for this reason, that since she is infused into the Matter of the world, she is thought to have commerce with matter.*

> *Finally, to speak briefly, <u>Venus is twofold</u>. One is certainly that <u>intelligence</u> which we have located in the Angelic Mind. The other is the <u>power of procreation</u> attributed to the World Soul"* (underlined for emphasis).

The virtuous Helen (an aspect of Heavenly Venus) is aided by her cupid (the Countess) in her descent from idea into action (from mind into body) and given help in her physical pursuit of Bertram. The Countess endorses Helen's love for her son and her journey (1.3.246-247; 248-249; 251)

> *Why, Helen, thou shalt have my leave and love,*

Means and attendants...

I'll stay at home

And pray God's blessing into thy attempt...

What I can help thee to, thou shalt not miss.

The Parisian Project

Helen follows Bertram to Paris. Her purpose there is to cure the king and negotiate a reward. This forms the basis of Act 2. Act 2 brings together two hopeless people. The King believes he is past all point of healing. He has given up on his doctors and they have given up on him. He has resigned himself to death. Helen too is engaged in a last ditch effort to bind Bertram to herself and find the love she is seeking. She goes to heal the King – if she fails she will be killed. She is willing to risk death to accomplish her goal.

The Heavenly Venus is connected to the Divine Mind and so the ability to heal the King is within her power. She pleads to the King for an opportunity to do so, stressing this heavenly conection (2.1.152-153; 156-157)

Dear sir, to my endeavours give consent;

Of heaven, not me, make an experiment...

But know I think, and think I know most sure,

My art is not past power, nor you past cure.

Shakespeare does not elaborate on the nature of Helena's ability to heal but Ficino provides more background (Ficino, Speech II, Chapter 7).

"Each Venus has as her companion a love like herself. For the former Venus [Heavenly Venus] is entranced by an innate love for understanding the Beauty of god. The latter [Vulgar Venus] likewise is entranced by her love for procreating the same beauty in bodies. The former Venus first embraces the splendor of divinity in herself; then she

244

transfers it to the second Venus. The latter Venus transfers sparks of that splendor into the Matter of the world."

These are the twin powers Helena possesses; the power to understand the Divine Mind and the power to pass this spark of knowledge into the created physical world. Her healing is based on understanding the roles that divinity plays within creation. There is a dual aspect, both the knowledge of god and the application of this knowledge to accomplish physical healing. The discussion that occurs among the various parties, after the king's healing, distinguishes rather than integrates these two positions (2.3.1-6)

They say miracles are past; and we have our philosophical
persons to make modern and familiar, things
supernatural and causeless. Hence is it that we make
trifles of terrors, ensconcing ourselves into seeming
knowledge when we should submit ourselves to an
unknown fear.

Lafew argues here for miracles and terror before God, whereas the King sees his healing as the result of technical expertise (2.3.29-31)

...he's of a most facinerious [wicked]
spirit that will not acknowledge it to be the –
Very hand of heaven.

The healing of the King was the first step in Helena's plan. She had negotiated with the King that if she healed him she would be rewarded with her pick of any available husband she chose (2.1.192-193)

Then shalt thou give me with thy kingly hand
What husband in thy power I will command.

The King assures her (2.3.56)

Thou has power to chose, and they none to forsake.

245

This action has turned tradition on its head, the woman is choosing the man. It is also upsetting the class hierarchy; a daughter of a physician is attempting to exercise power over a Count – Bertram in this case. This contravention of the rules of society is almost unimaginable (1.3.89-90)

> *That man should be at woman's command, and yet*
> *no hurt done!*

The King goes to great effort to lessen Bertram's resistance to the proposed marriage by pointing out that class distinction is an allusion and that money can transform inequity (2.3.117-120)

> *'Tis only title thou disdain'st in her, the which*
> *I can build up. Strange is it that our bloods,*
> *Of colour, weight, and heat, pour'd all together,*
> *Would quite confound distinction.*

The King wishes Bertram to look beyond appearances to the actions that make people worthy (2.3.128-131)

> *Good alone*
> *Is good, without a name...*
> *The property by what it is should go,*
> *Not by the title.*

Bertram's inability to see beyond appearances is part of his immaturity and it provides the basis for much of what occurs in the second half of the play.

The true idea of beauty was a Platonic concept and it involved seeing the divine, the god within another's soul. It was this inner longing – the good in one soul seeking the good in another's soul – that stirred the feelings of love and drove us to procreation (Ficino, Speech II, Chapter 7).

> *"These twin powers are two Venuses in us, accompanied by twin loves. When the beauty of a human body first meet our eyes, our*

intellect, which is the first Venus in us, worships and esteems it as an image of the divine beauty, and through this is often aroused to that. But the power of procreation, the second Venus, desires to procreate a form like this. On both sides, therefore, there is a love: there a desire to contemplate beauty, here a desire to propagate it. Each love is virtuous and praiseworthy, for each follows a divine image."

Helena's love is both intellectual and physical; both types of love are virtuous. This is why Parolles' discussion with Helena about virginity is not out of place in the story. It is also why the play is divided into two halves. The first half deals with the intellectual Heavenly Venus and her intellectual plan to marry Bertram. The second half of the play deals with the reality that results and the failure of her 'happy ever after' plan. The second half has more to do with the physical world, the Vulgar Venus, and the act of procreation. Both parts, the intellectual and the physical, are necessary in dealing with the different aspects of love. Helena is both the Heavenly and Vulgar Venus as both powers reside in all of us. Helena claims this dual nature of love, both the sensuous and the chaste (1.3.206-208)

> *Did ever, in so true a flame of liking,*
>
> *Wish chastely and love dearly, that your Dian*
>
> *Was both herself and love.*

Helena sets the example for love. She shows us how self-sacrificing love needs to be (2.3.102-104)

> *I dare not say I take you, but I give*
>
> *Me and my service, ever whilst I live,*
>
> *Into your guiding power. This is the man.*

As long as the beloved is equally self-sacrificing no harm comes to either party but in the case of *All's Well That Ends Well* Bertram, the object of Helena's affections, does not reciprocate. She is left abandoned (2.3.292)

I'll to the wars, she to her single sorrow.

Helena is always very deferential, perhaps overly so, with Bertram (2.4.45; 49; 52)

What's his will else?

What more commands he?

In everything I wait upon his will.

This shows the degree to which she has abandoned herself and it foreshadows the fictional death she concocts for herself later in the play. Ficino describes this type of behaviour as the consequence of love and the latter 'death' the consequence of unrequited love (Ficino, Speech II, Chapter 8).

"Certainly, since love is a voluntary death...whoever loves dies. For his attention, oblivious of himself, is always turned to the beloved...Therefore the soul of a lover does not exist in itself because it does not function in itself. If it does not exist in itself, it also does not live in itself. He who does not live is dead. Therefore anyone who loves is dead in himself. But at least he lives in another? Certainly.

There are two kinds of love: one love is simple, the other reciprocal. Simple love is where the beloved does not love the lover. There the lover is completely dead. For he neither lives in himself...nor does he live in the beloved, since he is rejected by him.

...Therefore the unloved lover is completely dead. Nor will he ever revive unless indignation should revive him."

In the case of Helena and Bertram; Bertram does not love Helena and so flees France. This flight response can be seen as a fear reaction. As Ficino has stated love is a form of death, a source of terror. This type of stimulus can induce two types of reaction (Ficino, Speech II, Chapter 6).

"Hence it also always happens that lovers <u>fear</u> and <u>worship</u> in some way the sight of the beloved " (underlined for emphasis).

Shakespeare has given us these two responses; Helena worships Bertram (1.1.95-96)

> *But now he's gone, and my idolatrous fancy*
>
> *Must sanctify his relics*

and Bertram fears Helena. Bertram's response is one of fear and flight, not unlike 'cold feet' before a wedding.

Helena and Bertram have much in common. They were raised and educated in the same household and grew up together (2.3.113-114)

> *I know her well:*
>
> *She had her breeding at my father's charge.*

Both were raised under the Countess's *"overlooking"* (1.1.36). This commonality of upbringing can lead to bonds of love; this Ficino comments on (ibid., Speech II, Chapt. 8).

> *"The natural and moral philosophers say that likeness of complexion* [astral influences at birth], *nourishment, education, habit or opinion is the cause of like affection. Finally where several of these causes occur together, there the interchange of love is found to be very strong."*

The fact that Helena has grown up to love Bertram cannot be denied and it can be argued that a basis for love between the two has been established. Unfortunately this fertile ground is left fallow for Bertram follows Parolles off to war and away from Helena.

Trapping Traitors

The second half of the play contains two traps. One set by Bertram and his men for Parolles and the other set by Helena and her women for Bertram. Both traps catch traitors.

Bertram and Parolles are connected characters, Parolles' affectations and deceitful nature are influential on Bertram's actions and reflect poorly on Bertram's judgment. Lafew sees Parolles for what he is and warns Bertram of his nature (2.5.42-45)

> *there*
> *can be no kernel in this light nut; the soul of this man*
> *is his clothes. Trust him not in matter of heavy*
> *consequence.*

Much of the latter half of the play is spent showing what a traitor Parolles is both to Bertram and other members of the company. This is done for several reasons. First, it highlights Bertram's poor judgment and more importantly forces him to acknowledge this aspect in himself. Second, it shows how Parolles betrays others which mirrors Bertram's own betrayals of the King, Helena, and Diana. Finally, within Parolles we see a microcosm of the themes that unfold in the rest of the play.

This last point requires some elaboration. Parolles' public undoing is a result of his own bravado. He brags he can recover the company's drum (comparable to a company's colours) that has been taken by the enemy (3.6.16-19)

> Ber. *I would I knew in what particular action to try him.*
> 2nd. *None better than to let him fetch off his*
> > *drum, which you hear him so confidently undertake*
> > *to do.*

Parolles is a very self aware though divided individual. He knows he is a coward and a liar but he readily accepts these aspects of himself (4.1.28-31; 34-36)

> *I find my tongue is too*
> *foolhardy, but my heart hath the fear of Mars before*
> *it and of his creatures, not daring the reports of my*
> *tongue...*
> *What the devil should move me to undertake the*
> *recovery of this drum, being not ignorant of the*

impossibility, and knowing I had no such purpose?

The Lords overhearing Parolles' self chastisement are amazed at his candor (4.1.44-45)

> *Is it possible he should know what he is, and be*
> *that he is?*

The consternation of the Lords is shared by Parolles himself. His mind proposes projects his body cannot deliver on. This separation between mind and body within Parolles parallels Helena's drama played out between the Heavenly Venus (Mind) and the Vulgar Venus (Body).

Helena solves her problem by employing the 'bed trick' to unite her intellectual love for Bertram with her sensual desire for Bertram.

Parolles is a 'self aware' scoundrel. He tailors his words and appearances to deceive. He literally is all appearance and false words with nothing underneath – the ultimate 'shallow man'. This is not, however, a source of embarrassment for him but he sees it as ultimately his source of strength for he cannot be shamed (4.3.322-323)

> *Simply the thing I am*
> *Shall make me live.*

Helena during the course of the story finds a way to unite her intellectual and physical selves. Parolles, though aware of these two aspects of himself chooses to leave them distinct, he chooses to remain a liar accepting that his actions will never match his words. Bertram, who began the story as a boy seeking physical adventure and as a fan of Parolles is now aware of his poor judgment. The Lords have shown him that Parolles is a scoundrel and not to be trusted. As the play proceeds towards its ending Bertram is shown with irrefutable evidence that he too has acted like a scoundrel. The trap set for Bertram is very similar to the trap he himself set for Parolles in that both are publicly caught in their lies. Parolles responds to his crime with indifference. Bertram has a chance to change. He now knows he has been too trusting and he also knows himself to be untrustworthy. Bertram has a chance to take his mother's words to heart (1.1.57-66) and become a man whose actions are as good as his word.

The Murder Trial

Shakespeare altered the ending of Boccaccio's/Painter's story by making it more serious and by bringing up the possibility that Helena was murdered. Bertram is put in fear for his life. In this way the play possesses a symmetry – the King at the beginning of the play was facing his own mortality and now Bertram at the end of the play is confronted with this same consequence. Helena in both instances provides relief from the fear of death.

Shakespeare may have introduced this aspect of murder into the storyline because he was using the plot to house an allegory on Ficino's insights. Earlier I quoted Ficino on non-reciprocal love, where he stated that *"the unloved lover is completely dead "*. Quoting further from this section of Ficino's commentary (Ficino, Speech II, Chapter 8):

"A murderer ought to be punished by death. Who would deny that a man who is loved is a murderer, since he separates the soul from the lover?

...Therefore, out of justice itself, whoever is loved ought to love in return. But he who does not love his lover must be held answerable for murder. "

In the King's eyes it is Bertram who is suspected of killing Helena (5.3.117-118)

> *...thou didst hate her deadly,*
> *And she is dead.*

As the play proceeds to its 'happy-ish' conclusion so too does Ficino offer a solution to the murderer's dilemma (Ficino, Speech II, Chapter 8).

"Hence it happens that like a...murderer...he can be killed by anyone with impunity, unless he himself should of his own accord, carry out that law, namely, that he love his lover.

...There is also that fact that the lover engraves the figure of the beloved on his own soul. And so the soul of the lover becomes a mirror in which the image of the beloved is reflected. For that reason, when the beloved recognizes himself in the lover, he is forced to love him."

When we examine Shakespeare's conclusion it proceeds along identical lines. First, Bertram, although under some duress, pledges his love for Helena by acknowledging her as both his wife and lover (5.3.301-303)

> Hel. *'Tis but the shadow of a wife you see;*
>
> *The name and not the thing.*
>
> Ber. *Both, both. O pardon!*

By claiming his love for Helena Bertram wishes to be pardoned of his previous sins. Shakespeare has also physically fulfilled Ficino's requirement for love, Helena is pregnant with Bertram's child; he literally can see his image reflected in Helena. This should assure us that Bertram's love is at this point genuine, that it has found a starting point to grow from.

The 'Bed Trick'

Helena and Diana are very similar characters, so much so, that they can stand in for one another during the 'bed trick'. Conceptually they are treated as the same 'type'. Both reflect the healing aspect of love; Helena healed the King's illness and Diana could heal Bertram's suffering desires (4.2.34-36)

> *Stand no more off,*
>
> *But give thyself unto my sick desires,*
>
> *Who then recovers.*

Bertram offers Diana the same vows of obedience that Helena offered to Bertram earlier in the play (4.2.52-53)

Here, take my ring;

My house, mine honour, yea, my life be thine,

And I'll be bid by thee.

Helena and Diana represent the verse and obverse aspects of love, being either 'the object of desire' or the 'desiring object'.

The 'bed trick' Helena designs allows her to exercise power over Bertram (in a loving way, for his own benefit) in a last ditch effort to claim him as her husband and to maintain his potentially lost honour.

The 'bed trick' is a version of catching a man with his hand in the cookie jar; it offers absolute proof of infidelity without its worst possible consequences. The case of seduction brought before the King by Diana forces Bertram to publicly acknowledge his worst possible nature but at the same time the 'bed trick' allows for mercy to be granted since no actual infidelity takes place. Intellectually Bertram was unfaithful and yet physically (because of Helena's intercession) he remained faithful. Helena, without Bertram's knowledge, was the true recipient of his family's ring and it was she who guarded his honour by using the 'bed trick'. Because of this Helena had the potential to restore honour to Bertram even though he had publicly exposed his dishonourable nature. She prevented his intent from becoming an actual crime.

Throughout the play the Mind/Body (Soul/Body) dichotomy has been exploited. It was played out within Parolles as well as in Helena's plotline. It also formed the basis for the 'bed trick' (intellectually guilty but physically innocent). Ficino concludes Pausanias' speech by discussing the harmony that can be achieved between a mismatched pair like the relationship between a wise old man and a beautiful boy. In

Shakespeare's play the mismatched pair are represented by a clever Helena and a handsome Bertram (Ficino, Speech II, Chapter 9).

"Finally among lovers beauty is exchanged for beauty. A man enjoys the beauty of a beloved youth with his eyes. The youth enjoys the beauty of the man with his Intellect. And he who is beautiful in body only, by this association becomes beautiful also in soul [mind]. He who is only beautiful in soul fills the eyes of the body with the beauty of the body. Truly this is a wonderful exchange. Virtuous, useful, and pleasant to both. The virtue certainly is equal to both. For it is equally virtuous to learn and to teach. The pleasure is greater in the older man, who is pleased in both sight and intellect. But in the younger man the usefulness is greater. For as superior as the soul [mind] is to the body, so is the acquisition of beauty of the soul superior to that of the body. This finishes the speech of Pausanias."

Shakespeare's play ends with a chastised Bertram who is actually relieved to find Helena alive and pleased that she is so clever. His family honour is newly restored, he cannot be accused of seduction, and he has a chance to now fall in love with Helena and become a wiser person through knowing her.

This is not a fairy-tale ending but rather a realistic starting point for a relationship to begin. Ficino can be quoted once more with regards to this last situation (Ficino, Speech II, Chapter 6).

"Moreover, some of the stupidest men are rendered more intelligent by loving."

The Two Venuses Within Us

Ficino argued that everyone had two Venuses within them; the Heavenly Venus serving the intellect and the Vulgar Venus serving our senses. Each of these Venuses is assisted by its own Cupid or passion that provides the impetus to achieve its desired goal.

255

G. K. Hunter in his introduction to the Arden Edition of *All's Well That Ends Well* (p. xxxiii) argues that Bertram is pulled between two forces: Helen representing an Angel and Parolles representing the Devil, like in a Morality play. This analysis is too simplistic and the characters more complex than this interpretation allows. Ficino's point was that within each of us were present these two forces, these two Venuses. This meant that Helena could employ qualities not unlike those possessed by Parolles – deceit and false appearances – to accomplish her 'bed trick'. Ficino did not see Vulgar Venus as evil but rather as an aspect of the Divine, as an aspect of the Creative force. The Vulgar Venus was the force of procreation active in the physical world. Helena is a virtuous character because she is a balanced character employing both the Heavenly and Vulgar Venuses in such a way that she is respectful of both the intellectual and physical worlds.

Parolles is an unbalanced character who prefers to ignore the divine and wallow in deceit and sensual pleasure. His indifference to the divine makes him an untrustworthy fellow but not necessarily bad company. Lafew warns Bertram not to trust Parolles in any situation of consequence but it is Lafew who takes Parolles in at the end of the play (5.2.50)

though you are a fool and a knave you shall eat.

Parolles finds employment with Lafew; Lafew is a man who knows Parolles is a knave and so can't be fooled by him. Lafew can enjoy Parolles' fictions for the stories that they are (5.3.316-317)

Wait on me home, I'll make sport

with thee.

Parolles is a poor role model because he ignores his inner Heavenly Venus and thusly guides Bertram into a series of bad decisions (3.2.87-89)

A very tainted fellow, and full of wickedness;

My son corrupts a well-derived nature
With his inducement.

Parolles, a specialist in retreats (1.1.196), has instructed Bertram in the bravery of cowardice and on how to run away from love and towards war (2.3.294-295)

A young man married is a man that's marr'd
Therefore away, and leave her bravely; go.

Bertram sinks to the same moral depths as Parolles, and like Parolles is publicly exposed as a dishonourable person. Parolles accepts his exposure with indifference (after all the truth is the truth) but Bertram appears willing to change, he can see that he exercised poor judgment and he can appreciate Helena's intellect (5.3.310)

I'll love her dearly, ever, ever dearly.

When Ficino translated Plato he understood that Love was an unsatisfied longing for the good. What Bertram has finally recognized in Helena is the presence of good, something he lacks in himself, a good that he now desires. This hunger for the good offers us some hope for their futures.

The play ends on this beginning, this hint of change, but it also begins a new cycle (of women having power over men) for the King promises Diana a dowry and the opportunity to pick a husband (5.3.322)

Choose thou thy husband and I'll pay thy dower.

In this way the play affirms the power of the twin Venuses, the power of women, within all of us.

Conclusion

In this essay I have proposed that Shakespeare used Ficino's *De amore* as a source to enrich his understanding of love and to inform and deepen his borrowed plot. The plot source is Boccaccio but I believe the philosophical source is Ficino.

Certain problematic aspects in the play disappear when *De amore* or more specifically a single speech within *De amore* is consulted and read in conjunction with the play. The unity that Ficino argues to exist between the Heavenly and Vulgar Venuses is perhaps the most important aspect utilized in the play. It means that Divine creation is mirrored in earthly procreation and that both aspects are considered to be holy.

Ficino's commentary is probably where Shakespeare sourced a completely unique set of ideas for his play. Shakespeare complicates Boccaccio's ending with an accusation of murder. This is understood within the context of Ficino's work for unrequited love was considered an act of murder – murder by stealing another's soul. This is why Helena perceived herself to have been reduced to a shadow. Bertram's refusal to return her love had resulted in the loss of her soul and reduced her physical self to a mere spectre of her former self. No source other than Ficino could introduce such a unique idea into Shakespeare's script.

Also indicative of Shakespeare's dependence on Ficino's work is the key role played by the women. The women drive the main storyline and continue to play a dominant part in its future iterations. This indicates that Ficino's concept of the twin Venuses was a major metaphor used in constructing the drama. The women control the action in the play because the twin Venuses control the actions within our world. The Divine Venus acting as the World Soul and the Vulgar Venus reigning over the act of physical creation.

Shakespeare's play does not end with the 'happy ever after' of a fairytale for it ends at just the very beginning of the recognition of love. The tentativeness of this ending may not be satisfactory for an audience but it is in keeping with Ficino's understanding of love as a yearning and constant unsatisfied longing for the good, the god within others and within ourselves.

Bibliography

1) *All's Well That Ends Well*, W. Shakespeare, edited by G. K. Hunter, The Arden Shakespeare, 3rd edition, Methuen and Co. Ltd., 1959.

2) *Commentary on Plato's Symposium on Love*, Marsilio Ficino, translated by Sears Jayne, Spring Publications Inc., 1985.

3) *Plotinus The Enneads*, translated by Stephen MacKenna, Larson Publications, 1992.

4) *Shakespeare's Imagery and What it Tells Us*, Caroline Spurgeon, Cambridge University Press, 19th Printing, 2005.

Abstract for *Julius Caesar*

Body, Blood and Spirit in *Julius Caesar*

Julius Caesar is a work that takes us on a 'fantastic voyage' through the workings of our own bodies. It examines our makeup, our ability to act and the inner workings that govern our actions. It does so primarily by focusing on Brutus, his nature, his decisions and the consequences that result from this one man's expression of his own free will.

Body, Blood and Spirit in *Julius Caesar*

"spirit is a most subtle vapour, which is expressed from the blood, and the instrument of the soul, to perform all his actions; a common tie or medium between the body and the soul, as some will have it..."

Robert Burton – *The Anatomy of Melancholy* (1621)

Introduction

Julius Caesar is a work of body, blood and spirit. Brutus opposes Caesar's spirit, sees it as tyrannical, but he knows no way of fighting this spirit without attacking Caesar's body. Brutus therefore decides that it is only by spilling Caesar's blood that he can free Rome of this malevolent spirit (2.1.166-170)

> *We all stand up against the spirit of Caesar,*
>
> *And in the spirit of men there is no blood.*
>
> *O that we then could come by Caesar's spirit*
>
> *And not dismember Caesar! But, alas,*
>
> *Caesar must bleed for it.*

The play employs the body, the blood, and the spirit as central metaphors and utilizes them to create its structure. The play is divided into two parts: before and after the assassination. The first part is governed by the metaphor of the body while the latter half utilizes the metaphor of the spirit (the will). The metaphor of blood holds the two halves together. The play's structure mimics our very makeup.

The Body

The first half of the play is rich in sensual imagery and as G. Wilson Knight points out it has a powerful apprehension of the human body as well as those things which nourish and refresh it, such as wine, food and sleep (*The Imperial Theme*, Chapter II, *The Torch of Life: An*

263

Essay on 'Julius Caesar' p. 40). Knight also sees this 'Roman body' as sick and suffering from afflictions.

When we examine the characters in this first half of the play we find most are touched with illness. Calphurnia is barren (1.2.6-9). Caesar is seen as both weak and ill for "*He hath the falling sickness*" (1.2.253) and experiences deafness in one ear (1.2.212). Cassius sees Caesar as infirm and recalls a time he had to save Caesar because he was a weak swimmer (1.2.102-115) and another when Caesar was overcome by fever (1.2.119-128). Portia is worried about Brutus' health and repeatedly asks "*Is Brutus sick?*" (2.1.260; 262; 267). She also shows herself to be unwell by voluntarily inflicting a wound upon herself (2.1.299-300). Caius Ligarius is another character introduced as "*Here is a sick man that would speak with you*" (2.1.309).

All this goes to show how weak or diseased the Roman State currently is. Since Caesar is unwell the State is unwell. Brutus and Cassius see Caesar as the source of the State's troubles and see the cure in his assassination. By bleeding Rome, killing Caesar, they hope to cure the State.

The Blood

Blood carried the human spirit. The body communicated with the soul through the blood. The blood carried three types of spirits. The veins carried the *natural spirit* responsible for our vegetative actions, our involuntary actions. The heart was considered the seat of the Passions, home to our desires, but it also acted on the natural spirit. The heart added heat and air from the lungs to transform this natural spirit into the *vital spirit*, the driving force for life, which was then carried in the arteries. This vital spirit, when delivered to the brain, was transformed this time into the *animal spirit* responsible for rational action. The brain was home to the Will.

The natural and vital spirits linked the body to the irrational part of the soul while the animal spirit, this highest part of the human spirit, linked the body to the rational part of the soul (*The Elizabethan World Picture*, p. 69; or *The Three Books of Occult Philosophy*, p. 730).

The spirit was an energy that both animated the material body and also stood between the material body and the immaterial soul as an insulator separating the two. The spirit was subject to input from both body and soul and was the intermediary instrument required for action. The passions, being the product of the heart, were concerned with desires and often opposed the choices made by the will, which was in touch with the highest part of the soul. This meant that the spirit was often torn between the needs of the body and the needs of the soul.

Brutus wished to separate Caesar's body from his spirit by spilling his blood. This desire is reflected in the storm sequence of the play. Not only is the storm a physical manifestation of Brutus' internal turmoil but during this storm we see that the spirit, an energy normally housed in the flesh, can also exist outside the body. Life forms and spirit forms walk together in this metaphysical storm;

"graves have yawned and yielded up their dead" (2.2.18)

"Men, all in fire, walk up and down the streets" (1.3.25)

"Fierce fiery warriors fight upon the clouds" (2.2.19)

"ghosts did shriek and squeal about the streets" (2.2.24).

The *"civil strife in heaven"* (1.3.11) during the storm is the same civil strife that Brutus is experiencing within his own body (2.1.62-69)

I have not slept.

Between the acting of a dreadful thing

And the first motion, all the interim is

Like a phantasma or a hideous dream:

The genius and the mortal instruments

Are then in council, and the state of man,

> *Like to a little kingdom, suffers then*
> *The nature of an insurrection.*

Brutus is torn between performing a physical act he has agreed is necessary while at the same time wishing to abstain from this act knowing that it is treasonous. Brutus' Will, the highest product of his animal spirit, his genius, is in contention with his body's Desire to act.

The Humours

The blood also carried the bodily humours. Thomas McAlindon (*The Numbering of Men and Days: Symbolic Design in 'The Tragedy of Julius Caesar'*, p. 380) points out that the four main characters in the play are broadly identifiable with the four blood humours. Brutus is melancholic, Cassius is choleric, Caesar is phlegmatic, and Antony is sanguine.

The four humours were associated with the four elements and their properties:

Melancholy was an *Earthly* humour considered cold and dry.

Choler was a *Firery* humour considered hot and dry.

Phlegm was a *Watery* humour considered cold and moist.

Sanguineness was *Airy* and considered hot and moist.

The four humours produced the four temperaments in humans. The melancholic personality resulted from excess black bile and produced a sad, discontented individual often lost in contemplation. This personality was considered to be ruled by Saturn. In the play Brutus is the one lost in contemplation *"with himself at war"* (1.2.46) to the point that he neither eats, sleeps or keeps company with his wife (2.1.249-251). He is the keeper of a *"sad heart"* (2.1.289) beneath *"sad brows"* (2.1.307) housed in a *"sober form"* (4.3.40). Brutus is associated throughout the play with introspection (1.2.37-47) and melancholy (1.2.28-29)

266

> *I am not gamesome. I do lack some part*
> *Of that quick spirit that is in Antony.*

The choleric personality resulted from excess yellow bile and produced a hot tempered, combative, rash, thoughtless individual who was often bold, brave, and full of initiative. He was considered to be ruled by Mars. Cassius easily matches this personality profile. It is Cassius who is the engine behind Caesar's assassination (1.3.121-124), it is Cassius who wishes to strike fire into Brutus (1.2.175-176). Cassius is *"lean and hungry"*, he is an ambitious and *"dangerous"* man (1.2.193-194; 207-208).

> *Yond Cassius has a lean and hungry look:*
> *He thinks too much: such men are dangerous.*
> *Such men as he be never at heart's ease*
> *Whiles they behold a greater than themselves.*

Cassius' rash nature also leads to his undoing (5.3.32-35) when he misinterprets the events around the greeting of a friend. Cassius, like Mars, is a soldier (4.3.30-31) and associated both with the colour red and with blood (5.3.62)

> *So in his red blood Cassius' day is set.*

The phlegmatic personality was considered stolid (not easily stirred or moved) and belonging to a pale sickly type. It was a personality type ruled by the Moon. McAlindon (ibid., footnote 19, p. 381) referenced the phlegmatics' associations with palsies and feebleness and remarked on its association with water. Caesar is easily associated with this type through his epilepsy (1.2.253) and the water imagery that surrounds him. Calphurnia dreams of him as a fountain (2.2.76-77) and Cassius tells of saving him from drowning (1.2.100-115). Caesar himself proclaims his stolidness describing himself as *"constant as the northern star"* (3.1.60-65). This immovable nature would have been recognized by the Elizabethan audience. It would have confirmed in their minds that Caesar was fixed in his desire to become Emperor. Cassius recognizes this as well and at various times refers to Caesar as being a tyrant (1.3.103) or a god (1.2.115-116). He has no doubt about Caesar achieving his goals. He believes wholeheartedly that if Caesar is not assassinated he will become king – Caesar's nature makes this assumption true.

Finally Antony completes this group. His sanguine nature is mapped out in his optimistic, kind, cheerful demeanor (2.1.187-188)

for he is given

To sports, to wildness and much company.

He is seen as companionable, *"a masquer and a reveller"* (5.1.61). It is said that Jupiter rules over the sanguine. The sanguine were believed to be both passionate and just. Antony's eulogy brings both of these characteristics to life. Antony engages with the crowd as one of their companions as *"a plain blunt man / That love my friend"* (3.2.211-212) and then he employs his sense of justice to *"stir men's blood"* (3.2.216-217). Antony's hot-moist-airy nature unfolds in a rich, emotional, and passionate speech which contrasts with Brutus' cold-dry-earthly nature and rational oratorial style.

Brutus tries to reason with the people's intellect, through their brains, while Antony engages with their emotions, through their hearts. Antony is not perceived as a threat by Brutus because of Antony's companionable nature (3.1.220)

Friends am I with you all, and love you all.

Caesar also never feared Antony as he viewed him as a contented happy man who loved life and engaged with it through his love of theatre and music (1.2.202-203).

Shakespeare has presented us with the picture of Rome as an ill body; he has introduced the people of Rome as its blood – they are the humours which are out of balance.   Moving this blood, lying at the still centre, is the heart of Rome, Caesar (3.1.207-208)

> *O world, thou wast the forest to this hart,*
>
> *And this indeed, O world, the heart of thee.*

He is the fixed point around which the play moves. Motion occurs around Caesar like the motion around the centre of a wheel. Caesar is the 'unmoved mover' of the play and in this sense he is like the god he yearned to become.

Caesar, the heart, is the centre of the play's passions. Cassius' hate of Caesar fuels his plans of assassination; it motivates him to organize the senators and helps him to inflame even Brutus' subdued passions to his cause. Antony's love of Caesar fuels the latter half of the play and it is his passion for justice that drives his actions and this gives form to Caesar's revenge.

Shakespeare has personified Rome as sick with disease and employed a violent phlebotomy as its cure. Political assassination has removed an ordered but tyrannical government and replaced it with civil war and chaos. When the conspirators severe Caesar's body from his spirit by spilling his blood they unwittingly release Caesar's spirit into the world. It is Caesar's revenging spirit that guides Antony's loving hand to wreak havoc in the latter half of the play (3.1.270-273)

> *And Caesar's spirit, ranging for revenge,*
>
> *With Ate* [1] *by his side come hot from hell,*
>
> *Shall in these confines, with a monarch's voice,*
>
> *Cry havoc and let slip the dogs of war.*

The Spirit and The Will

The spirit is not only a life force but is also connected to our passions (vital spirit) and in its highest form (animal spirit) is linked to our will. The spirit is the power source for the body and the will.

Because of this connection Cassius has trouble seeing Caesar's spirit as anything grander than the weak body it is housed in (1.2.90-160). Cassius cannot imagine one person's spirit as being more inspirational than another's. In this way he is an egalitarian; he thinks the name Brutus will inspire men as easily as Caesar's did (1.2.132)

> *'Brutus' will start a spirit as soon as 'Caesar'.*

Portia also shares this belief that a weak body contains a weak spirit. She fears that her own spirit may be weak because her body is that of a woman's. She challenges this understanding by cutting herself and so proves to herself that she can be strong (2.1.295-300).

The storm scene confirms Portia's new insight by showing that the energy of one's spirit can exist independently from one's body and is therefore not limited by it. The storm scene also suggests that the conspirators' plans for killing Caesar's spirit by killing his body are naïve.

The conspirators have a faulty understanding of the power associated with a 'spirit' but they correctly link it to the will, in this case Caesar's will to achieve his purposes (2.1.167)

> *We all stand up against the spirit of Caesar.*

The senator's oppose Caesar's intended actions, the exercise of his free will, as those actions will in turn limit the free will of others. The mistake the group makes is in thinking that killing Caesar will end the threat of tyranny. Tyranny is not altered by a single death but only by education, a change in those conditions that inform people's wills.

Generally speaking in the play the word 'spirit' refers to one's will, the power to choose one's own actions. Spirit and free will are synonymous. In specific incidents however spirits become manifest, as in the storm scene and in the scene where Brutus encounters the 'physical spirit' of Caesar (4.3.272.1). Here the ghost identifies itself as "*Thy evil spirit, Brutus*" (4.3.279).

The correct use of free will was to do God's Will, i.e., to make just decisions but because humans had free will they could choose to act against this urging of the soul. Humans could act immorally.

When the ghost of Caesar (a physical manifestation of a metaphysical idea) identifies itself as 'Brutus' evil spirit' he is saying he is a manifestation of 'Brutus' evil choices', of the fact that Brutus has failed to act justly (4.3.19)

> *Did not great Julius bleed for justice' sake?*

It is Brutus' nagging doubt that haunts Brutus.

Justice

Aristotle wrote that (*Nicomachean Ethics,* V.i.15)

"Justice then in this sense is perfect virtue, though with a qualification, namely that it is displayed towards others. This is why Justice is often thought to be the chief of the virtues...

'In Justice is all Virtue found in sum'.

Virtue was the product of the intellectual virtues (Wisdom, Knowledge and Prudence) and it manifests itself in the moral virtues (Justice, Courage and Temperance). Justice and Virtue were linked and they were in turn related to honour. The relationship is best described in a quotation from *The French Academie* (1586), p. 247.

"For this cause the ancient Romans built two Temples joined together, the one being dedicated to Virtue, and the other to Honour: but yet in such sort, that no man could enter into that of Honour, except first he passed through the other of Virtue...Therefore that goddess and excellency which proceedeth of wisdom and good instruction is the first step to come to honour, because from that as from a lively fountain floweth every virtuous and praise-worthy action practiced by a prudent man" (spelling and alphabet have been modernized from original for ease of reading).

Justice is Virtue and Virtue is an exercise of Prudence. It can be argued that Brutus is not prudent. Those that are prudent remember their pasts, plan their present and foresee their future. Brutus recalls his past (2.1.53-54), he helps plan the present assassination (2.1.168-171), but he makes no preparations for the future. This Seneca remarks on (*Moral Essays*, Vol. III, On Benefits, II.xx.2)

"How forgetful, in truth, he was, either of the law of nature or of the history of his own city, in supposing that, after one man had been murdered, no other would be found who would have the same aims."

Seneca was astonished that Brutus didn't foresee the civil strife he would unleash or the ambitions he would ignite in others.

Wilson Knight points out (*The Imperial Theme*, Chapter III, *The Eroticism of Julius Caesar*, p. 73) that Brutus thinks in terms of cold abstract reason and that he fails to make any emotional connection with the reality around him and it is because of this that he is always misjudging both men and women and how they will behave. He lacks prudence (practical wisdom). Brutus is an intellectual living in a world controlled by passions and because of this he constantly misreads situations.

Seneca sees Brutus' lack of prudence as the weakness that compromises his virtue, his justice, and his ability to act honourably.

Brutus' Honour

Thy honourable mettle may be wrought
From that it is disposed.
For who so firm that cannot be seduced?
(1.2.308-309; 311)

Brutus claims to be an honourable man. Cassius plans to use Brutus' sense of honour to manipulate him. Antony plans to use

Brutus' sense of honour to discredit him. It is therefore worth looking at this concept of honour to see how it applies to Brutus.

Aristotle provides us with an understanding of honour that was certainly common knowledge amongst Elizabethans (*Nicomachean Ethics*, IV.iii.10-11)

"Now the greatest external good we should assume to be the thing which we offer as a tribute to the gods, and which is most coveted by men of high station, and is the prize awarded for the noblest deeds; and such a thing is honour, for honour is clearly the greatest of external goods. Therefore the great-souled man is he who has the right disposition in relation to honours and disgraces...it is honour above all else which great men claim and deserve".

Brutus' primary motivation is honour, *"I love / The name of honour more than I fear death"* (1.2.88-89). He chooses honour over love, friendship, and all else in his life. He is described by Ligarius as the *"Soul of Rome"* (2.1.320). There is no doubt that Brutus sees himself as Aristotle's *"great-souled man"* who is in the correct relationship with respect to honour, but is he?

(ibid., IV.iii.15)

"For instance, one cannot imagine the great-souled man...acting dishonestly"

(ibid., IV.iii.28)

"He must be open in both love and in hate, since concealment shows timidity; and care more for the truth than for what people will think; and speak and act openly".

Brutus, however, does not act openly. Caesar is deceived by Brutus, fooled by his love (2.3.126-127) but he is not deceived by Cassius who does little to hide his distaste for the man (1.2.312). Portia too has trouble reading Brutus' intensions; she expects a husband's love and is distressed at his lack of kindliness (2.1.266-274). Brutus, like all the other conspirators, hides his intensions beneath a mask of *"smiles and affability"* (2.1.79-82). He is not honest with Caesar over his concerns.

We are also told in Aristotle that the great-souled man is not easily flattered (ibid., IV.iii.17).

"Honour rendered by common people and on trivial grounds he will utterly despise, for this is not what he merits."

Yet, in the play, Cassius plans to send notes to Brutus (as from several citizens) expressing their great opinion of him (1.2.314-318). This Cassius does in order to seduce Brutus to the conspiracy. He recognizes Brutus' vanity and exploits it, for Cassius is insightful (1.2.201-202)

He is a great observer, and he looks
Quite through the deeds of men.

Cassius needs Brutus to legitimize his cause. He needs the citizens to associate the assassination with their version of an honourable man (1.3.157-160)

O he sits high in all the people's hearts:
And that which would appear offence in us
His countenance, like richest alchemy,
Will change to virtue and to worthiness.

Finally we learn that the great-souled man (ibid., IV.iii.30)

"...does not bear a grudge, for it is not a mark of greatness of soul to recall things against people, especially the wrongs they have done you, but rather to overlook them".

Yet in the quarrel scene we see Brutus does hold a grudge against Cassius for siding against him in the case of Lucius Pella (4.3.1-6).

So Brutus may be a man trying to do the right thing and although he is regarded by others as honourable his actions reveal that he is neither great-souled nor honourable.

Brutus' Ingratitude

When Antony delivers his speech he attacks the conspirators by attacking Brutus' honour. He does this by showing Brutus to be ungrateful (3.2.179-184)

For Brutus, as you know, was Caesar's angel.

Judge, O you gods, how dearly Caesar loved him.

This was the most unkindest cut of all:

For when the noble Caesar saw him stab,

Ingratitude, more strong than traitor's arms,

quite vanquished him.

Seneca also saw this failing in Brutus. Seneca felt ingratitude was the source of all crime (*Moral Essays* Vol.III, On Benefits, I.x.3-4)

"Homicides, tyrants, thieves, adulterers, robbers, sacrilegious men, and traitors there always will be; but worse than all these is the crime of ingratitude, unless it be that all these spring from ingratitude, without which hardly any sin has grown to great size" (underlined for emphasis).

Seneca felt ingratitude was not only Brutus' weakness (a traitor) but was also Caesar's (a tyrant) and perhaps even the Roman people's major flaw (1.1.55-56)

Pray to the gods to intermit the plague

That needs must light on this ingratitude.

Gratitude is the response to a freely offered gift. Caesar had pardoned Brutus after his and Pompey's defeat in a previous civil war. Brutus owes Caesar his life. To plot against Caesar is certainly an act of ingratitude regardless of whether Caesar was a tyrant or not.

Brutus' public act of ingratitude effectively destroys the harmony in Rome and undercuts the foundation of civil law (ibid., IV.xviii.1).

"To prove to you that the sentiment of gratitude is something to be desired in itself, ingratitude is something to be avoided in itself because there is nothing that so effectively disrupts and destroys the harmony of the human race as this vice. For how else do we live in security if it is not that we help each other by an exchange of good offices?"

So from Seneca's point of view Brutus was not prudent, grateful, or honourable (ibid., II.xx.1-2).

"It is an oft-debated question whether Marcus Brutus ought to have received his life from the hands of the deified Julius when in his opinion it was his duty to kill him. The reason that led him to kill Caesar I shall discuss elsewhere, for, although in other respects he was a great man, in this particular he seems to me to have acted very wrongly, and to have failed to conduct himself in accordance with Stoic teaching."

Seneca saw Brutus as a Stoic as did Shakespeare (4.3.143-144). What Seneca says about Stoics reveals much to us about how Brutus is depicted in the play. It helps explain his obsession with honour (ibid., V.xii.5).

"According to us Stoics there is only one sort of good, the honourable."

This belief system also helps explain the distance Brutus places between himself and Portia (ibid., IV.ii.4)

"...for virtue despises pleasure, is its enemy, and recoils from it as far as it can, being more acquainted with labour and sorrow, which are manly ills."

It also helps explain his quarrel with Cassius over what might be regarded as a trivial matter (ibid., V.xv.2).

"I am merely voicing the grumbling of the Stoics, who count every act as most evil and wrong that falls short of the standard of righteousness."

For Seneca as well as Brutus the most important aspect of the human was their mind (ibid., II.xxxi.1)

"...we Stoics refer every action to the mind, a man acts only as he wills."

Brutus' Will

Brutus intended to bestow a benefit upon the Roman people by killing Caesar. It was an action he performed with no intension of personal gain (5.5.69-71). If Brutus acted wrongly it was because of an error he made in his understanding of the situation. This should come as no surprise since Brutus has made logistical mistakes throughout the play [2].

Faulty understanding could arise from any of several missteps. The Understanding had the job of sifting through the evidence of the senses which had been organized in the Common Sense. The Understanding had to employ the Imagination to construct all the possible ways this information could be arranged or accounted for. By summoning memories, recalling knowledge and utilizing one's wisdom it was then possible to inform the Will as to what was the most desirable action to be taken.

It was the job of the Will to make a just decision. Justice often required God's Grace or love to direct it. Love is the one thing lacking in Brutus, he uses the word when talking about Caesar, the Roman people and Portia but we see little evidence of his showing love.

The French philosopher Jamyn described a Roman picture (*The French Academies of the Sixteenth Century*, Yates, p. 144) while discussing why the temple of Honour was built directly behind the temple of Virtue:

"In Roman pictures there was always a little Cupid leading Honour towards Virtue".

What this indicates is that love guides the person seeking honour towards virtue or justice, since it is the whole of virtue.

Cornelius Agrippa also spoke of love as a critical guide to the Will (*Three Books of Occult Philosophy*, Chapter XXVIII, p. 355-356).

"Grace therefore, which divines call charity, or infused love is in the will, as a first mover; which being absent, the whole constent (consonance) *falls into dissonancy."*

Agrippa felt love guided the will, as first mover, and if it was absent then destructive choices would result. Agrippa related love to harmony and its absence with evil. Agrippa so believed in the strength of love that he felt it could dispel evil.

"...there is nothing more efficacious to drive away evil spirits than musical harmony...as David by his harp appeased Saul being troubled with an evil spirit."

In Shakespeare's *Julius Caesar* Brutus too is troubled by an evil spirit and he employs his boy Lucius to play music to comfort him. Unfortunately Lucius falls asleep and the evil spirit makes its entrance (4.3.272.1). When Caesar's ghost leaves, Lucius, prior to waking, cries out from his sleep (4.3.289)

The strings, my lord, are false (gone out of tune).

Lucius is intuitively aware of the dissonance, the lack of love, that accompanies 'Brutus' evil spirit'.

Love is the missing piece in Brutus' personality. It is why he is incapable of making a just decision. Love is so moderated in Brutus and so overwhelmed by his concern for honour that it has little chance to guide his will. This is the source of Brutus' error; he is immoderate with respect to honour (*Nicomachean Ethics*, VII.iv.5-6)

"...money, gain, victory, honour...excessive devotion to them is bad and to be avoided".

Brutus is also deficient with respect to love and this has led to the dissonance in his soul. The unjust action that led to Caesar's execution is 'Brutus' evil spirit'. Brutus, ironically, has become the tyrant he feared Caesar to be (2.1.18-19)

> *Th'abuse of greatness is when it disjoins*
> *Remorse from power.*

Brutus' lack of love, his cool detachment that separated love from logic, led to this unjust action; an action so unjust and so devoid of compassion that it haunts him.

The Great Debate: Reason vs. Passion

When Brutus and Antony eulogize Caesar, Honour is pitted against Love. Brutus' cold intellectual honour attempts to justify the killing of Caesar to the Roman people while Antony's hot emotional love stirs their passions into seeing the injustice of the act.

Brutus' stoicism biases him into believing that reason controls people's actions. His address (3.2.12-47) is devoid of emotion. Unfortunately he presents himself as a cold blooded killer who could stab an unarmed man to death for abstract reasons (3.2.20-24)

> *why Brutus rose against*
> *Caesar, this is my answer: not that I loved Caesar less,*
> *but that I loved Rome more. Had you rather Caesar*
> *were living, and die all slaves, than that Caesar were*
> *dead, to live all freemen?*

His audience does not see itself as enslaved nor do they see the threat of becoming slaves as a real possibility. Brutus' reason for his action does not resonate with them; it lacks emotional truth. They do not see, feel, or fear enslavement. Brutus has only appealed to their reason, he has only presented an abstract argument that Caesar was ambitious and that by becoming King he would, by logical extension, enslave them all. They are willing to accept Brutus' argument because Brutus has always been a man of honour (3.2.14-16)

> *Believe me for*
>
> *mine honour and have respect to mine honour, that you*
>
> *may believe.*

When Brutus finishes his speech they are nonetheless willing to crown him Caesar (3.2.51-52). This behaviour confirms Cassius' fear that the Roman people are sheep wanting only to be led (1.3.105).

When Antony speaks he addresses Brutus' two central points: that Caesar was ambitious and that Brutus is honourable. In the process of praising Caesar he points out that Caesar brought income to Rome (3.2.89-90), was empathetic to the poor (3.2.92-93) and had refused the crown three times (3.2.97-98). Antony asks the crowd *"Was this ambition?"*; the implication being that if Brutus could so misjudge Caesar's intensions then could he have acted justly?

Antony pauses to let this sink in; he then promises to show them Caesar's will, a will that would reveal the truth of what Caesar felt towards the Roman people, a written confirmation of his intensions, a will that would, by the natural laws of gratitude, tie the Roman people to Caesar.

Antony constructs his speech by engaging the crowd's emotions. He uses imagery to excite their feelings. He shows them Caesar's corpse, Caesar's robe, the knife-holes, the blood spray. He knows things seen are more moving than descriptions heard. He has engaged the power of mnemonic theory in his speech. He is making it sensual and memorable and finally he locks the images in place by adding the horror of ingratitude (3.2.183-184)

> *Ingratitude...burst his mighty heart.*

Having dismissed Caesar's ambition, having discredited the conspirators' honour (honourable people are not ungrateful), Antony now unveils Caesar's will. He shows the people how much Caesar loved them, the gifts he bestowed on them. He has put them in Caesar's debt and they know they must do the only thing they can, as grateful citizens, to repay this debt (3.2.236)

> *Most noble Caesar, we'll revenge his death.*

Antony accomplishes all this while staying quietly in the background as "*a plain blunt man*" that only loved his friend (3.2.211-212). Antony promises the people nothing and claims no honour for himself. The crowd does not act on his behalf but only on their own initiative. He has unleashed pure passion and at this point takes no steps to guide it (3.2.251-252)

> *Now let it work. Mischief, thou art afoot:*
> *Take thou what course thou wilt.*

Horse and Rider: Passion and Reason

> (4.1.29; 31-33) *...my horse...*
> *It is a creature that I teach to fight,*
> *To wind, to stop, to run directly on,*
> *His corporal motion governed by my spirit.*

Here Antony is speaking of his horse but he could just as easily be speaking of his own body. It is a continuation of Brutus' metaphor about the division between "*The genius and the mortal instruments*" (2.1.66), the mind and the body.

The passions (the sensual appetite) were not seen by all as evil but rather as part of the driving force necessary to help us accomplish 'the good'. The passions, like a horse, just needed to be guided by our reason to perform good service.

Plutarch, Shakespeare's primary source for the play, (*Julius Caesar*, Arden 3rd Series, p. 86-92) argued for the moderation of the passions through instruction and not for their extirpation. Through the exercise of virtue Plutarch felt the overstraining impulses of each passion could be moderated and trained to accomplish good ends (*The Middle Platonists*, p. 195-196).

In the speeches delivered by Brutus and Antony it is clear that Brutus has divorced his mind from his passions as any good Stoic would. Any love he harboured for Caesar was not given the voice it deserved. He let abstract concerns over Caesar's future behaviour take precedence over both his gratitude and his love for Caesar. His feelings were shut out of his decision making process. This also is true in his actions with Portia.

Brutus' bad decisions are a result of his ignoring the input from his passions. His passions could have moderated his cold logical mind into making more prudent choices. Prudence is the exercise of practical wisdom to help make moral choices in a physical world.

Prudence, as in Antony's metaphor, harnessed the passions to the guiding mind. In this way the understanding had access to more information and was better enabled to make proper choices.

Antony acts much more prudently than Brutus. He has more successfully integrated his passions to his guiding mind. He achieves the only goal he has aimed for; to avenge Caesar's death. We see him release the energy of the passionate mob without direction but he is more careful in governing his own passions. He does this right from Caesar's death where he forces himself to declare his friendship with the assassins while secretly despising everything they did (3.1.255-256)

> *O pardon me, thou bleeding piece of earth,*
> *That I am meek and gentle with these butchers.*

He controls but does not ignore his passions. He does what Brutus fails to do. Brutus ignores his love for Caesar whereas Antony merely sublimates his hate for the conspirators till a more appropriate time arises.

Brutus is intellectually arrogant, valuing only the input from his mind, and this is his undoing.

Brutus ignores not only the input of his passions but also the input of others. Brutus ignores Cassius' advice both about how to handle Antony (2.1.154-157) and about how to wage the war against him (4.3.197-200). He also ignores Portia's pleas to have input into his decision making (2.1.254-255; 267-269; 271-274) and (2.1.297)

Tell me your counsels. I will not disclose 'em.

Brutus is also ungrateful and unjust in his treatment of Caesar. He never talks to Caesar about his concerns nor does he ever point out to Caesar the dangers Caesar's may face. Brutus does not, in fact, take his own advice (5.1.29)

Good words are better than bad strokes.

Brutus is arrogant because he takes no steps to increase his understanding. He ignores the input of others and chooses self-sufficiency over consultation (*Nicomachean Ethics*, III.iii.10)

"when the matter is important, we take others into our deliberations, distrusting our own capacity to decide".

Free will cannot be properly expressed if it is insufficient in knowledge or understanding and particularly if it ignores love, a force that directs us towards the good.

Antony is a passionate man; his speech shows us he knows how to stir passions and his actions tell us he can control them. In (4.1) we see him building ties with Octavius and Lepidus. The favours they exchange are the deaths of those close to them. They are purging the Senate of conspirators and sympathizers but in the process must give up people they care for. The exchange is a dark form of gift-giving and the bonds of mutual pain bind the Triumvirs together (4.3.172-173)

Octavius, Antony and Lepidus
Have put to death an hundred senators.

Antony never presents himself as an honourable or even a good man, only as a plain blunt man. He is not a better man than Brutus only a more balanced man and because of this a more capable man.

Brutus agonizes over how to act but his Stoic beliefs deprive his understanding of the information he needs to make the correct choice. The lack of balance seen in Brutus can also be seen in Cassius only this time the balance tips in favour of the passions, the senses.

Cassius is an Epicurean, *"You know that I held Epicurus strong"* (5.1.76). This meant that Cassius believed in the supremacy of the senses, like Epicurus he felt that our ability 'to know' or 'to think' all hinged on the input from our senses (*Lucretius On The Nature Of Things*, ll 469-480, p. 313-315)

"...how he knows what it is to know or not to know as the case maybe, what gave him the concept of true and false, what evidence proved that the doubtful differs from the certain.

You will find that it is from the senses in the first instance that the concept of truth has come, and that the senses cannot be refuted ".

Epicurus believed that reasoning rested on the senses and that reasoning therefore could not refute the senses. For Epicureans sensation was the primary standard of truth (ibid., ll 482-484, p. 315)

"What, moreover, must be held to be of greater credit than the senses? Shall reasoning, derived from false sense, prevail against these senses, being itself wholly derived from the senses?"

Epicurus felt the mind could be deceived. He felt this routinely happened in such instances as relative motion, in observing refraction, with reflections, in dreams and in seeing ghosts (ibid., p. 305-313). Epicurus held the belief that (ibid., ll 465-468, p. 313)

"...because of opinions of the mind...things are held to be seen which have not been seen by our senses".

Epicurus trusted the senses like modern day scientists trust their instruments (which are extensions of the senses). Epicurus held the belief that 'data does not lie' and that the problem was always in its interpretation.

Epicurus felt reasoning had to be built on a foundation of sensory information and not just on conjecture, for the mind was easily deceived (ibid., ll 513-521, p. 317)

"as in a building, if the original rule is warped, if the square is faulty and deviates from straight lines, if the level is a trifle wrong in any part, the whole house will necessarily be made in a faulty fashion...all betrayed by false principles at the beginning".

Epicurus would see Brutus as possessing a mind that was deceived and would view his resulting actions as being betrayed by their false beginnings.

Cassius, when viewed separately from Brutus, consistently made the correct decisions but he always betrayed his own beliefs by acquiescing to the judgments of Brutus' mind. Near the end of the play Cassius finally gives up his Epicurean views and starts adopting a more superstitious attitude (5.1.76-88). Epicurus held that the gods did not participate in the lives of humans and so believed that signs and omens revealed nothing of coming events (ibid., ll 44-49, p. 7)

"for the very nature of divinity must necessarily enjoy immortal life in the deepest peace, far removed and separated from our affairs...needing us not at all, it is neither propitiated with services nor touched by wrath".

Cassius wants to believe this but he now has his doubts. His own mind starts to betray him or more precisely his imaginings start to betray him. Cassius now, like Brutus, becomes an example of the bad things that happen when the mind is given supremacy.

Cassius' last impulsive act is to end his life (5.3.12-46). Pindarus tells Cassius what he sees but Cassius interprets it wrongly, he misjudges the greeting of friends for the attack by enemies. The memory of Caesar's betrayal by his 'so called friends' perverts Cassius' judgment of the unfolding events. Cassius driven by his rash nature (4.3.39) and the coloured judgment of his mind makes a dreadfully wrong decision. Cassius, whose senses never failed him, is ultimately betrayed by his mind's imaginings.

Cassius' Epicureanism (primacy of the senses) and Brutus' Stoicism (primacy of the mind) are both extreme positions taken around Antony's pragmatism. Each adds a nuance of understanding to the debate of Passion over Reason.

Neither Brutus nor Cassius is self-aware; they do not know themselves. If they did they could adjust their behaviours to accommodate their natures and avoid acting in error (5.3.69-71)

> *O Error, soon conceived,*
>
> *Thou never com'st unto a happy birth*
>
> *But kill'st the mother that engendered thee.*

Sadly, neither man makes such an adjustment and dies as a result of his mistakes.

The Free Will

> *The will, the will. We will hear Caesar's will.*

This chant (3.2.140) could ring out throughout the play. Caesar's physical will, what Caesar wills to do and what Caesar will do in the future play a central part in the drama. Each character in the play acts in response to Caesar.

Caesar's actions reveal a man that behaves responsibly. Even Brutus acknowledges this (2.1.20-21)

> *I have not known when his affections swayed*

More than his reason.

Brutus sees balance between Caesar's affections (passions) and his reason but he still fears what Caesar may do in the future (2.1.32-34); he fears that he will make himself King. He fears this action will put everyone else's free will in jeopardy and so he decides to kill Caesar pre-emptively. He kills him before Caesar can manifest the actions of his own free will. Caesar is deprived of the expression of free will which Brutus wishes to protect for the Roman people.

In the first part of the play Brutus is consumed with thoughts about the expression of free will. He is worried about both Caesar's expression of free will and the free will of the Roman people.

Antony is the loving friend of Caesar. He does not fear Caesar and from his love freely performs acts in Caesar's interests (1.2.10)

When Caesar says 'Do this', it is performed.

Antony, like Caesar, understands and maintains the correct relation between his passions and his will

"Appetite is the will's solicitor and will is appetite's controller" (*The Elizabethan World Picture*, p. 74).

Antony loves Caesar and would not have usurped his position but upon Caesar's death Antony's interests change. Antony intends to do what's best for Antony. He will avenge his friend's death but he no longer feels obliged to follow Caesar's will (4.1.8-9)

Fetch the will hither, and we shall determine

How to cut off some charge in legacies.

Antony is using his free will and acting according to his interests and so chooses to reduce the size of Caesar's gift to the Roman people. Brutus' actions have freed Antony's ambitions.

Pindarus is another character of interest. His story provides an example of 'structural rhyming'. He is a slave to Cassius but he finds he is given his freedom against his will. Cassius reminds him *"to keep his oath*" and to "*do whatsoever I bid thee do*" (5.3.36-46). Cassius then asks Pindarus to kill him. Pindarus is a mirror of both the Roman people and of Antony who were willingly enslaved to Caesar and would not wish their freedom at the cost of his death (5.3.47-48)

> *So, I am free; yet would not so have been*
> *Durst I have done my will.*

Pindarus' true expression of free will would have been to disobey Cassius and not strike him down. Pindarus would have preferred to remain a slave to a living Cassius than to be a free man without him.

Free Will That's Not

Free will is a concept which dominates the play but it too is subject to other forces: Chance and Fortune. Pindarus' will is limited by his oath and his position. Earlier in the play a poet, Cinna, finds his free will too has been compromised by Fate (3.3.1-4)

> *I dreamt tonight that I did feast with Caesar,*
> *And things unluckily charge my fantasy.*
> *I have no will to wander forth of doors,*
> *Yet something leads me forth*

(underlined for emphasis).
Cinna is fated for death and his free will apparently cannot restrain him.

Caesar too acknowledges the role of Fate (2.2.27-28) and tries to comfort his wife with its inevitability

> *What can be avoided*
> *Whose end is purposed by the mighty gods?*

But Fate and Chance are sometimes difficult to distinguish from one another for sometimes they are intertwined (2.3.14-15)

> *If thou read this, O Caesar, thou mayst live;*
> *If not, the Fates with traitors do contrive.*

Even Cassius understands the role of chance in life. He has tied his fate to Brutus' and must obey orders (5.1.72-75)

> *Give me thy hand, Messala:*
>
> *Be thou my witness that against my will*
>
> *(As Pompey was) am I compelled to set*
>
> *Upon one battle all our liberties*

(underlined for emphasis).

Cassius understands that his free will and that of all those who serve under him are suspended at this moment for all must obey their orders which come from Brutus. A soldier's will is not his own.

Brutus too feels his free will compromised. He always believed in living and seeing what providence had in store for him (5.1.100-107) yet now feels that if he suffers defeat (the role of chance) he will have no choice but to commit suicide as Cato did (5.1.108-112) [3].

The expression of free will and the suspension of free will structure the action in the play (Plutarch, *Table Talk* (*Quaest. Conv.*) IX.5 (740C); *The Middle Platonists*, p. 209)

"...the operation of Fate mingles and interweaves with that of Chance, while our free will in its turn combines with one or other of them or with both simultaneously".

In the beginning of the play Cassius and Brutus freely act to kill Caesar. Caesar's free will falls victim to theirs. At the end of the play Cassius and Brutus both feel deprived of their free will and find themselves forced into actions not strictly of their own choosing. This is also true of the Roman people who find their free will compromised by Brutus' actions – instead of being free to carry on with their lives under Caesar's benevolent dictatorship they find their freedoms compromised as they are thrust into the turmoil and instability of a civil war.

Conclusion

Julius Caesar is an examination of human weakness and the expression of human will. The play begins by examining our weak human flesh and the illnesses that pervade our bodies. The play reveals to us the biases we carry in our blood through our humours. These cloud and shape our judgments. The play makes manifest our spirits as something distinct from our bodies, as something that can be greater than our physical selves. It is this spirit that is finally the subject of *Julius Caesar*.

All the characters in the play have tyrannical tendencies (my will over your will). The play begins with Murellus and Flavis trying to impose their wills over those of the crowd assembled to celebrate Caesar's return. Caesar hopes to impose his will over the whole of Rome. Cassius cunningly shapes Brutus' will to match his own. Cassius wishes to assassinate Caesar; essentially imposing his will over Caesar's right to exist. After the assassination Antony begins to flex his will. First he tests to see if the will of the people is in line with his own. Then he begins to impose his will over the wills of Octavius and Lepidus in order to gain control of the Empire.

Each character's expression of free will is challenged. Caesar wishes to be Emperor but he tempers this ambition to the mood of the crowd. Caesar finds that when he refuses the crown (1.2.243-244)

> ...the rabblement hooted, and clapped their
> chopped hands, and threw up their sweaty nightcaps

and (1.2.262-263)

> ...he perceived
> the common herd was glad he refused the crown.

Caesar lets the will of the people inform him and so he re-thinks his immediate actions.

Cassius' plans are constantly vexed by Brutus. Cassius desperately needs Brutus' legitimacy in order to lend credence to his action. Brutus is slow to come on board so Cassius must cajole him to the cause. Once enlisted Brutus limits the scope of Cassius' plans to just include the assassination of Caesar and no others. Later in the play Brutus imposes his military plan over Cassius' which again proves disastrous.

Antony is forced to work with both Octavius and Lepidus so compromise is essential to all their ambitions but comments made to Octavius show an Antony that is set at gaining more autocratic control. Antony speaks of Lepidus as "*a property*" for their use (4.1.24-25)

> *And having brought our treasure where we will,*
>
> *Then take we down his load and turn him off.*

Antony plans to impose his will on Lepidus, who is stripped of his own, to this Octavius agrees (4.1.28)

> *You may do your will.*

Octavius is not just a patsy and he quickly learns to deal with Antony. He is not going to let Antony take control (5.1.16-20)

> Ant. *Octavius, lead your battle softly on,*
>
> *Upon the left hand of the even field.*
>
> Oct. *Upon the right hand I. Keep thou the left.*
>
> Ant. *Why do you cross me in this exigent?*
>
> Oct. *I do not cross you: but I will do so.*

Brutus is the primary focus of the play. It is his expression of free will that we see most clearly examined. It is Brutus' assessment of the situation we see questioned; Brutus is not thinking clearly. We see Cassius, through subtle means (flattery and messages of propaganda), manipulate Brutus. We see Portia, his wife, offer him true partnership and collaboration only to have her input rejected. Brutus' free will we find expressed without the benefit of a clear understanding of the situation. His nature and other's input or lack thereof have deprived him of the information he needs to make an informed choice (3.2.105-106)

> *O judgment, thou art fled to brutish beasts*
> *And men have lost their reason.*

Brutus in Latin means 'stupid' or 'unknowing beast' and Brutus' stupid decision condemns Rome to years of civil war. Eventually Brutus is deprived of the very thing he killed Caesar to protect - his free will.

At the heart of Brutus' decision-making ability is his will. Brutus' will is a manifestation of his spirit, in that it is his spirit that bridges the gap between the body and the soul. The spirit allows information to be passed from one to the other. The spirit ensured that our minds were always informed by both the physical and spiritual worlds. The spirit allowed for this flow of information so that our will would be capable of doing God's will. To make prudent choices, the input of both had to be considered. Practical wisdom is what is needed to make moral decisions, decisions about life in the physical realm. Brutus ignores his love of Caesar as well as the role of gratitude in his decision-making. He chooses Stoic ideology over balance. Brutus' error is our warning, and education our only salvation.

Footnotes

[1] Ate was a goddess that created delusions in men and prompted them to commit irresponsible acts. Shakespeare's use of this goddess in association with Caesar indicates he felt Caesar was deluded in his wish to become Emperor. Shakespeare's association of Caesar with the phlegmatic personality also indicates he felt Caesar was not to be deterred from his plans. That Shakespeare depicted Caesar in the same way that Brutus and Cassius perceived him does not however mean that Shakespeare was sympathetic to his assassination.

[2] A few of Brutus' tactical mistakes (not necessarily moral mistakes) are as follows:

a) He refuses to let Antony be slain (2.1.179-182).

b) He agrees to let Antony speak at Caesar's funeral (3.1.244-246).

c) He expects the citizens of Rome to accept cold reason as to why Caesar had to die (3.2.12-34).

d) He abandons Portia even though she feels isolated and estranged from him (2.1.281-286).

e) He chooses to come out of the defensible hills and meet Octavius and Antony on the plains for battle (5.1.1-4).

f) He attacks Octavius too early and fails to provide back-up for Cassius' troops (5.3.5-8).

[3] The play presents suicide as the final expression of free will. Portia, Cassius, and Brutus all intentionally take their own lives. All feel they are out of options and view suicide as a final honourable protest against a life lacking in free will (1.3.96-97)

> *But life being weary of these worldly bars*
> *Never lacks power to dismiss itself.*

Bibliography

1) *Julius Caesar*, edited by David Daniell, The Arden Shakespeare, 3rd series, Thomson Learning, 1998.

2) *The Imperial Theme; Further Interpretations of Shakespeare's Tragedies Including The Roman Plays*, G. Wilson Knight, Methuen and Co. Ltd., 1954.

3) *The Wheel of Fire; Interpretations of Shakespearian Tragedy*, G. Wilson Knight, Routledge Classics, 2001.

4) *Shakespeare's Imagery and What it Tells Us*, Caroline Surgeon, Cambridge University Press, 19th printing, 2005.

5) *Studies in Philology*, Vol. 81, No. 3 (Summer, 1984), p. 372-393, *The Numbering of Men and Days: Symbolic Design in 'The Tragedy of Julius Caesar'*, Thomas McAlindon, Published by University of North Carolina Press.

6) *The French Academie* (1586), P. de la Primandaye, Georg Olms Verlag, 1972.

7) *The French Academies of the Sixteenth Century*, Frances A. Yates, Routledge, 1988.

8) *Three Books of Occult Philosophy*, Henry Cornelius Agrippa, transl. James Freake, edited and annotated by Donald Tyson, Llewellyn Publications, 2004.

9) *Seneca Moral Essays*, Volume III, On Benefits, transl. John W. Basore, Harvard University Press, 2006.

10) *Nicomachean Ethics*, Aristotle, transl. H. Rackham, Harvard University Press, 1934.

11) *The Elizabethan World Picture*, E.M.W. Tillyard, Vintage Books, 1958.

12) *The Middle Platonists, 80 B.C. to A.D. 220*, John Dillon, Cornell University Press, 1996.

13) *New Larousse Encyclopedia of Mythology*, The Hamlyn Publishing Group Ltd., 1982.

14) *Lucretius On The Nature Of Things*, translated by W.H.D. Rouse, revised by Martin F. Smith, Loeb Classical Library, Harvard University Press, 2006.